# Common Ground, Contested Territory

## Examining Roles of English Language Teachers in Troubled Times

### Mark A. Clarke
University of Colorado at Denver

### Foreword by Diane Larsen-Freeman
University of Michigan

*Surviving Innovation, Volume 2*

Ann Arbor

THE UNIVERSITY OF MICHIGAN PRESS

# Dedication

*For Evan Benjamin, Hannah Rose, and William Austen, the next generation. And for their teachers.*

2010    2009    2008    2007        4    3    2    1

ISBN-10: 0-472-03213-5
ISBN-13: 978-0-472-03213-6


Library of Congress Cataloging-in-Publication Data

Clarke, Mark A.
    Common ground, contested territory : examining roles of English language teachers in troubled times / Mark A. Clarke.
        p. cm. — (Surviving innovation ; v. 2)
    Includes index.
    ISBN-13: 978-0-472-03213-6 (pbk. : alk. paper)
    ISBN-10: 0-472-03213-5 (pbk. : alk. paper)
        1. Teaching—United States—Philosophy. 2. Teachers —United States. I. Title. II. Series.

    LB1025.3.C5346  2007
    371.102—dc22                                              2006048074

Cover art: *Tell Tale Apple*, bead embroidery by Amy Clarke Moore. This piece is inspired by the William Tell folktale of Switzerland where Tell was forced by an oppressive dictator to shoot an apple off his son's head. He held a second arrow in his hand, meant for the dictator if the first arrow harmed his son. Amy Clarke Moore is the editor of *Spin-Off* magazine (Interweave Press).

# CONTENTS

# FOREWORD

By Diane Larsen-Freeman
University of Michigan

It has been said that the 20$^{th}$ century was the century of physics and that the 21$^{st}$ century will be the century of biology. As the 21$^{st}$ century has barely begun, it may seem premature to be characterizing it. Nevertheless, the following excerpt from a recent editorial in the journal *Science* (Kafatos & Eisner, 2004, p. 1257) makes it clear why such a characterization is apt.

> Scientific progress is based ultimately on unification rather than fragmentation of knowledge. At the threshold of what is widely regarded as the century of biology, the life sciences are undergoing a profound transformation. They have long existed as a collection of narrow, even parochial, disciplines with well-defined territories. Now they are undergoing consolidation, forming two major domains: one extending from the molecule to the organism, the other bringing together population biology, biodiversity studies, and ecology. Kept separate, these domains, no matter how fruitful, cannot hope to deliver on the full promise of modern biology. They cannot lead to an appreciation of life in its full complexity, from the molecule to the biosphere, nor to the generation of maximal benefits to medicine, industry, agriculture, or conservation biology.

Although *Common Ground, Contested Territory* is a book for teachers of English language learners, not biologists, there are themes in the book that resonate with statements in this editorial. Mark Clarke argues against seeing education in a fragmented way. He realizes that we need to take a long view—from the "molecule" of a teaching technique (which he, tellingly, conceives of as an event, p. 160) to the "biosphere" of education on a national level. If we do not do so, we do not appreciate the full complexity of schools and schooling, nor will teachers of English language learners be able to hold their own in "contested territory." Above all, given the zeitgeist and given the extent to which global environmental challenges confront us, it is not surprising that scholars like Mark Clarke have adopted ecological metaphors to help us understand the nature of our work. Seeing teaching from an ecological perspective, we acknowledge and share Clarke's discontent "with responses to situations that ignore the complexity" (p. 202). The ecological perspective, as he writes, forces "the awareness of the interconnectedness of individuals, institutions, and communities—systems within systems within systems" (p. 24). Indeed, the interconnectedness of classrooms within schools within communities cannot be ignored—at whatever level of scale. Any system that is conceived to be "irreducibly self-contained cannot meaningfully relate to the world 'outside'" (Leather & van Dam, 2003, p. 6).

Indeed, there is a growing awareness among language acquisition/language socialization researchers and educational linguists (Larsen-Freeman, 1997; van Lier, 2000; Kramsch, 2002; Leather & van Dam, 2003) that the foci of their investigations cannot be studied apart from the contexts in which they operate—cannot be seen as autonomous objects of any kind. Furthermore, such scholars have come to realize that the study of complex, contextualized systems is made more difficult by the fact that such systems are often dynamic, continually being transformed over time, shaped by their environments and shaping them in a reciprocal manner (Larsen-Freeman & Cameron, forthcoming). The dynamics themselves are nonlinear, and therefore unexpected consequences sometimes emerge. The operation of such stochastic systems is not revealed by searching for simple proximate, linear causality; instead, what is of interest are "relationships and processes, not products and outcomes; our focus is on the ways that new patterns of organization and knowledge emerge in a situation of change; we are concerned with the quality of the educational environment and the learning opportunities it affords—and explicitly with the values and ideals we wish to promote in our educational work" (van Lier, 2003, p. 51).

Drawing on these ideas in systems theory and other sources for his inspiration, Mark Clarke offers an approach for dealing with seemingly intractable problems in education. As Clarke puts it, "Simple, straightforward causal explanations for human phenomena are rarely useful. People are complex, and organizations even more so. Whether you are attempting to understand a particular event or situation or trying to change something, you need to abandon causal thinking—Event A causes event B—and adopt ecological thinking—Event B can be understood as the (expectable) outcome of a convergence of factors. How to influence these factors to create an environment for change becomes the focus of your efforts" (p. 198).

This is the only kind of thinking that will meet with any success in these "troubled times" in my opinion. In keeping with this orientation, Clarke encourages teachers to acknowledge the influence of their mentors, all the while becoming generators of their own knowledge, through a process of action research and reflection. He knows that the learning of teachers is well served when they cultivate "attitudes of inquiry" (Larsen-Freeman, 2000) because prescriptions and proscriptions will be of little assistance in situations where "all human interaction, including that encountered in the classroom, is unique to the moment" (p. 159).

Hanks (1996, p. 15, cited in Leather & van Dam, 2003) suggests that approaches to linguistics can be characterized conceptually in terms of two basic foci: the degree to which language is seen to exist as an autonomous system versus the extent to which language is cross-linked to the circumstances of its utterance (its "relationality"). In such terms, an ecological approach will clearly be high on relationality and low on autonomy. Adopting an ecological approach to understanding teaching, Clarke emphasizes relationships—not only in explicating the circumstances of interest—but also in the relationships that teachers establish with their students. As Mark Clarke states, "First and foremost, good teaching involves human relationships. Good teaching involves authentic engagement between people around things that matter" (p. 22). Furthermore, in order to be successful, teachers need to establish relationships outside of the classroom because "significant problems cannot be solved at the level they are encountered" (p. 181). Finally, it is clear that Clarke has undertaken very seriously a mission to establish an authentic relationship with us, his readers.

Although he says that he has worked to remove it, there is still a lot of Mark Clarke in this book. And I say, all for the better. We need more of his kind of thinking if we are going to deal effectively with the times that we live and work in. While it is true that humans cannot help learning (although I do find his definition of learning—"change over time through engagement in activity"—curiously broad), it takes a level of commitment for the learning to be purposeful and helpful. Clarke seeks to experience the ideal of coherence—"that fleeting state where my philosophical commitments align with the mundane decisions I am making on a minute-by-minute basis" (p. 31). He adds "we are all seeking coherence in the world—ways of aligning our behavior with our convictions—and we want to avoid being compromised by the pressures that seem to dominate the profession these days" (p. 200). I can think of very few individuals who achieve coherence in their lives. Mark Clarke is on the short mental list that I maintain; certainly, he is among those who embody the conscience of the field.

Surprisingly, he does not use the term *awareness* often in this book; yet, to my mind, this book is centrally concerned with awareness. Having been a long-time faculty member at the School for International Training, where we organized our curriculum for language teachers around knowledge, skills, attitudes, and awareness, I find the absence of the term "awareness" striking. For instance, Clarke asks, "Do students emerge [from a particular activity] with the knowledge, skills, and attitudes that contribute to their immediate success and long-term life chances?" (p. 123). Of course, he is not alone in not mentioning awareness explicitly. Nevertheless, I am quite sure that he would agree that awareness is essential for moving "from merely seeing the world toward seeing ourselves in the world, from being embedded in the problems we are trying to solve toward gaining perspective on them" (p. 195). With awareness comes choice. One can think and act differently—with a level of intentionality that being a teacher of English language learners in troubled times requires. Mark points out, and I agree, that it is important to acknowledge one's intellectual debts. Caleb Gattegno, the originator of the Silent Way, is one of my mentors. And Gattegno impressed upon me the fact that only awareness is truly educable. To this end, I am already conceiving of a course that with good fortune I might get to teach one day—one that uses this book as its text in order to nurture the awareness essential for teachers who work in contested territory.

## REFERENCES

Hanks, W. (1996). *Language and communicative practices.* Boulder, CO: Westview Press.

Kafatos, F., & Eisner, T. (2004). Unification in the century of biology. *Science, 27,* 1257.

Kramsch, C. (Ed.) (2002). *Language acquisition and language socialization: Ecological perspectives.* New York: Continuum.

Larsen-Freeman, D. (1997). Chaos/Complexity science and second language acquisition. *Applied Linguistics, 18,* 141–165.

———. (2000). An attitude of inquiry: TESOL as science. *The Journal of the Imagination in Language Learning, 5,* 10–15.

Larsen-Freeman, D., & Cameron, L. (Forthcoming). *Complexity theory and applied linguistics*. Oxford: Oxford University Press.

Leather, J., & van Dam, J. (Eds.) (2003). *Ecology of language acquisition*. Dordrecht, The Netherlands: Kluwer Academic Publishers.

Van Lier, L. (2000). From input to affordance: Social-interactive learning from an ecological perspective. In J. P. Lantolf (Ed.), *Sociocultural theory and second language learning* (pp. 245–259). Oxford: Oxford University Press.

———. (2003). A tale of two computer classrooms: The ecology of project-based language learning. In J. Leather & J. van Dam (Eds.), *Ecology of language acquisition* (pp. 49–64). Dordrecht, The Netherlands: Kluwer Academic Publishers.

# INTRODUCTION: WHOSE QUESTIONS COUNT?

---

The question is, "Who commands?"
—*Alice in Wonderland*

---

Greetings and welcome.

In this book I pose questions about teaching and learning as I grapple with the issues that we face today in education. My primary audience is the classroom teacher who is working with English language learners, but I welcome all teachers for whom these questions seem important:

❐ Who is in charge of lesson plans and of organizing classroom activities?

❐ Who places students in classes?

❐ Who selects the books? The tests?

❐ How are students evaluated, and who determines this? What consideration is teacher opinion given in decisions about student progress in school?

My answer is that you *should* play an important role in *all* of these activities. As a classroom teacher, you *should* have the final say in most of these cases, and your opinion *should* weigh heavily in all of them. Recently, however, I have been

struck by how difficult it is for teachers to exercise their professional prerogatives. Consider the following incidents, for example:

❏ A teacher at North High School in Denver, Colorado, was told by the district
superintendent (and the exchange was published in the newspaper) *how* she
should be teaching her class—what she could or could not do and how she was
to use the instructional materials brought to class. This occurred in response
to public uproar over her displaying the Mexican flag at the same height as
the U.S. flag in her classroom.

❏ Another teacher reported that she could not give a passing grade to a student
because he was not reading "on grade level"; both the criteria and the mea-
surement tools had been determined by school policy.

❏ The dean of our Initial Professional Teacher Education program announced
that graduate students who received a B– or lower for a class would not get
program credit for their work.

❏ The National Council for Accreditation of Teacher Education, in conjunction
with the professional organization TESOL (Teachers of English to Speakers
of Other Languages), has issued guidelines for graduate programs that require
courses to have assignments that are "performance based"; in other words,
learning has been defined as behavior—if you can't see it, it isn't learning.

I hasten to add that a reasonable case can be made for the decisions reported in
each of these situations, and I am not arguing for unilateral control by teachers
of all features of the curriculum. But what these cases all have in common is the
fact that the locus of decision-making in teaching—lesson plans, tests, methods
and materials, teacher/student interaction—has moved away from the classroom; increasingly, important decisions are being made by individuals who are
removed from day-to-day contact with students.

So, in spite of the fact that the territory is unambiguously demarcated—
after all, most teaching is still done in classrooms—the number of individuals
and special interests involved in decision-making has increased dramatically. If
teachers are to maintain any semblance of influence in the profession, we cannot exclude or ignore the other players; *we have to find common ground* and negotiate our positions.

At the same time, *it is clear that the territory is contested.* That is, given the diversity of individuals who have a say in educational matters, we are not all going
to agree on what needs to be done or how it should be accomplished. We need
to be clear on our roles and responsibilities, and we need to work to maintain
our professional prerogatives.

The problems teachers face are manifold. History and global events press in on all sides. I am writing these words in the summer of 2006, under the long shadow cast by events of 9/11/01 and the subsequent war on terrorism. Newspapers carry stories every day that directly impact me—news of war casualties that include the names of people I know or spouses of my students, visa restrictions and anti-terrorist laws that threaten to bankrupt the schools with whom I collaborate, letters and emails from friends and family abroad that recount the stresses of living in a global village where English speakers are increasingly viewed with suspicion or hostility. It is not difficult to make the case that everything is connected to everything else (Diamond, 1999, 2005; Friedman, 1999, 2005).

This book continues the argument developed in *A Place to Stand: Essays for Educators in Troubled Times* (Clarke, 2003), which is that classroom teachers hold the key to the future of education and, without exaggeration, to the future of society and the civilized world.

"Hold on!" you say. "I've got enough going on without some crackpot casting me in the role of superhero! Who are you to be telling me what my roles and responsibilities are?"

Good question.

In these days of barnstorming politicians and self-proclaimed gurus, it pays to be cautious when someone attempts to convince you that he or she has the answers to your problems. And in an increasingly partisan atmosphere of decision-making, it is important to scrutinize the credentials of people who present themselves as having answers to your questions (whether you asked them or not). And because I am not a fellow classroom teacher but a university professor, it is important for you to be clear on the claims I make on your time.

In Colorado, we have had our share of acrimonious exchange around the subject of professorial privilege. Consider this, for example: On Friday, September 10, 2004, I awoke to an overcast sky and chilly temperatures and the story on page 4 in the *Denver Post*.

I do not know any of the professors involved in this case and I have no opinion on this particular controversy, but I bring the story to your attention for two reasons.

First, it is indicative of the climate within which teachers work today: Debates are becoming more and more shrill and accusatory, characterized by a singular lack of charity. Educational decisions are increasingly being made in the press, with political commitments playing as important a role as questions of teaching and learning. And that fact prompts a central message of this book: *Teachers need to participate in the exchanges around education, especially as these concern*

# 3 New Claims of Prof Bias Are Heard by Panel[1]

Three new accusations of political bias by college professors emerged Thursday in a special hearing before state lawmakers investigating the issue....Some Democrats, while denouncing the acts, likened the hearing on political indoctrination to a "witch hunt" and said the episodes—if they are true—are isolated and are being investigated by the colleges....

The professors were not present to defend themselves during the hearing, and attempts to reach them Thursday were unsuccessful. The new accusations come on top of allegations that emerged in two previous legislative hearings....

"The allegations seemed to have some credibility; however, it's hard to be sure whether or not a problem really exists because we were given testimony by three or four students, and we have tens of thousands of students," said Sen. Ron Tupa, D-Boulder, who likened the hearing to a witch hunt.

"I don't see a pattern, I don't see a trend, and frankly I'm not sure I see a problem. You may have a few bad apples among the otherwise thousands of fine, dedicated faculty."

Students with differing views on either the professors or the ideological debate said they were told Wednesday they would not be allowed to testify.

Senator John Andrews disputed that, saying, "Our announcement made clear that public comment would be received."

Thursday's hearing stemmed from a memorandum of understanding signed this year by college presidents who promised to update lawmakers periodically on their progress in protecting students from political discrimination and indoctrination.

The issue rose to the forefront a year ago after Andrews and other Republicans met with David Horowitz, a Los Angeles conservative pushing for an "Academic Bill of Rights" for students.

*freedom of speech and professional prerogative. We need to define the territory of education, and we must find common ground with both our allies and our adversaries.*

Second, I want to assure you that I do not condone the use of the professor's lectern as bully pulpit for personal political or ideological views. This book has been crafted in my graduate classes over three decades, and I have worked hard to present a balanced view of the problems that face us as English language teachers. I have successfully (according to course evaluations) orchestrated conversations among individuals from both ends of the political spectrum, among conservative Christians, confirmed atheists, and devout Muslims, and between adherents of opposing pedagogical and ideological perspectives. I hope that individuals from all walks of life will be able to read the book without feeling attacked.

At the same time, it is impossible to present an objective view of learning and teaching, so you have a right to know who I am and what my biases are. In the spirit of full disclosure, I hereby assert the following to be facts:

❐ I was born in 1947 in a small mountain town, Gunnison, Colorado. I have one younger brother, Andrew J. My parents were both college educated and together ran the Clarke Agency, real estate and insurance. I was the third generation of Clarkes and Bomers to live in the town; my aunt still lives there. My father died of a heart attack when I was 16.

❏ I am married and have three adult children and three grandchildren.

❏ I live in an urban neighborhood in Denver, Colorado, and I belong to the large and racially diverse Park Hill United Methodist Church.

❏ I received my B.A. from the University of Colorado, Boulder, my M.A. from the American University in Cairo, Egypt, and my Ph.D. from the University of Michigan. At Colorado I was on the varsity wrestling team.

❏ I have taught at the University of Colorado at Denver since 1977 M.A. courses in the Language, Literacy, and Culture program and in the Initial Professional Teacher Education Program and doctoral courses in Educational Leadership and Innovation.

❏ I speak English (native), Spanish (fluent), and Arabic (basic).

❏ I am a registered Democrat. I am pro-choice and anti-war.

Therefore, to the extent that labels are informative, the following might be accurately applied to me: *native English–speaking multi-lingual white middle class educated progressive passivist anglo-saxon protestant heterosexual able-bodied jock urban academic male.*

I have dinner with my mother every Monday night and have lived in the same house for thirty years; you might reasonably conclude that I am pretty set in my ways.

However, I have traveled enough to know that there are as many ways of looking at the world as there are people living in it; I believe it is possible for people with profound and irreconcilable differences to live and work peaceably together.

These essays constitute an account of my experience as a language teacher and teacher educator. I began writing a number of them some many years ago— my ongoing effort at understanding teaching and learning, particularly as this involves me and English language learners. I do not intend for them to be read as professional prescription or as personal memoir; rather, they are my best effort at making sense of the world, and I figure you will take what you can use.

I believe that we all make up our own minds about important issues in language learning and teaching, and that the best way to understand an issue is to explore the details of others' experiences that lead them to have different perspectives, opinions, and commitments.

One teacher took issue with that assertion. "I don't agree," she said. "I believe we need to understand our own experience with regard to the issue and form our own conclusions."

Yes and no.

I agree that we need to be clear on who we are and what we believe, but I note that today people seem to be doing more talking than listening, especially when they are engaged with others who are different or whose perspectives are different from their own. What I am saying here is that there is much to be learned by knowing other people's life experiences and the basis on which they have made their decisions. It doesn't mean we have to agree with them, but it will help us understand why our points of view differ.

So, in order for you to understand my point of view, allow me to continue with my own story.

My first teaching experience was as an undergraduate tutor for Chicano youth in a summer program at the University of Colorado in Boulder. I had no idea what I was doing, and I seriously doubt that my efforts benefited the young women assigned to me. Later that summer, my wife and I boarded a plane for Egypt, and I soon found myself enveloped by the intoxicatingly exotic mélange of sounds, sights, and smells of Cairo. I now find it amusing that I was cast as the teacher in my evening encounters with English language learners—secretaries, embassy employees, mid-level government administrators—at the Department of Public Service because they were actually my mentors, amazingly tolerant guides to Egyptian life and culture, the intricacies of Arabic, and Islamic views of the world. Since then I have taught in a variety of settings in Latin America, the Middle East, North Africa, and Europe, but since 1977 most of my teaching has been an extension of my responsibilities as a professor at the University of Colorado at Denver.

Over the years I began to consolidate what I believe about teaching and learning. I have come to a number of conclusions:

❒ Learning is not limited to a change inside the skull; it is not merely a cognitive thing. Learning involves the "whole person"—changes in attitude, behavior, and thinking are all involved in one way or another.

❒ All learning involves adjustments in identity, whether the individual is learning to throw a pot in a weekend arts-and-craft class or picking up gardening techniques from a neighbor. Learning a second (or third, or fourth) language requires fundamental changes in one's sense of self.

❒ For this reason, language learning always involves some element of risk and anxiety. School is the site of tender negotiations for everyone, but it is an extremely risky place for English language learners.

❒ I have long since let go of the notion that I can make people learn what I want them to learn, and I have relaxed in how much detail I use to organize my lessons. I have concluded that teaching is a matter of creating environments for learning.

❐ Everyone is learning something all the time but very rarely the same thing. The best I can do is influence the direction of the learning. I cannot specify in advance *precisely* what is going to be learned, but I can increase the probability that some things will be learned by the way I organize classroom activities.

❐ Relatively recently, I tumbled to the fact that I was the individual doing the most learning in my classes. I am, after all, the individual who is always present semester after semester, who responds to events and adjusts techniques and activities according to what has occurred, who gives the most time and thought to how class time is used and how assignments relate to learning goals.

❐ I don't have to know all the answers to be a good teacher, and confusion—mine as well as that of the students—is not necessarily a bad thing. In fact, creating opportunities for students to teach each other and me might relieve some of the tension that often creeps into courses where everyone has learned to be just a bit defensive about what they know and don't know. My grandfather was fond of saying that we are all ignorant of something, and some scholars believe that it is important to savor your problems and confusions as opportunities of learning.

These are some of the ideas that I explore in this book. I realize that you are at a different stage of your career than I am and that you arrive with your own questions and problems. It is impossible to write a book that anticipates every reader's experience and point of view. But I can offer advice on your approach to the book; to that end, I encourage you to adopt four rules of thumb as you wrestle with the ideas and activities in these essays.[2]

❐ Be *critical*. Adopt a stance of thoughtful skepticism as you explore ways of teaching and learning. Step back, psychologically, and ask yourself, "What is the logic of this? Why should this be so? What are the assumptions behind this activity or that requirement? What are the merits/demerits of this idea? Who benefits from this view of reality?" Also, learn to question your own reactions to things: "Why am I feeling this way? How did I come to have this attitude?"

❐ As an extension of this critical stance, require that decisions and interpretations be *grounded* in reality. If someone (including me, a colleague, or an author of another text) makes a claim, ask yourself, "What sort of experience might support this assertion? How does this relate to my reality?" Of course, be prepared always to offer evidence in support of your own opinion. And, just as important, be prepared to yield to others if their experience is more authoritative than yours. This admonition requires you to look back, to evaluate ideas against your understanding of the past.

❏ Be *pragmatic* as you think about applications of ideas to the classroom (or to life in general, for that matter). As ideas or suggestions are offered, test them against your view of the world and your experience in schools to evaluate if they would be practical and reasonable ways of altering practice. This admonition requires you to look forward, to evaluate ideas according to their likelihood of success in the future.

❏ Be *prepared* to stretch your understanding of the effects of your actions; think broadly about your work and your spheres of responsibility. As you focus on a lesson, for example, think not only about what students are learning at the moment, but how that learning might carry over into their futures and into their lives outside of school. As you organize your teaching, think beyond the classroom to the ripple of your efforts in your school and community. In other words, assess your work according to the *scale* of effects that you may have. *Scale* refers to dimensions of space and time, and it is crucial that we understand that we are always working in the here and now, but our actions reverberate in places and events beyond the present.

The book is a work in progress (a somewhat disingenuous statement, given that you have paid your hard-earned money to acquire it), and I welcome your candid evaluations as you proceed. You can keep me informed of your thoughts, questions, and confusions by posting your comments on the website *www.press. umich.edu/esl/bookclub/*.

## Overview of Essays

All of the essays address questions faced by teachers as they work to solve problems encountered in the course of the day. The classroom is the most common point of departure and teaching decisions are the most closely scrutinized phenomena, but I also examine educational reform and institutional innovation. I am particularly interested in the intensely personal nature of language learning and cross-cultural communication, especially as these surface in classrooms as pedagogical problems or possibilities.

A theme that runs throughout the book concerns the importance of recognizing the range of choices we have as we work, and I repeatedly invoke the mantra of "teacher knows best." I trust that you will find this an affirming stance. At the same time I argue that the only person over whom you have any control is yourself, so if you are going to change things, you will have to start with who *you* are and how *you* teach.

Let me be clear on this point: If you want to exercise your proper authority as a teacher, you will have to change the way you think and the way you interact with others. I believe good teachers are always reflective practitioners and that they should also see themselves as theorists, philosophers, action researchers, and political activists. It is important for teachers to take an active role in school and community politics.

In other words, I think you'll find that reading this book will require more work than typically expected by teacher reference books.

And finally—perhaps most important—I believe teachers should cast themselves as learners in their classrooms and work to create environments in which the most frequently asked question is, "What have we learned here?"

Other questions arise as I consider the various arenas in which teachers are engaged. In what follows, I preface brief summaries of the essays with some of the questions addressed in the essays.

## 1. Ecological Perspectives of Teaching: Making Choices in a Complex World

❒ How do I organize my decision-making as I plan my teaching? How does one prioritize the work of the day?

❒ What are the choices I make for myself as I work, and what are the choices that others make for me?

❒ How do we achieve some modicum of agency, of professional discretion? What is the meaning of *agency* in this complex world or worlds?

Here I develop the framework within which all of the essays are organized. I believe we are plagued today by causal thinking—variations on "carrot and stick" approaches to teaching that cast both teachers and learners as balls on a billiard table, reacting unthinkingly to external forces. I argue that we need to adopt an ecological perspective of our work.

Succinctly stated, an ecological perspective uses the garden as a metaphor, rather than the assembly line or the theater. Teachers are seen as creators of environments that promote the healthy growth of their charges, rather than managers of learning or performers. Learners are seen as unique individuals whose curiosities require our attention and whose efforts require scaffolding. The implications of this approach are profound, and they impact all aspects of our work. Among the most significant is recognition of the fact that we cannot force students to learn. Just as the gardener provides a trellis for the rose bush, we provide activities that guide learners to focus on what we believe to be important. A related implication is that the content of the curriculum is less important than our relationships with students and the decisions we make as lessons proceed.

I tell the story of Gwen Hill, a veteran ESL teacher at CU Denver, as she negotiated a lesson with a group of Vietnamese refugees in the early 1980s. Gwen dumped her lesson plan in favor of a letter-writing campaign prompted by her students' discovery that the state legislature was considering limiting financial aid for studying English. The story illustrates why lesson planning is less important than planned listening. Gwen harnessed the energy of her students as she crafted a lesson that not only furthered her agenda and the curriculum but also taught valuable lessons in citizenship.

## 2. On Learning and (Therefore) Teaching

❒ What is learning?

❒ How do you know when someone (including yourself) has learned something?

❒ What is the relationship between your teaching and what your students are learning?

❒ How do your lessons reflect what your students are ready to learn?

❒ How do your lessons reflect what is expected of you by the curriculum?

It may seem too obvious to mention, but because teaching is all about fostering learning, teachers must have a clearly articulated theory of learning and be able to explain how their teaching promotes student learning. These sorts of questions frame the work of the day—lesson preparation, materials development, student assessment, etc.—but they also provide the basis for others' evaluation of your teaching. You need to be confident in your answers to questions such as these in order to participate effectively in school decision-making and in the debates that surround teaching today.

I use the story of Aimee Trechock's reading lesson to illustrate this point. She and seven children explore the motivations and adventures of a little boy and a mouse as they become friends in the children's book, *The Mouse and the Motorcycle.* I videotaped the lesson as part of a research project, and I have returned to one sequence again and again as I attempt to understand the relationship between focused grammar instruction on the one hand and communicative language teaching on the other. Here, I am interested in exploring the relationship between theories of learning and the classroom activities teachers develop to promote learning. I argue that there is no "ultimate" theory, that what matters is your own grasp of how your teaching fits with your theory of learning. I believe teachers need to be able to answer questions such as those listed in ways that both satisfy their sense of what is correct and that meet the expectations of parents (or corporate sponsors), administrators, and policy-makers.

## 3. Teaching as Learning, Learning as Life

❐ How do you organize your time with students? What information do you use to make teaching decisions?

❐ How do you adjust what you do tomorrow based on what you did today? How do you reflect on your daily practice so that it goes beyond thoughtful pondering in the shower or on the commute to work?

❐ How does one make decisions now that still seem like good ideas weeks and months from now?

❐ What are the "adjustments" required of you and others (colleagues, administrators, community members, for example) to improve the environment for learning?

No matter what lofty motivations brought you to the profession, if you cannot get organized for the day, you will be miserable as a teacher. Teaching may be about nurturing the minds and souls of learners, but it is also about the relentless assault of minutia, and once the school day is launched you have little time to catch your breath, much less engage in philosophical pondering about the value of one activity over another.

So it seems important to have a grand plan, an overall vision of your work that is grounded in worthy philosophical principles and sound theoretical perspectives. My recommendation is that you see yourself as a reflective practitioner and action researcher. I use a story of a colleague working with Latino children in rural Colorado to make the point that serious problems can rarely be solved at the level on which they are encountered.

Maria is a conscientious sixth grader who suddenly begins arriving late, missing school, and failing to do her assignments. The teacher faces some difficult choices—follow school policy and fail her or discover the source of her problems and work to improve conditions for her. What originally seemed like a straightforward set of pedagogical decisions turns out to be an extended quest for budgetary support for small-scale educational reform. The teacher succeeds in changing the system by doggedly asking questions and pursuing the answers with what can be described as action research at its best.

## 4. Philosophy as Autobiography

❒ What is a philosophy of teaching? Of what use is it and to whom? Who dictates what constitutes an adequate philosophy?

❒ Who are the authorities whose teachings guide my decision-making?

❒ How do I integrate my classroom experience into my philosophy?

❒ And a number of tactical questions: What should one include? What options are available for organizing it? How to maintain it, keep it fresh and relevant?

Most teachers I know are heartily sick of the teaching philosophy. It has become the symbol of bureaucratic intrusion, required in teacher education courses, job interviews, and school accreditation visits. No one reads them, and they serve no discernible purpose apart from institutional window dressing. If there ever was a professional equivalent of "Spare the rod and spoil the child," the teaching philosophy is the rod that the teacher has not been spared.

My response has been to take it on as my own personal project. After many years of resisting the requirement, of reluctantly dusting it off and grudgingly updating it every year for my annual review, I decided that this was a ridiculous farce. If I was going to spend so much time complying with the requirement, perhaps I should make it work for me rather than letting it work me over.

What I do in this essay is tell my own story and use it to illustrate an important point that none of us can escape: Who we are as teachers is a variation of who we are as human beings. If you are going to be an effective educator, you need to cultivate the habits of the philosopher and the autobiographer; you need to become more aware of who you are and how you learned to be you. I explore the assertion that personality and identity are socially negotiated entities and that you can expand your consciousness by reflecting on the relationships that have shaped your life. I trace my own propensities as a teacher to my rural Colorado upbringing, my love of books, the quiet serenity of libraries, and my wanderlust. I organize some activities that encourage you to discover how you learned to be you.

## 5. Authenticity in Language Teaching: Working Out the Bugs

❏ How can we harness the curiosity and enthusiasm that learners bring with them so that they master the knowledge and skills required by society?

❏ What can we do to create meaningful, authentic activities within the constraints of the required curriculum?

❏ What can we do to mitigate the pressures of school that often provoke resistance from students?

This essay recounts a class in which I taught from a newspaper as I tried to coax students into authentic conversation about a pleasingly bizarre event: the seven-year cycle of the cicada invasion in central United States. I use the story to examine the concept of *authenticity* and to develop principles for lesson preparation that improve our chances of authentic teaching.

I define *authenticity* as any experience that connects in meaningful ways with student experiences, interests, and aspirations. It is not a *thing;* it is an event. Authenticity emerges in the conduct of the lesson, the result of the focused, sensitive response of the teacher to the efforts of the students. It permits the individuals involved to experience the activity as having value *in and of itself,* apart from whatever significance it may have for the lesson.

I develop seven principles for lesson preparation and orchestration. Key among them is keeping one's core values in sight and establishing a rhythm and routine. I elaborate on Earl Stevick's criteria of *strong, transparent, and light,* and I emphasize the importance of nudging students toward critical thinking using activities that appeal to both head and heart.

## 6. Authenticity Revisited: Rhythm and Routine in Classroom Interaction

❏ How do I find the time to create authentic lessons as I cope with all the pressures of the day?

❏ How can I make lessons authentic when I am teaching with mandated curricula, textbook, and materials?

❏ How do I know if a lesson is authentic?

There are two problems with conventional thinking about authentic teaching: First, it is generally assumed that extensive planning and elaborate materials are required, and second, that the activities involved must be drawn from "real life," not the classroom.

I argue that authentic classroom experiences emerge from meaningful interactions between teacher and students, and that the key element is in the teacher managing to make a "shift of consciousness," getting inside the students' heads, in effect, and discovering how they see the world. This is the ultimate example of "starting where the learner is," and it gives the teacher a chance at orchestrating authentic lessons regardless of the materials being used.

I illustrate my points with excerpts from an ESL text, attempting to show how subtle adjustments as the lesson unfolds permit the teacher to move in close to the students, focusing on the language being learned and checking and extending comprehension as relationships deepen.

## 7. Teachers and Gurus

❒ How do we get students to take responsibility for their learning—how do we balance control and initiative in activities?

❒ How does one keep up with the scholarly work in the field? How do you integrate the advice of experts into your teaching?

❒ How does one respond to educational mandates from administrators and policy-makers?

Perhaps all professions are the same, but it seems to me that teaching has more than its share of bandwagons and gurus. In the current climate of accountability, teachers are required to implement "scientifically based" teaching and to defend their practices by citing the authorities on which their classroom activities are based. It is impossible to participate effectively in curriculum decisions or even coffee shop discussions about teaching without being up to date on the latest acronyms and professional personalities. I know from working with novice teachers that this is a daunting aspect of entering the profession, but I can assure you neophytes that it is not a piece of cake for veterans either.

In this essay I argue that you need to balance the dictates of gurus with your own common sense understanding of what works. For many years I have used a technique called "the blackboard composition" as a way of teaching writing. I tell the story of one lesson in which international students were trying to make sense of contemporary values surrounding love and courtship in the

United States, and I argue that the success of that lesson depended more on the choices I made than on the wisdom of gurus. I use this experience as the basis for arguing that you need to develop a "higher consciousness" about your work, one that permits you to see yourself as a shaper of the trends and fashions of educational discourse rather than as a consumer. You have to become your own authority for your teaching.

## 8. Teaching to Standards: How to and Why Not

❏ What are standards? Where do they come from, and how do they influence our thinking and behavior?

❏ Whose standards count?

❏ How can I position myself to balance external mandates against my own sense of what is right?

Given the realities of education today, how do teachers cope with the demands under which they work, and how do they maintain some semblance of professional discretion? My answers to the questions posed in the title are simple: Do your best work for the benefit of your students, use the standards as a checklist after the lesson to assess what you have accomplished, and decide how you are going to proceed. The "why not" portion of the answer revolves around the age-old tension between internal and external authority: Do NOT organize your teaching merely to comply with a mandate; maintain your own view of what is required for your students. Work as if you were self-employed.

## 9. Changing Schools: Creating Disturbances and Alarming Your Friends

❏ How can schools adjust policies and procedures—and even more important, norms, routines, and daily rhythms—to provide a healthy learning environment for English language learners?

❏ What are the roles and responsibilities of the individual classroom teacher in promoting the larger systemic changes of the sort required by these questions?

❏ How does one adjust one's thinking and daily activity to move oneself and the school toward these goals?

My argument here is simple: You need to be teaching in a school that values your contributions and that is organized around your priorities. If you discover this is not the case and you decide that change is unlikely, it is time for you to change schools.

I do not find it surprising in general that institutions are slow to change or that schools and universities espouse values that they have difficulty putting into practice—it is the nature of systems to resist change. In fact, if you were to adopt an aggressive approach to the democratic inclusion of non–English speaking students in your school, you would indeed alarm your friends and colleagues because the smooth functioning of the institution and the habitual calm of everyone involved depend on practices that assume that everyone speaks English and shares the broad cultural assumptions of the mainstream English-speaking world.

It is clear to me that changing this situation is a gargantuan task, and not one that English language teachers are going to accomplish in my lifetime, perhaps not for generations to come. However, I provide an opportunity for contemplation about how you might approach a project of linguistic democracy in your school, and I offer some ways of thinking about the issue that you might find intriguing….or not, depending on how you feel about alarming your friends.

## 10. It's All One Thing

In this chapter I reiterate my argument that there is only one thing: life. All human beings and all enduring collections of human beings—families, communities, classrooms, schools, etc.—are open systems functioning according to a handful of principles. If we understand those principles, we stand a chance of achieving some peace of mind as we grapple with the overwhelming complexity of the problems we are trying to solve. I summarize the principal arguments of the book, and I offer three suggestions for coping with the complexity: Identify the boundaries of your efforts; work within yourself; focus on what you are doing *now.*

**One last word or two….**

You will have noticed that all the essays are keyed to questions. I have amended them countless times in response to readers' comments and confusions. I'm not confident that I have, in fact, captured the most important ones, but I remain convinced that the questions matter as much, if not more, than the answers. As we work to create dialogues with others, I think our most important behavior may be this act of constantly questioning. And, of course, listening to the answers we get.

On reading the essays: The way I have organized the book puts the more general arguments first—the ones that address theory, philosophy, and action research—followed by essays in which classroom teaching and school activism are the focus. But I intended for each essay to constitute an argument unto itself, so you should be able to read them in any order that strikes you as interesting.

You will, of course, follow your own inclinations in any case....

## REFERENCES

Clarke, M. A. (2003). *A place to stand: essays for educators in troubled times.* Ann Arbor: University of Michigan Press.

Clarke, M. A., Davis, A. W., Rhodes, L. K., & Baker, E. D. (1998). Principles of collaboration in school/university partnerships. *TESOL Quarterly, 32,* 592–600.

Diamond, J. (1999). *Guns, germs, and steel: The fates of human societies.* New York: W.W. Norton & Co.

———. (2005). *Collapse: How societies choose to fail or succeed.* New York: Viking.

Friedman, T. L. (1999). *The lexus and the olive tree: Understanding globalization.* New York: Farrar, Straus and Giroux.

———. (2005). *The world is flat: A brief history of the twenty-first century.* New York: Farrar, Straus and Giroux.

Kegan, R., & Lahey, L. L. (2001). *How the way we talk can change the way we work: Seven languages for transformation.* San Francisco: Jossey-Bass.

## NOTES

1. Excerpted from an article by Dave Curtin, *Denver Post* staff writer, Friday, September 10, 2004. (Full article available at *www.denverpost.com* archives.)

2. These admonitions are excerpted from an article that appeared in *TESOL Quarterly* some years ago. From "Principles of Collaboration in School/University Partnerships," by M. A. Clarke, A. W. Davis, L. K. Rhodes, & E. D. Baker, 1998, *TESOL Quarterly, 32,* pp. 592–600.

# ❶ Ecological Perspectives of Teaching: Making Choices in a Complex World

In this essay I set out my understanding of the way the world works and begin to make a case for how we might more effectively approach our responsibilities as teachers of English language learners. I address these questions:

❒ How do I organize my decision-making as I plan my teaching? How does one prioritize the work of the day?

❒ What are the choices I make for myself as I work, and what are the choices that others make for me?

❒ How do we achieve some modicum of agency, of professional discretion? What is the meaning of agency in this complex world or worlds?

My responses to these sorts of questions are grounded in my understanding of systems theory, with liberal borrowings from anthropology, social psychology, cultural/historical perspectives, and critical theory—all of which is pretty abstract, I admit. So I use anecdotes and narratives to anchor my explorations as I struggle to achieve a balance between theoretical clarity and scholarly rigor on the one hand, and believability and usefulness on the other. I have found stories of personal experience to be helpful in clarifying issues and focusing my decision-making. The story that follows, for example, helps me understand how teachers might balance the demands of the curriculum with the interests and anxieties of students.

### GWEN HILL'S CHOICES

A number of years ago I was observing Gwen Hill's ESL class at the University of Colorado at Denver when she responded to a situation in a remarkable way—"remarkable" because it illustrates the complexity of teaching English language learners, not because it was in any way out of the ordinary for her or, I suspect, for most accomplished teachers.

My observation was part of the requirements of the graduate program Gwen was completing, so technically I was there as her mentor. However, I had been looking forward to the observation as an opportunity to learn more about her and her students. She was one of the first ESL teachers I met when I arrived in Denver, and I knew her to be a seasoned veteran. And she was working with a group of students with whom I had had relatively little contact—Vietnamese refugees.

Gwen had prepped me on what she had planned for the morning, and the truth is I can't remember exactly what she was intending to do, but it probably had to do with the usual stuff of English classes—subjects and predicates, topic sentences and paragraph structure. And I'm sure she was using a textbook, but that too has slipped from memory. The point is that she had done her customary job of preparing her lesson—perhaps even more than usual because I was going to be there—and she was ready to go.

Most of the students were already in the classroom when we arrived, but they were oblivious to our arrival. They were gathered around one student's desk, and the raucous nasality of Vietnamese and Chinese echoed off the walls of the old Tramway Building where the class met. The students had just learned about legislation pending on the Hill (state government) that would limit the number of years that state funds would be available to support English instruction for immigrants and refugees. They were attempting to make sense of the newspaper article, but it was a struggle because of their limited English proficiency. When they saw Gwen, they swarmed around her demanding that she tell them what the story said.

She declined.

But she quickly organized the lesson around the newspaper. While the students returned to their desks to get ready for class, she skimmed the article and got the drift. I don't remember if there were multiple copies of the newspaper in the class or if she cut the story into pieces, but the next scene is clear in my mind's eye: Small groups of students huddled around several desks, intensely engaged in deciphering the story guided by the questions Gwen had written on the board— basic comprehension questions that focused on main ideas, vocabulary, and implications for the students.

Gwen then orchestrated a discussion by the whole class using what each group of readers had learned. The students calmed down a bit when they realized that they were not facing immediate loss of scholarships and loans; the legislative process had just begun and the proposal to limit funds was in the preliminary stages. In other words, there was a chance of influencing the legislation. "Perhaps you should write letters to your representatives," Gwen suggested.

A major hullabaloo followed, composed of equal parts civics lesson on the progress of a bill toward law in the Colorado legislature and an English lesson on how to write a persuasive letter. Native languages figured in as much as English, but the energy never subsided, and by the time the class ended the students had their rough drafts and their deadlines for revision. I don't know what followed in subsequent sessions, but I would not be surprised to learn that the students sent the letters or that Gwen engineered a trip to the Capitol to hear the debates on the bill. I do know that the outcome was far less dire than the students originally feared it would be, and that the students finished their English studies and continued their education.

## On Seeing Our Choices: Teaching as Decision-Making

It was the sort of class teachers dream of—totally focused students engaged in an authentic convergence of personal priorities and curriculum goals. We should all be so lucky, every day of the week.

But—and this is my point—it wasn't a matter of luck.

Or, rather, as my wrestling coach used to say, "Luck is when opportunity meets preparation." Gwen had planned for the class; she had a lesson plan that fit in the general trajectory of the semester's curriculum. And, she knew her students—both their linguistic competence and their life challenges. But her preparation was much more profound; it was a combination of technical competence and opportunistic attitude. To an inexperienced teacher or uninformed observer, the scene that day might have appeared chaotic and unproductive. It *was* chaotic, but it was certainly *not* unproductive.

Gwen saw the students' energy and anxiety as an opportunity to be exploited, not an obstacle to her lesson plan. She made a number of strategic choices that went beyond the details of English grammar and vocabulary, and she permitted the lesson to emerge rather than trying to force the students to comply with her lesson plans.

She saw that her choices were not limited to the immediate world of the classroom. In addition to responding to students' anxieties, she orchestrated activities that both addressed the curriculum she was responsible for teaching and permitted students to get a glimpse of how they might participate in civic debate.

In order for this story to be more than a pleasing anecdote about a resourceful teacher, I need to shift focus slightly and examine what happened on a more abstract plane. The story permits me to introduce themes that shape this book. Let me elaborate on elements of this lesson that I believe all of us in education need to understand, especially those of us working with English language learners.

First and most important, teaching involves human relationships. Good teaching involves authentic engagement between people around things that matter. *Things that matter*—both to the students and to the teacher. Gwen responded to the students not as a teacher with a plan that required everyone to postpone their emotions and focus on the lessons of the day, but as an ally and fellow citizen, someone who was aware of the students' lives beyond school and who understood how the political debate brewing in the legislature and in the newspapers was going to affect their lives. Make no mistake—Gwen was in charge of the class. She *was* the teacher, and they *were* the students. But she was able to balance the constraints of her *role* as teacher with the more pressing demands of her *relationship* with the students as she improvised the session. She covered the curriculum that day, but she adjusted her approach to accommodate the interests and energies of the students.

Second, just as teaching involves more than didactic presentation of subject matter content, learning involves more than mastery of the material. The students in Gwen's class were learning important lessons about themselves as human beings even as they were learning facts about the English language. They were discovering that they were citizens in a democracy as well as learners of English. In this book I define learning as *change over time through engagement in activity*, and I position English language teachers as shapers of identity and culture by virtue of the fact that, day in and day out, they are creating activities in which learners gradually come to define who they are. The stance may strike you as a bit grandiose, but I argue that the mundane business of getting through the day involves us all, willy-nilly, in the task of negotiating our own identities and those of our students in multiple worlds—classroom, school, and community. This is particularly true of teachers working with English language learners.

Third, I want to frame Gwen's approach to her teaching as "ecological," although I'm confident that this is not how she thought about it at the time. Ecologists study the relationship between organisms and their environment, and when Gwen acknowledged the importance of the pending legislation to the welfare of her students, she accurately assessed the relative importance of politics and school; she understood that the opportunities available that morning required her to step away from the curriculum and her lesson plan and to move toward the realities of her students' lives.

Among other things (the recognition that we cannot unilaterally force students to learn, for example), an ecological perspective of teaching asks us to understand our classrooms as open systems, functioning to maintain stability, and loosely coupled with other open systems—the school, the community, and larger social and economic contexts. This view permits us to see opportunities for learning and options for teaching that otherwise might not be visible.[1]

These three assertions about the lesson seem merited by the facts as I have told the story. What is less visible is the role that Gwen played in the institution and in the profession. I believe that her leadership at the university and in the English language teaching community played an important part in the way she conducted the class. She knew that she had the authority to modify the lesson to respond to the students' interests. And, I suspect, her views on language teaching were having an impact on the profession in Colorado.

Times were simpler then, it is true, and accreditation standards and institutional mandates did not intrude on the daily business of teaching to the extent that they do now. But in the context of the times, Gwen's discretion in how she conducted the lesson and her inventiveness in responding to student concerns were a function of the fact that she viewed herself as a leader, both in the university and in the field of English as a second language. Gwen had a voice in how English was being taught to the waves of refugees at the university because she was part of a small group of professionals working to increase the chances of these students as they arrived in the Denver area.

She was also active in CoTESOL (Colorado Teachers of English to Speakers of Other Languages), the state affiliate of the international organization, TESOL (www.tesol.org; www.colorado.edu/iec/cotesol/). Gwen served on the board of CoTESOL, and she regularly presented papers and workshops at the annual conferences. She served as the publisher liaison for the organization and worked to make sure that local teachers had access to the latest ideas in the profession. I will return to this point on many occasions, hoping to convince you that, however distant they may seem, institutional policies and societal politics are legitimate territory for teacher activity.

Let me now move through the same territory with a more analytical lens, constructing an argument for viewing teaching as a scholarly activity involving active participation in a number of overlapping contexts.

## An Ecological View of English Language Teaching

A key element in an ecological perspective is the awareness of the interconnectedness of individuals, institutions, and communities—systems within systems within systems. In order to work effectively, the teacher-as-ecologist recognizes that problems encountered on one level—the classroom, for example—are inextricably intertwined with elements of school policy and community politics. The ecologically minded activist realizes that problems are rarely solved at the level they are encountered.

For example, you may be dismayed to learn that you have too many students or that the range of language ability of your students is too great for you to effectively teach. You will probably not be surprised to learn, however, that you cannot solve the problem by sending a group of the students down the hall to the director's or principal's office to be reassigned to other classrooms. Nor are you likely to tell the students to go home because you would rather not deal with their problems in your classroom. In other words, community demographics and school policy dictate the composition of your classroom; if you are going to have a say in the profile of your learners, you will need to become involved in decision-making before the first day of school.

If you concede this point, you will agree that teachers need to exercise leadership roles in schools and in the broader social and educational communities if they are going to be successful. In other words, teaching is not merely a classroom activity.

You may greet this assertion with skepticism, so let me elaborate.

There was a time, we are told, when teachers merely had to close their classroom doors to focus on the education of their charges. This is no longer the case, if in fact it ever was. The noise that assails English language teachers today is not merely the raucous exchanges of students in the hallway; added to this relatively benign distraction are suspicions of foreigners (and anyone who works with/for them or who speaks up on their behalf), public and political clamoring for high test scores, administrative mandates to comply with standardized curricula, professional pressures for teaching to reflect research, and the urgent, if often inarticulate, pleas from students to respect their cultural and linguistic heritage.

Which is to say that the pressures teachers face are complex and inextricably intertwined. The most obvious ones come from the classroom. Being an effective teacher requires technical competence in planning and orchestrating lessons. But today we are forced to cope with a bewildering array of external demands, and if we are to do more than merely comply with someone else's mandates, we will have to become school leaders, community liaisons, and political activists. Although the details vary depending on one's position and locale, it seems to me that this is a requirement of everyone in the profession. Since it is not possible to give all these roles equal attention all of the time, a principled stance toward the powerful forces that shape our lives is required. It is helpful therefore to try to get a handle on those forces and to conceptualize the problems in such a way that we can deal with them. What are the sources of pressure on educators these days? Here is my take on the situation.

First and foremost, there are the students—adults or children, speakers of one or many languages, literate or illiterate in their native tongue, educated or not in their home country, small classes or large classes. This is the center of teacher attention. We spend most of our days preparing lessons and orchestrating classroom activities. These are the pressures that seem most immediate, most real. The fact that we have signed contracts to meet this responsibility is only part of the story; having to face individuals every day who have paid for our services and whose futures are at stake assures that we will spend significant time and energy on class preparation. In addition, because of the multiple demands on students as newcomers to an English-speaking world, the sense of responsibility often extends beyond the formal requirements of the school. Most English language teachers have logged many hours helping students and their families with the pressing problems of transportation, shopping, and child care. The difficulties for immigrant students have become more serious in recent years, and today teachers may find themselves working on visas, testifying at deportation hearings, and writing letters to immigration authorities.

Institutional and societal pressures are also changing. For a variety of political and economic reasons, the diversity of the student population in schools has increased dramatically. The inevitable difficulties caused by this demographic change directly affect teachers in classrooms, but it has also shifted the harsh glare of the political spotlight onto schools, exacerbating the pressures for accountability from the public, policy-makers, and politicians. Laws are written to cover areas that traditionally were left to professional discretion.

This pressure is passed along to teachers in the form of standardized curricula, high-stakes testing, accreditation reviews, and other forms of institutional accounting.

Less direct, but increasingly more insistent, are the expectations of society in general and the response by politicians to those expectations—tighter immigration controls, restriction of services to immigrant families, increased scrutiny by public officials of matters that have traditionally been considered the province of social workers and community volunteers.

The official response to these sorts of educational mandates comes from professional organizations in a variety of forms—standards for instruction and assessment, guidelines for evaluating programs, research on teaching and learning that establishes norms for professional conduct. At first glance this seems reasonable and helpful—nationally (and perhaps internationally) recognized groups of individuals whose responsibility it is to speak for teachers everywhere. But this service is not without risk to the individual teachers because the decisions made by such groups contribute to a generalized pressure for conformity that teachers experience in a variety of ways—restricted choices of texts and materials, official and unofficial sanction of teaching methods, expectations of professional conduct. This often seems to be a combination of professional fashion and political correctness. The shifting trends of research and scholarly writing may seem far removed from the realities of the classroom, but they contribute to the educational climate, and we need to pay attention to this arena of action if we want to influence the environment within which we work.

Laid out like this, the educational scene appears to be a stormy sea and teachers castaways grasping for flotsam just to keep our heads above water. I don't want to promote an alarmist perspective, but I also do not want to minimize the threats to our daily work. The task is to figure out how to align ourselves to the winds that are blowing across the educational seascape, which can be captured by focusing on five contexts of activity.

❐ *Person-to-Person:* Teaching always boils down to a not-quite-simple fact of human contact, of relationships with learners. Whether I have 15 or 150 students, the quality of their learning hinges on my ability to foster authentic connections with each of them.

❐ *Classroom:* The group is more than the sum of the parts, so I cannot count on the fact that good relationships with individuals will translate into a smoothly operating classroom. But it helps. Effective instruction depends on my being able to organize activities that engage students' attention and occupy their time. Methods and materials figure in to this in a major way as do models of classroom management, but I argue that these are merely tools in the hands of the resourceful teacher, not answers to problems.

❏ *School:* Healthy interpersonal relationships cannot be fostered in an unhealthy school climate. Teaching is, in fact, as much an institutional accomplishment as an individual *tour de force.* Good teachers can be rendered ineffective by a bad school, and inept teachers become better in a good school. It is up to us as individuals to provide leadership in our schools if we want policies and procedures that support our vision of learning and teaching.

❏ *Community:* Schools exist in the public sphere, buffeted by anxiety about educational achievement and drooping test scores, international terrorism, and global economic and military tensions. More and more these pressures bear directly on schools and teachers. It is important to participate in debates that once seemed distant from our responsibilities as teachers. Take two examples: School vouchers that permit students to attend schools of their choice disproportionately increase the discretion of the affluent and powerful. Centralized decision-making and legislated educational decisions aimed at distributing resources across all students also work to reduce the choices of teachers in their daily work. We must work to ensure that educational issues are understood, not merely as planks in political platforms, but as the foundation of basic human rights and the basis for daily decision-making that directly affects students' and teachers' lives.

❏ *Professional Organizations:* The discourse shapes the climate within which we work, and we cannot afford to cede expert commentary to professional pundits. When legislation about school funding is pending, when public disputes about school boundaries or immigration laws hit the newspaper, when teacher contracts become the focus of debates about how to deal with linguistic and cultural diversity in the classroom—policy-makers and newspaper columnists turn to "experts," and very often the only individuals available for comment are the luckless souls who are in charge of organizing the annual conference of the local professional organization. They didn't think of themselves as "experts," but they suddenly realize they know more about the issues and have more opinions about the solutions than lawmakers and school administrators. We must look upon volunteer jobs in professional organizations as opportunities to shape public policy, rather than merely taking responsibility for organizing the book raffle at the publishers' exhibit.

Imagine five concentric and overlapping force fields that influence your decision-making on a regular basis (see page 28). That's you in the middle, the tall figure, and the smaller figures represent your students. Each sphere represents the five contexts that I just sketched, five sets of options from which you choose your next move as the day unfolds. The ovals extend to the left indicating the past and to the right signifying the future.[2]

Most of the school day is spent in dealing with students—individually or in groups—and our success depends greatly on our ability to adjust responses in ways that improve the quality of the relationships we have with them. The inner oval represents the immediate demands of the interpersonal constraints on our teaching. These are typically brief exchanges during class or in the halls, but they also include extended conversations about school and life.

The next oval represents the classroom—fifty minutes or all day, depending on your situation, of focused attention to the flow of action from blackboard to textbook, from didactic presentation to small group work and individualized instruction.

The third oval is meant to invoke our work in the school. The rhythms of our involvement in school activity typically follow longer cycles—perhaps a weekly staff meeting or periodical conferences with supervisors or colleagues around student problems or curricular decision-making. The extent to which these are pleasant or onerous depends on a variety of factors, among which issues of power—gender, ethnicity, seniority, etc.—are probably the most salient. Most teachers view these responsibilities as "administrivia"—tiresome chores around mundane matters such as student placement, grading policies, curriculum modification, and testing—but they represent important fulcrum points for influencing decisions that impact our teaching.

The fourth and fifth ovals represent the cycles associated with the sociopolitical and professional forces in our lives. These may be more difficult to envision, and their effects may be harder to see in the daily grind than the first three ovals. They revolve around the political and academic calendar. For example, election years increasingly bring scrutiny of schools and teachers, and there is a frenzy associated with late summer that can be easily connected to the academic calendar. Our awareness of professional issues will depend on how involved we are in the organizations; the arrival of a monthly newsletter or quarterly journal may signal opportunities to stay abreast of current funding opportunities or the latest teaching techniques, and the annual or semi-annual pilgrimage to conventions may be a time of rejuvenation or time off from the grind.

I suspect that you haven't thought about your life this way. Maybe it's just "one day at a time" or "if I can just get through this crisis and move on to something better." Or, "I'll get to that when the dust settles from this latest crisis." We experience life as an onslaught of events, and we often feel overwhelmed by the sheer number and intensity of experiences.

However, we are not dealing with new challenges every day, but rather, points in recurring cycles of activity. Each moment has its elements of novelty and surprise, but it is rare for something to happen that is not an example of a situation we have dealt with before. Recognizing the pattern, appreciating the cycle, permits us to learn from experience and to accumulate strategies for dealing with the recurrent facts of school life.

Back to the concentric ovals for a minute: Notice that they are all touching at a particular moment. That moment is now. The smallest oval represents a cycle of a few moments, and the other ovals represent larger loops of time. Yes, I am dealing with this group of learners at this particular moment, but each of us represents a history and a potential future. There is a natural rhythm in the world of school, one that is punctuated by class sessions, break time, out-of-school activities, the school week, and the school term. There is also the rhythm associated with the major holidays and exam schedule of the year. As I make decisions and react to situations, I am aware of all these loops. I am aware of the political climate in which I am teaching—strained economy, military confrontations, growing ethnic and religious tensions—and the educational environment of mandated curricula and high-stakes testing. And I am also aware of the more amorphous cycles of professional discourse—the rhythms of theoretical and methodological trends that shape institutional and personal decision-making.

It is important to avoid thinking too literally about the graphic, but at the same time the illustration does depict an important aspect of reality—it is cyclical, and some events come around more quickly than others. My success in moving learners toward my goals will depend on my ability to respond appropriately in the moment. I have an infinite number of options at any moment, but the actions I take will be shaped by my understanding of the myriad constraints emerging from those cycles. And it is not merely the response of the moment but the long-range ripples of the actions I take today and their effect on the future.

Which brings us back to the title of this book—*Common Ground, Contested Territory.*

Let me bear down on this point a bit: We are involved in a noble endeavor—teaching—and we need to be active players in the education game. We need to be heard in the debates that shape the lives of learners, whether those debates occur in the teachers' lounge, staff meetings, or larger political and professional arenas. There is wide agreement on the importance of education; that is the *common ground* we share with virtually all thoughtful individuals on the planet. At the same time, the goals of formal learning, the importance and nature of schools, the content of curriculum, and the conduct of teachers and learners all represent the *contested territory* that I want to examine in this book.

I would like to avoid bellicose metaphors and aggressive stances, and I believe that it is important to resist polarization and politicization as we attempt to forge agreements on what is important and how to proceed. Ours is a sacred trust. Parents send their children to us. Countries entrust their future leaders to our care. Individuals, desperate to participate in the prosperity they see all around them, spend disproportionate amounts of their scarce resources for tuition so that they can better themselves. It seems important to do our work with humble awareness of the importance of our charge.

But this is not a candidate's speech intended to get you involved in new and different activities; I am not encouraging you to drop everything you have been doing and rush out and volunteer for a campaign or to throw your body in front of a curriculum reform train.

Rather, I hope to engage you in a pleasurable and thought-provoking journey over familiar terrain. You are a learner, this I know, because you are, or soon will be, a teacher. So you will recognize the landscape—classrooms and schools, primarily. But I am also interested in exploring the imagination of teachers and learners and the multi-faceted world of cultural identity and interpersonal interaction that makes teaching such an exciting and exacting profession. I am assuming that if you are reading this book you believe in the capacity of learners to respond creatively to the world with all its demands. And I trust that you would agree that teachers are among the most influential participants in shaping that response.

## Conclusions and Provocations

From an ecological perspective teaching is seen as a matter of creating environments and nudging people toward your goals. It is a matter of creating activities and, once things are under way, responding to what students are doing in ways that you view as productive. Viewed from a distance, such behavior might easily be confused with a commonly held notion of teaching as a procedure, and there are some days that do flow in uncomplicated ways within the framework you have established. But, in fact, it is a much more nuanced view of teaching than the one provided by a methods and materials perspective.

The significance of this approach is that it underscores the role of the teacher as decision-maker. Let me conclude by ruminating on the questions with which I began this essay.

❏ How do I organize my decision-making as I plan my teaching? How does one prioritize the work of the day?

The trick is to make decisions that not only respond to the exigencies of the moment, but that also stand up to scrutiny over time. I develop this idea in more detail in subsequent essays, so here it is only necessary to invoke the ideal of *coherence*, that fleeting state where my philosophical commitments align with the mundane decisions I am making on a minute-by-minute basis (Clarke, 2003). I need to be clear on my core commitments, and I need to understand how the details of my behavior right now will map onto the longer temporal landscape of the semester and school year. So, I work to keep the larger picture in mind as I deal with the immediate pressures of the school day. At the very least, I want to avoid crass expediency and comfortable routine as the day unfolds. I remind myself that situations that seem compelling may not, in fact, turn out to be all that important, and I work to distinguish between the two.

❏ What are the choices I make for myself as I work, and what are the choices that others make for me?

Of course, the important thing to keep in mind is that I do, indeed, have choices, and that those choices are not all at the same level of scale; that is, some decisions affect only the immediate situation, while others have implications for longer periods of time and space. I am responsible for what happens next in a lesson, with almost total discretion in my response, but if I choose to ignore curriculum mandates in the next few minutes I will need to adjust my behavior in the coming days. Or, if I decide that a particular unit or chunk of text does not merit the attention it has been allotted, I may need to volunteer to serve on the curriculum committee so I have a say in the mandates. But merely understanding that all these decisions involve choices and that I need to partici-pate in their formulation is an important step in the right direction.

❏ How do we achieve some modicum of agency, of professional discretion? What is the meaning of agency in this complex world or worlds?

In other words, how do we carve out territory, and how do we negotiate healthy decision-making? And how do we create common ground with others? The key element of effective decision-making and incisive action is recognizing our spheres of influence and working sensitively within them. Related to this is the importance of being clear on our convictions and knowing what we want. I'm not talking about grandiose public gestures here, but rather, the day-to-day stuff of schools and classrooms—decisions about curriculum, tests, and grades, discipline, parent-teacher conferences, hallway bulletin boards, agendas for faculty meetings, textbook adoption, and hallway passes.

*Agency* and *professional discretion* refer to the range of choices available to us, and our ability to act decisively in ways that are consistent with our core values and in concert with what we believe is important for our students. In other words, we need to attend to the minute particulars of our daily responsibilities even as we keep our eyes on the larger issues.

## REFERENCES

Bateson, G. (1999). *Steps to an ecology of mind*. Chicago: University of Chicago Press.

Brown, H. D. (2007). *Principles of language learning and teaching* (5th ed.). New York: Longman.

Clarke, M. A. (2003). *A place to stand: Essays for educators in troubled times*. Ann Arbor: University of Michigan Press.

van Lier, L. (2000). From input to affordance: Social-interactive learning from an ecological perspective. In J. P. Lantolf (Ed.), *Sociocultural theory and second language learning* (pp. 245–260). Oxford: Oxford University Press.

———. (2004). *The ecology and semiotics of language learning*. Dordrecht, The Netherlands: Kluwer Academic Publishing.

## NOTES

1. Ecology as a metaphor for understanding teaching and learning has received considerable attention, and it is a central theme in this book. See, for example, Brown (2007) and van Lier (2000, forthcoming). The topic is developed in more detail in the essay on pages 62–83.

2. This presentation is based on the definition of context developed by the anthropologist Gregory Bateson (1999, p. 289): "we may regard 'context' as a collective term for all those events which tell the organism among what *set* of alternatives he must make his next choice." Every day, all of the time, we make decisions based on the alternatives presented by a situation that is in our face at the moment as well as our understanding of larger issues and distant situations.

# ❷ On Learning and (Therefore) Teaching

From the file of stories I would like to see on the front page of the *New York Times* and *Washington Post*:

---

## Scientists Discover Humans Cannot *Not* Learn!

No matter what we are doing, we are learning, according to the report. The question is, are students learning what is being taught or are they learning that they do not want to play the game? The research calls into question mandated curricula and methods and throws the educational community into turmoil.

BOSTON, MA—The *New England Journal of Education* today released a report on three centuries of scientific research that conclusively refutes the notion that there are "best practices" or "proven methods" of teaching, throwing legislative committees into marathon sessions to reapportion funds earmarked for mandated curricula and high-stakes testing.

The research team, led by the eminent philosopher/educator John Dewey, and assisted by such notables as Gregory Bateson, Maria Montessori, and Margaret Mead, reviewed masses of test data and conducted hundreds of hours of ethnographic observation of learners of all ages. They concluded that the subject matter being taught was less important than the way lessons were conducted.

"It's actually common sense," said Dewey, speaking from his book-lined office. From birth, the human being is taking in data and making sense of it, adapting to events and situations and changing according to circumstances. This is the essence of learning and should be used as the model in our teaching; unfortunately, we have become so engrossed in the institution of teaching that we have forgotten to attend to learning.

---

The clipping is fictional, but the story is true. Human beings are mean-ing-making animals, constructing sense out of all experience and using that understanding to attain their goals. This is a good news/bad news situation. The good news is that we cannot stop our students from learning; to be alive and active is to be learning. The bad news is that they may not be learning what we think we are teaching; that is, our carefully prepared lesson plans and the curriculum that we are following may not be the focus of their attention. This has at least three important implications.

1. You should attend as much to the activity your students are engaged in as to the subject-matter content of the lesson.
2. Informal assessment—your observation of learners—is just as important as formal evaluation (including standardized tests) in determining what students have learned.
3. Your theory of learning must be constructed as much from an analysis of your ongoing classroom experience as from the writing of eminent theorists.

This is not to say that you should throw out curriculum guides and text-books, or that you should ignore the data from standardized tests, or that you cannot benefit from educational research and the proclamations of experts.

But it does mean that you should be just as thoughtful about the activi-ties you organize for your students as you are about the facts you want them to learn. And the scrutiny needs to be both backward and forward; you need to spend equal time evaluating the day as you do in planning it. Some of the learning occurring in your classroom will include the usual fare of subjects and verbs, main ideas and topic sentences, of course, but students will also infer from your lessons what sorts of people they are, what it means to be a learner, and what their responsibilities are as citizens of the world.

As teachers we need to be clear on what we think about learning. It is what we get paid to promote in our classrooms, and it is the basis on which we are evaluated. We need to be able to define it, show how our practice promotes it, defend our perspective with scholarly citations, and argue for curricular and programmatic changes based on that perspective.

This has always been the case, I suspect, but today teaching positions and school accreditations hinge on the answers to questions such as these:

❏ What is learning?
❏ How do you know when someone (including yourself) has learned some-thing?

❐ What is the relationship between your teaching and what your students are learning?

❐ How do your lessons reflect what your students are ready to learn?

❐ How do your lessons reflect what is expected of you by the curriculum?

In this essay, I want to examine possible answers to questions like these, and I want to explore the climate in which the questions are asked. In particular I'm interested in the issue of who gets to frame the debate. We need to be working toward a time when the people closest to the students are the ones whose answers count and whose voices are heeded when disputes arise.

To ground the effort, think of a lesson you taught recently and use your memory of it to scribble your answers to the questions in the box that follows. If you do not yet have a teaching position, think of a situation in which you informally taught someone something—how to use a piece of software, how to mulch a rose garden, how to adjust a tennis swing, for example. You should be able to give rough answers to all but the last question, and later on I will discuss the meaning of "curriculum" in a way that will permit you to respond to that as well.

If you found the task difficult, take heart. In spite of the fact that everyone agrees that the primary purpose of teaching is to foster learning, the task of defining learning and connecting it unambiguously to teaching is not at all straightforward. Part of the reason is that there is considerable debate among scholars about what constitutes learning. Experts from different eras emphasize different aspects of the process, technology improves and permits different data to enter the debates, and theoretical perspectives change as researchers adjust their views of the purpose and uses of research.

The scholarly debate about the nature of learning is only part of the difficulty, however. A bigger issue has to do with who is doing the asking and what personal or political stake she or he has in the answers. For example, put yourself in the position of the teacher being asked questions like these, and imagine the different ways you would feel if the questioner is a friend at a dinner party compared with, say, your immediate supervisor, the irate parent or employer of one of your students, or the local investigative reporter for the tabloid newspaper. Definitions of learning, whether explicit or implicit, influence political and administrative decision-making, and it may be the case that your definition, while perfectly adequate for you in the classroom, is considered irrelevant by administrators or politicians who shape the environment in which you teach.

Each of us has to answer questions like these for ourselves first so that we can use the answers to guide our own classroom practice. Then, we need to examine the various situations in which our perspective might be used to shape decisions of larger scope—school discussions of curriculum development and student evaluation, or presentations to community members on the rationale for student placement, program development, or discontinuance, for example. It would be nice if we didn't have to pay attention to these debates, but we cannot do an effective job in the classroom if policies about what gets taught and how it is evaluated prevent us from doing the work we need to do.

You might not even have a job to do if you do not attend to the larger contexts. It is conceivable, for example, that immigration authorities would decide to deny visas to your students because their definitions of "student progress" are determined by criteria that you have not been attending to. Or, in a public school environment, your students might be mainstreamed into regular classrooms as a budget-trimming tactic by well-intentioned administrators seeking ways to balance the ledger by reducing the number of English language specialists required at the school.

Teachers need to be heard in these sorts of discussions, but not as a faint protest after decisions are made. We need to fashion our own understanding of this most fundamental of considerations—how students learn and therefore how we teach—so that we can do our jobs, and then use the same rationale as the basis for principled participation in the larger debates in our institutions, the community, and the profession.

Did you actually scribble anything in the box? Did you compare your answers with a friend or colleague or think about the various ways you might answer each question? If so, I imagine that you have already said, "It all depends..." and then listed factors that affect the answers:

❏ on the nature of what is being learned—fact, skill, attitude

❏ on the age, culture, language, education of the learner

❏ on the constraints of time, space, materials

❏ on the way "curriculum" is defined

❏ etc.

Which, of course, is always true. The answers depend on the details of the situation. And the situation that matters most to you is your own; all of this speculation about the nature of learning and the purpose of theory and the relationship of theory to practice is a monumental waste of time if it does not serve you in your daily work.

So, let us turn our attention to the classroom for a minute. Consider a lesson I observed in an elementary school classroom.

Aimee Trechock is a veteran English language teacher in an elementary school in the Denver area, and she has mastered the delicate balance between teacher control and student initiative; her classroom is an engaging place, an enticing mélange of colorful bulletin boards, gardens, science projects, chicken hatcheries, art work, and academic accomplishment. I describe a portion of a reading lesson and examine the ways that she works back and forth between conversational interaction with the students and didactic attention to conventions of print, grammar, and vocabulary.

This transcript is taken from the videotape I shot of a class of third, fourth, and fifth graders (8–10 year olds) working with Aimee on Chapter 5 of *The Mouse and the Motorcycle* (Cleary, 2000). Aimee sits at a kidney-shaped table close to the chalkboard with seven children, speakers of Spanish and Russian (an aide is working with another group of children on a similar lesson at the same time). Her back is to the board, and from time to time she reaches back and writes grammar points or vocabulary examples on the board. They are reviewing yesterday's reading using a page of questions that Aimee has prepared. This occurs in a teacher-orchestrated conversation with much exchange of opinion, questions about vocabulary, spelling, punctuation, etc. The routine consists of Aimee calling on a student to read a question. After they have discussed the question, they all write the answer in the blanks, conferring and checking among themselves and with the teacher.

*The Mouse and the Motorcycle* is about a boy named Keith, his toy motorcycle, and a mouse named Ralph who wants to ride the motorcycle. Keith and Ralph become friends and have a number of adventures together. The children had reviewed several books together and voted to read this one. For Anna, Mark, Olga, and Rosa, the book is about right in terms of level; for Eduardo, Juanita, and Sara, it is a bit difficult. I videotaped the lesson from about ten feet away. Aimee sits at the top of the frame, and the children are arrayed clockwise around the table: Eduardo, Mark, Anna, Juanita, Sara, Olga, and Rosa. We enter the session about halfway through as the children are answering a question about Ralph's encounter with Keith's dog.

### THE MOUSE AND THE MOTORCYCLE[1]

1. *Aimee:* "Number four! Juanita."
2. *Juanita:* "Wait."
3. *Aimee:* "Oh, you're almost done. Let's wait. Let's wait for Juanita." (Hubbub: everyone talking at once as Juanita finishes writing her answer to number three.)
4. *Juanita:* "Okay." (Everyone quiets down and focuses on the sheet as Juanita begins to read.) "What did Ralph do to the dog?" (More hubbub as they all offer opinions; Aimee decides to summarize that portion of the story for them.)
5. *Aimee:* "Do you remember when...when the man was holding the dog? Right? And Ralph says...first he's afraid? But then he learns that the dog can't get away? Right? And then, what does he do?" (Aimee points to Anna who is making faces with thumbs on temples and wriggling fingers.) "That's right. So what did Ralph do to the dog?"
6. *Mark:* "Ralph made the face."
7. *Aimee:* (Nods.) "Uh huh, and what did he do with his (pointing to her tongue) tongue?"
8. *Mark:* "He push it out."
9. *Aimee:* "He pushed it out. That's right. So, here's Ralph, who was afraid.... now he's making faces at the dog. So how can you answer it? What did Ralph do to the dog?"

10. *Sara:* (Sara raises her voice above the other students who are also giving answers.) "Ralph was doing faces to the dog."

11. *Aimee:* "Good. Ralph made faces at the dog." (The students all begin writing the answer on the sheet.)

12. *Juanita:* (General hubbub concerning making/doing faces.) "I don't know how to spell <u>faces</u>."

13. *Aimee:* (Speaks to Juanita, sounding out <u>faces</u> for her.) "Ey, ey, fey, ey." (She turns to the board and writes, chalk poised so that the children have time to speculate about the way that the sounds are written. **Then returns to Juanita**: She is focused on Juanita, but several of the students are if-ing and ey-ing and contributing to the discussion about how to spell faces.) "What's another one that has that sound?" (Hubbub: all the students are writing and vocalizing looking at the board or writing on their papers.) Finally, she writes <u>faces</u> on the board for the students to refer to if they have not already figured out the spelling.

14. *Rosa:* "Can I read number six?"

15. *Aimee:* To Rosa, "Mm Hmm." (Aimee straightens up over table and speaks to the group, emphasizing <u>at</u> slightly as she speaks.) "Ralph made faces *at* the dog."

16. *Olga:* "<u>At</u> the dog? To the dog!"

17. *Sara:* "To the dog! Ehh?" (She makes a gesture of impatience and erases her answer.) "To the dog."

18. *Aimee:* (She shrugs shoulders and makes a slight grimace.) "All right, now! Number five. Who didn't read one? Yes." (She indicates Rosa who is raising her hand.) "Go!"

You'll have to take my word for it—this was a marvelous lesson enjoyed by one and all. The portion you see here was merely one example of focused engagement by children in which everyone was paying attention, vying to participate, and making visible progress with reading and writing skills in the service of conversational enjoyment of the story. I would quite happily assign my children and all my children's children to Aimee for their elementary school careers.[2]

But, my personal enthusiasms notwithstanding, the question remains, "What have the children learned?" And, almost as important, "How did they learn it? How do we know what they have learned? And, what did Aimee learn in the lesson? How might she build future lessons around what she learned about their learning? And how might she convince parents, administrators, and policy-makers that the children's learning is significant?"

To answer these questions we need to examine the lesson carefully, looking both at content and the activity. Bear with me a minute as we go back through the transcript to accomplish this.

I have a limited amount of data from which to present my case, so your judgment about the reasonableness of my position will depend less on the comprehensiveness of my argument and more on the extent to which my points resonate with your experience. That is, I am appealing to your sense of reasonableness and to your ability to see yourself using these ideas in your own teaching. I am not attempting to build a grand theory of learning and teaching for language theorists; I am constructing a tool for everyday use by everyday teachers. You can be the judge of my efforts; take what you can use and leave the rest.

It is difficult to portray the richness of Aimee's classroom on paper. The transcript only hints at the complexity of the interaction among the teacher and students—brief exchanges, questions and answers, and give and take that show the students are mastering aspects of the language. At the same time, there is no mistaking the fact that this conversation occurred in a school setting. This is definitely an English language class, and the transcript gives us an opportunity to examine several features of Aimee's conduct that provide insight into how she views language teaching. Among the aspects of the class that I find most interesting are the following.

❒ *Focused language lesson versus communicative interaction:* In the professional discourse there is a tension between language teaching as direct didactic event and as conversational accomplishment. One sometimes gets the impression that English language classrooms should be snatches of real life rather than teacher-orchestrated environments. It is doubtful that this could be accomplished, even if it were desirable, which I suspect it is not. In the first place, there is the institutional reality: We cannot escape the fact that we are participating in a formal, often compulsory, environment and that we have responsibilities to students and to the school that prevent us from eliminating all trappings of the classroom. In addition to the requirements of curriculum and evaluation, the students look to us to create a safe environment, to organize their time, and to help them learn the language. The school and community (parents or sponsors, depending on the setting) expect us to fulfill our contractual obligations as teachers. In other words, we need to accept the fact that the language classroom is not a coffee shop or sandbox conversation where English happens to be acquired as the by-product of interaction. And even if that were not the case, we have abundant evidence from generations of immigrants that many people do not learn the language if merely exposed to it.

So the issue is not whether or how to control the interactions of students, but to what extent we can balance the studied attention to details of the language with an air of informality and functional communication, which Earl Stevick has characterized as the tension between control (by the teacher) and initiative (by the student) (Stevick, 1996, 1998). And this is what Aimee has accomplished in this lesson. The conversational turn always comes back to her; she determines who is to speak, and she provides key support on mechanics, vocabulary, and grammar work. But this occurs in an atmosphere of joyful exchange among engaged learners where it is quite obvious that everyone is communicating about things that matter to him or her and, not coincidentally, having fun.

Examples of her orchestration of events are visible in Lines 1 and 3 where she calls on Juanita and has the group wait for her to finish writing. She takes over the telling of the story in Line 5, and she moves things along in Lines 13 and 18. The role of teacher control is central to an understanding of all successful teaching and no less so in communicative language teaching. The important point, I think, is that it is not necessary to relinquish control of the rhythm and flow of the activities as we attempt to move students toward relevant, functional use of the language.

❐ *Grammar work:* Aimee makes several important decisions concerning grammar in the course of the lesson, and in the portion of the class that appears here she chooses to correct errors by providing the correct form. For example, in Line 7 she asks the group "What did he do with his tongue?" and Mark replies "He push it out." Aimee corrects his answer by repeating it correctly, in a conversational tone: "He pushed it out."

Later (Line 10) Sara says, "Ralph was doing faces to the dog," and Aimee provides the correction, *made*, with slight emphasis, as the children continue writing on their worksheets. She apparently notices that several of the children persist in using the wrong preposition with the verb *make*, so she repeats the correct sentence, "Ralph made faces *at* the dog" (Line 15), before she pushes on to the next item on the worksheet. This is grammar correction, but it is done so subtly that it seems like conversation.

Perhaps just as important as these examples of correction are the opportunities for correction that she does not take. For example, in Line 6, Mark says, "Ralph made the face," and Aimee merely confirms the accuracy of the information, ignoring the grammatical form, when she says (Line 7), "Uh huh." In other words, she does not correct errors on every occasion. It may be that Aimee was sensitive to some aspect of the class rhythm or to this particular student that indicated to her that correction was not necessary or advisable at that point.

❐ *Spelling, punctuation, and pronunciation work:* On several occasions in the course of the lesson, Aimee responds to children's requests for help with mechanical aspects of the language (for example, in Line 12, where Juanita asks how to spell *faces*). Her tendency is to both provide assistance and to give hints to the students as to the correct answers. In this portion of the videotape, she cues the correct answer by making noises to remind students to sound out the words they do not know how to spell, and by asking them to think of other words they know that sound the same.

What is significant is that Aimee responds to the request for help but in such a way that the children are thrown back on their own resources and reminded to use strategies they have learned earlier. In addition, she does this without interrupting the flow of the class or distracting students for whom the spelling of *faces* is not a problem.

❐ *Comprehension work:* The book was selected by the students from several that Aimee had recommended. As a result, there was a high level of interest in it, even though it is somewhat above the level of three of the seven students. As they work on the answers to the questions, Aimee helps the students understand events in the story and express them in English. In one section of the transcript (Line 5) she uses a favorite technique, summarizing group responses, to do this. She retells a portion of the story with animation and engaging gestures, while eliciting participation from the students until she is certain that the whole group understands what happened in that portion of the story. In the course of a few minutes, she reviews the text, reinforces vocabulary, models representative sentences, and engages the students in a spirited exchange as they relive events from the story. In other words, she not only checks their comprehension, but she also extends it through conversation.

❐ *Conversation work:* It is necessary to underscore something that might not be clear from a reading of the transcript: Aimee has managed to achieve a relaxed atmosphere of camaraderie and enjoyment while at the same time keeping everyone focused on the language work at hand. That is, it is clear from watching the tape that the children are having a good time, yet it is equally clear that they are working diligently on the worksheet and on mastering the English of the book and the conversation. It seems to me that this is precisely the task of the teacher working with English language learners (and perhaps with *all* learners), but it is also the accomplishment that is least available to inspection and analysis. It is impossible to prescribe the particular behaviors that accomplished this feat, but it is also true that if one is not able to accomplish it, the ideal of communicative proficiency will not be achieved. So, on this point I have little of value to contribute apart from the observation that we should pay attention to our students and make sure that they are relaxed and interested in what we are doing.

However, there is one rule of thumb for language teaching of this sort, and that is to step softly in the role of "teacher." Aimee provides a good example of this in the last half of the transcript (from Line 11) as the students work to express the idea that Ralph made faces at the dog. It is clear from the gestures the children are making and from what they are saying that they understand what happened between Ralph and the dog, but a language point emerges as they work to answer the question: Several are struggling with the expression to *make faces at*. Aimee notices this, and in Line 11 she provides a model, emphasizing the verb *made* rather than *do*, which is the word Sara had used. Then, as the children are writing, she sees at least two (Olga and Sara) still have the wrong preposition, so she repeats the sentence stressing *at* slightly as she does so (Line 15).

## What Has Been Learned?

Based on this very brief glimpse of one lesson, what do you observe about what has been learned here? Jot a few observations in the box that follows. (Of course, you don't have to jot anything in the box; you can merely skip down to the next piece of text to discover what I think the answer is. However, I think you would benefit by reading the transcript aloud, maybe having different people take roles to see if you can make it come alive.)

*Here's what I think:* The children have learned a great deal. They can read and follow directions. They can write within the lines. They have mastered the rudiments of sentence-level punctuation. They know about the connection between the sounds of words and the written symbols used to convey them in print; they are learning how to sound out words as they attempt to spell them. They know how to participate in the reading lesson as Aimee has organized it, and they know how to take turns in the conversation. Achieving this sort of classroom rhythm is a significant accomplishment.

But in addition to these school skills, I would argue that Aimee's students have learned a number of essential lessons about themselves and about school that will serve them well in their academic careers and beyond. They have learned that school is an interesting place to be and that learning is fun and rewarding. They have learned how to assert their prerogatives in group inter-action by asking if they can take a turn or by contesting an answer to a question. They have learned that there are adults who are prepared to organize interesting activities for children and to guarantee their participation in those activities.

And, by participating in Aimee's class they have learned an important lesson—that they are entitled to their opinion in spite of the fact that they are merely children, and nonnative English–speaking children at that. This is an essential lesson if they are to become successful students in school and informed citizens in the world. It will not be learned in lectures delivered once and evaluated on a midterm exam; these are the sorts of lessons they learn in the mundane details of everyday negotiations with their teachers and their peers.

They are learning how to be learners. And, by extension, they are molding their identities as learners and language users.

I want to linger over this assertion for a moment because it is central to my belief that everyday events shape us in ways we do not always appreciate and because there is so much going on in the lesson that it would be easy to overlook it.

*The key point is this:* Whatever else is being learned in this lesson, everyone—children, teacher, researcher—is learning how to be him- or herself.

A basic tension that characterizes all human learning—the struggle between becoming a competent member of a group and exercising your autonomy, between knowing confidently that you are accepted by the powerful people in your life, that you are part of a community, *and* that you are unique—characterizes the lesson being played out in this little snippet of videotape. I want to turn your attention to a small struggle between the teacher and a few of the children to illustrate this point.

I wonder if you caught the significance of the exchange between Olga and Rosa and Aimee in Lines 16, 17, and 18 as they were attempting to answer the question of what Ralph did when he was confronted by the dog.

> 15. *Aimee:* To Rosa, "Mm Hmm." (Aimee straightens up over table and speaks to the group, emphasizing <u>at</u> slightly as she speaks.) "Ralph made faces *at* the dog."
> 16. *Olga:* "<u>At</u> the dog? To the dog!"
> 17. *Sara:* "To the dog! Ehh?" (She makes a gesture of impatience and erases her answer.) "To the dog."
> 18. *Aimee:* (She shrugs shoulders and makes a slight grimace.) "All right, now! Number five. Who didn't read one? Yes." (She indicates Rosa who is raising her hand.) "Go!"

What has happened here?

One thing that is clear is that the children have answered the question to Aimee's satisfaction—they have understood that the mouse, who used to be afraid of the dog, is now taunting him. Aimee draws everyone's attention to Anna, who is making faces with thumbs stuck in her ears and wiggling her fingers—showing everyone what was happening in the story. They all get it, and collaboratively, they translate their understanding into English.

But their understanding is not quite acceptable English; the answer they come up with is, *Doing faces to the dog.* Olga and Sara, in particular, like *to the dog,*—that is what they are writing. They object when Aimee corrects them by musing conversationally over the heads of the children, saying, "Ralph made faces *at* the dog."

Olga says, "*At* the dog? *To* the dog!" and Sara echoes her protest—with feigned indignation, clenching her fists and making as if to hit the table in defiance. They assert their opinion about how to express in English what they have learned in the story. They hold their ground in the face of the teacher's authority. Aimee merely shrugs her shoulders as if to say, "Have it your way" and continues with the lesson.

The girls are left to their own devices. They can leave the answers as they have written them, or they can change them. Aimee does not insist on a particular response at that moment. She is moving on with the lesson, and she is focused on the whole group.

The girls do, in fact, change the answers on their sheets, so the instructional goal of the lesson has been met. But this occurs in a way that has potential reverberations far beyond the selection of a preposition.

Aimee created a small space and provided choices. The girls made their choices within the space, on their own, so to speak. A small step, perhaps, but when the pattern is reenacted again and again throughout the day, day in and day out, the children gradually come to think of themselves as decision-makers.

The protest is insignificant in the flow of the day and something that would not have been caught and singled out if I had not been there with the camera, but it would have occurred in any case because this is the way Aimee conducts business with the children. I believe it is an important feature of a conversationally oriented classroom, and one that leads learners toward competence, not only in English, but also in important interactional rituals that characterize daily life.

But, how did they learn this lesson?

Ah, now we're getting to the nub of the matter. It is one thing to agree on what has been learned. It is quite another to arrive at a consensus about how they learned it. But you can relax. Because there is vigorous debate on this matter among the "experts," you are free to construct your own theory of learning, which is what I am recommending, and what I am about to do here.

In order to do this I first need to briefly review the major learning theories that have guided education in the past three or four generations. I do not pretend to be an expert in these matters, and if you have studied educational psychology in depth, your review might differ from mine. The goal here is not to construct a detailed picture of the field; rather, I want to sketch the major assumptions that undergird most contemporary educational practice. I believe that we all need to know the broad sweep of knowledge that shapes the discourse so that we can recognize assumptions behind the directives, explicit and implicit, that we have to deal with.

## What Do Learning Theories Contribute to Our Understanding?

An important first step is to make sure we are in agreement about what *theory* means. The *Random House Dictionary* defines theory as "a coherent group of general propositions used as principles of explanation for a class of phenomena." I am working from the simple idea that a theory is a set of assertions about the nature of reality and the way the world works. A theory of learning provides us with a principled basis for organizing activity and evaluating our efforts.

The history of attempts to define learning and to understand teaching dates back to antiquity. For most of that history, education was the province of philosophy and politics because the writers were concerned with governing the masses of uneducated subjects (Ulich, 1954). Since the early 1900s, especially in the United States and western Europe, the debate has been shaped by discipline-based disputes about human growth and development, the nature of school, and the roles and responsibilities of the state in educating the nation's young people.

As I read the literature, I identify five distinct characterizations of learning — Behavioral, Cognitive, Humanistic, Constructivist, and Sociocultural (Bateson, 1979; Bateson, 1994; Cole, 1996; Kegan, 1994; Leonard, 2002; Wenger, 1998). Because debates in education today are shaped by assumptions that are derived from these perspectives, it is helpful to review the principle tenets of each before moving to my rationale for defining learning as "change over time through engagement in activity."

*Behaviorism* is built on the work of Harvard psychologist B. F. Skinner, whose research with pigeons and rats yielded a view of learning based on stimulus-response sequences between the learner and the environment (Skinner, 1976, 2002). Behaviorists focus on observable phenomena and on shaping behavior through reinforcement and punishment. They are not concerned with the mental or emotional state of the learner. They would argue that to get students to learn something, you have to organize lessons around rewards and punishments that gradually shape their behavior in the direction you desire.

Behaviorists would speculate about the gradual shaping of the children's behavior in the class. They would probably assert that Aimee had organized the system of rewards and punishments so that the children's behavior was gradually shaped in the desired direction. They would point out that this lesson is just one example of the habitual turn of events in the classroom, and that Aimee and the children engage in this sort of ritualized behavior every day.

Behaviorism remains a powerful force in schooling today. Lesson plans and curricula that are structured around narrowly specified objectives and class sessions that are organized to build in gradually increasing difficulty where students are controlled by rewards—these draw on behaviorist tenets. In fact, it is not an exaggeration to argue that most modern legislation about education—mandated tests and curricula, funding rationales, programs of incentive and sanction—is founded on behaviorist concepts of learning.

*Cognitivism* is based on the belief that human thinking is analogous to computer information processing. Learners identify patterns in the external world and build mental constructs that guide their decision-making. Learning is seen as primarily a mental process that occurs inside the head. Scholars in this tradition attempt to identify the symbolic representation of ideas that constitute the database individuals access as they solve problems (Ausubel, 2000; Bloom, 1969; Gagne, 1985; Miller, 1969; Shannon, 1958). Teachers working within this tradition emphasize the accurate transmission of knowledge using advanced organizers and precise definition of the cognitive features of learning. Lessons are carefully orchestrated, very often with visual concept maps that help learners understand how ideas are related to each other.

Cognitivists analyzing *The Mouse and the Motorcycle* lesson might argue that Aimee was successful because she had been able to establish a "positive set" for the lesson in previous activities. They would point out that Aimee's behavior indicated that the children had learned the meanings of key words before the comprehension activity, and that they had also been taught the basic format of the story—beginning, middle, end, hero and villain, danger and escape, etc.

*Humanism* is based on the conviction that learning is a matter of personality development and personal realization that involves the whole person; it is not merely a cognitive phenomena nor a response to external stimuli. Humanists emphasize freedom and autonomy in making life-affirming choices morally, spiritually, emotionally, physically, and mentally. The work of Abraham Maslow and Carl Rogers provides the foundation for this approach, which continues to be an important source of ideas for educators. Maslow believed that humans struggle with experience by attending to a hierarchy of needs ranging from the basics of survival to those associated with belonging and self-actualization (Maslow, 1970, 1993). Rogers developed a client-centered approach to counseling based on similar convictions. He believed that people needed only guidance in discovering the answers to their problems within their own experience (Rogers, 1951, 1983).

Educational practices that reflect a humanistic bias include activities intended to foster confidence and self-regard, autonomy and informed decision-making, tolerance for ambiguity and self-directed learning.

Humanists would assert that Aimee had established a nurturing environment for "whole-person" learning in her classroom. Although only visible by implication in the transcript, her classroom attracts children like flowers attract bees. Before the bell rang on the days I was there, students of all ages surged in and out of the classroom talking excitedly, reporting the latest news, and inquiring about projects they had going. One group clustered around the incubator examining the eggs to check on the progress of their brood. Another gaggle of nature watchers was expressing dismay that all the cocoons collected on a recent field trip seemed to be moths rather than butterflies. The greenhouse against the west bank of windows fairly surged with new growth, and the bulletin boards sagged under the weight of child art. The tone of the noisy exchanges was gleeful and yet respectful; it was clear to me that this was a room where they all knew the rules and in which they took considerable personal pride.

*Constructivism* developed out of the work of Jean Piaget (1998) and Lev Vygotsky (1962, 1978) and has been elaborated by a number of scholars, including Jerome Bruner (Bruner, 1966, 1986), Jean Lave (Lave & Wenger, 1991), Michael Cole (Cole, 1996; Cole & Cole, 1996), and Robert Kegan (Kegan, 1982, 1994; Kegan & Lahey, 2001; Wenger, 1998). Piaget's developmental learning theory is structured by stages of development, each with its own particular accomplishments and abilities. Development is seen as dependent on two important processes: *accommodation*, where existing cognitive structures change to make sense of the new events occurring in the environment, and *assimilation*, where the individual interprets environmental events based on existing cognitive structures.

The Soviet psychologist Lev Vygotsky, a contemporary of Piaget's who died in his thirties from tuberculosis, emphasized the social nature of learning. He underscored the importance of working within the learner's "zone of proximal development"; that is, adjusting instruction so that it is just a little bit beyond the individual's independent problem-solving ability.

Jerome Bruner believes that learners are more likely to remember concepts if they discover them on their own, apply them to their own knowledge base and context, and structure them to fit into their own backgrounds and life experiences.

Jean Lave focuses on the specifics of context that influence learning; she sees individuals adjusting to the social demands of the communities they are striving to enter.

Michael Cole has developed an extensive network of school/community activists and researchers who believe that learners need to have freedom within structure. They have organized after-school clubs called The 5th Dimension in which learners play games and learn social and academic skills in the process of constructing their own "curriculum." They learn to identify their own tasks and to proceed at their own pace.

Robert Kegan and his colleagues and students have extended constructivism into adolescent and adult learning, arguing that human beings experience life as a series of identity crises occasioned by recurring demands on one's ability to negotiate increasingly complex situations.

Constructivists reject behaviorist tenets of learning that presented the child as a passive recipient of knowledge and the mind as a tabula rasa, waiting to be shaped by external stimuli. Piaget, Vygotsky, and their successors recognize that children do not internalize adult knowledge directly. Instead, they actively form their own cognitive schema through interaction with the physical world and with other people, and these representations initially differ greatly from those of adults. Constructivist educational activities are structured to promote learner initiative and exploration. Teachers organize instruction around key experiences, and students are encouraged to experiment and draw their own conclusions. Goals for lessons are identified in terms of values and direction of learning, and teachers encourage emergent understandings of concepts and skills.

Constructivists might point to the fact that Aimee models reading and writing for the students and encourages them directly and indirectly to adopt her approach to literacy and learning. She provides a risk-free environment that encourages the children to express opinions and draw their own conclusions. The children are free to make mistakes and to profit from those mistakes.

These four perspectives grow out of psychology, the traditional source of theories about learning. In the past fifty years or so, a number of other theoretical perspectives have addressed learning either directly or indirectly and merit consideration. These can be grouped together as sociocultural theories, because all expand the focus beyond the individual.

*Sociocultural theory.* What all sociocultural approaches to learning have in common is the awareness that we cannot ignore the contexts of learning. They differ in the extent to which they emphasize the interpersonal, institutional, and historical scope of their analysis, but they all recognize that learners are always interpreting and negotiating realities that extend beyond cognitive phenomena. They are interested in the fact that all human activity is structured by tradition and history, and that individuals are always negotiating norms that have been developed, consciously or unconsciously, over time (Wertsch, 1998). They are interested in the fact that all humans are becoming *socialized* into norms and values of their community (Holland, Lachicotte, Skinner, & Cain, 1998; Parsons, 1962; Rogoff, 2003; Wenger, 1998). They draw our attention to the fact that learning is characteristic not only of individuals but also of groups such as companies and schools. They are interested in the ways that organizations adjust to changes in the environment (Argyris & Schon, 1978; Senge, 2000). Theorists in this tradition draw on insights from ecology and focus on the natural sciences for metaphors and models. Ecologists recognize that the individual or the organization must always be understood as part of a larger context, and that learning is always cyclical, with gradual adjustments of behavior and understanding occurring over time as part of an ongoing adjustment to circumstances (Bronfenbrenner, 1979; Kramsch, 2002; Leather & van Dam, 2003).

Sociocultural theorists would say that Aimee's classroom reflects society's values and that the children are learning important lessons about time and space in the way lessons are organized. Knowledge comes from books and from the authority of the teacher, and skills are learned in didactic lessons. The children are being socialized into dominant western cultural traditions that emphasize the importance of telling stories in linear, causal fashion, and in working back and forth between oral and written language.

## Constructing a Personal Theory

So, getting back to the question of "How did the children learn what they learned?" the answer is, "We won't ever know." If I had constructed my research differently, I might have been able to answer that question, but I was not focused on comparative analysis of learning theories when I was in Aimee's classroom. I was attempting to understand how she orchestrated her instruction and how the children responded.

But it does not matter. You are not interested in the grand theory of *how humans learn.* You are concerned with a workable theory about how your students learn.[3] By "workable" I mean something useful—a theory to guide your decisions in the classroom that can be used to organize your professional decision-making in other situations as well. What is required is a personalized learning theory that you construct using available resources and your own experience.

All of the perspectives discussed can contribute to an understanding of what was going on in Aimee's classroom that spring morning, but they are important only if you can organize them for your own use. The first task is to overcome the reticence that most teachers feel in thinking of themselves as theorists.

If you feel compelled to assert that, in fact, you *are* a teacher and a practitioner, *not* a theorist or a scholar, consider the possibility that this is the natural and expectable outcome of being a teacher in modern times. Teachers are generally *not* paid to think; if you were to peruse most teachers' contracts you would undoubtedly discover that there is no explicit mention made of thinking in any of its guises—reflection, research, publication, conference presentation, etc. You might find a "preparation period" as a sanctioned category of behavior, but in some schools even this is closely scrutinized and teachers are required to demonstrate that they are using the time wisely. I will not tarry here to ponder what all this tells us about our society or our institutions of learning—that will come in later essays.

For now, all I want to do is assure you that it is quite normal for teachers to believe that they are not theorists, and that this is nothing to be apologetic about. However, I want to argue forcefully against this sentiment and encourage you to actively engage in the rest of this essay as a theory-builder. If you already consider yourself a theory-building scholarly practitioner, my apologies for trying your patience. Bear with me as I add these two bits of rationale to the argument.

First, if you do not build your own theory you have to use someone else's, and very likely this will be filtered through the lens of your administrators, a textbook selection committee, or distant policy-makers. In any case, you will find that you have to adjust your ideas about teaching and learning to the interests and preferences of others whose positions of power may create problems for you if you discover aspects of their theory that you do not agree with.

Second, the primary reason for theory in education is to improve practice, and as teachers we are not interested in improving practice in general, but in improving our own practice. It is therefore obvious that our theory has to be built on the daily activity of our own experience.[4]

If this is the case, and if we also attend to the legacy of learning theorists, then building a personal learning theory (and writing it down) would seem to be a relatively straightforward matter. The following steps constitute a modest but respectable beginning.

1. Identify a number of classroom techniques and activities that you believe to be effective. These might be taken from your experience as a learner or as a teacher, but in any case they will lead you naturally to the next step.

2. Articulate the key elements of a successful learning experience. What is required to promote learning in the classroom?

3. List the important attributes of the learners with whom you work that must be attended to if you are to be successful.

4. Identify key tenets of established learning theories that support your convictions.

5. Adopt a critical stance toward yourself and your practice that permits you to constantly revise all of these ideas as you experiment with classroom techniques and as you continue to read, attend conferences, and engage in collegial exchanges with other teachers. This will include all of the conventional assessment techniques that teachers regularly use to evaluate student work and to assign grades, but it will also include systematic attention to your own behavior and attitudes.

It might be helpful to see how this approach would apply to the lesson on *The Mouse and the Motorcycle*. As I reflect on this particular class, the following constitute an example of the type of analysis I am suggesting.

1. *Techniques and activities:* Aimee used small group, round-robin reading sessions punctuated by focused comprehension activity. She encouraged and animated by exchanges of opinion about the characters and action in the story.

2. *The successful learning experience:* The result was a relaxed lesson that had, nevertheless, a clipped pace—enjoyable for the students but also productive for the teacher. This resulted in a scaffolded discussion of the story that permitted her to assess what each student has understood from the story and permitted them to attend to elements of the language as they expressed their understanding.

3. *Attributes of learners:* The children were clearly interested in the protagonists of their age level and the stories of adventure and excitement. They were engaged in the tasks that affirmed their competence and permitted them to learn. The activity permitted them to interact with their friends and receive teacher attention and approval. The lesson provided structured tasks with clear guidelines for success at a pace that was appropriate for their attention span.

4. *Support of established learning theorists:* I did this in the brief paragraphs after reviewing each of the learning theories above. I indicated how individuals from each tradition might explain the success Aimee has a teacher. Because all learning theories have merit, the primary condition of this step in the process is that you be clear on why you are using a particular technique and what you would take as evidence of its effectiveness.

5. *Critical stance:* Ah, now we get to the important step in the process. It is important that we not use this approach as a means for rationalizing our habits and personal preferences. This is where we need to raise our heads from our own classrooms and attend to the curriculum we are required to teach, to the standards that are invoked as we and our students are evaluated. But even more important for our own benefit and that of our students, we need to be as clear-headed and objective as possible as we assess the effects of our work. At the very least, we need to keep records of student achievement and notes on lessons. We need also to attend to our own prejudices and inclinations as we examine our teaching.

   a. In my case, I know that I enjoy literate activities and talkative students, so I would need to make sure that I balance this sort of reading/writing activity with, say, art lessons, science experiments, and out-of-doors excursions.

b. I would need to develop techniques that force me to attend to the quiet or compliant student to make certain that he or she is, in fact, understanding the material. Too often, I am so focused on the progress of the lesson that I assume people are learning rather than stopping to confirm it.

c. And, I sometimes have difficulty with the resistant or rebellious student. I am often content with sullen silence or feigned compliance when what I need to do is probe to see if I can help the individual make sense of what we are doing.

This approach to teaching may strike you as haphazard and iconoclastic. "Surely," you might be saying, "we cannot have all teachers running around constructing their own theories of teaching and learning! Why, that would result in chaos and confusion! How will we ever attain any semblance of order or organized instruction?"

And I believe you are right.

The illusion of control that each era of pedagogical wisdom brings with it is merely that—illusion. Teachers are individuals with personal histories and preferences who get into the profession because of their own success in school and their desire to help others learn. They are as much influenced by their experiences in school and by their memories of the teachers they had as they are by the theories and methods they studied in their teacher preparation courses. Even if they believe they are following the dictates of particular theoreticians or pedagogical authorities, they will adjust the prescribed activities to suit their own learning styles.

I say this with rueful confidence. In the early 1990s my colleagues and I were engaged in a study comparing "whole language" approaches to literacy with other approaches. We used interview and observation techniques to identify teachers in different pedagogical camps, and we had great difficulty making connections between what teachers said they believed and how they conducted their classes. That is, we observed some teachers who used practices that were very similar to those of other teachers, but whose theoretical allegiances were diametrically opposed to each other. And vice versa—teachers whose theoretical proclamations were very similar but whose classroom practices differed so dramatically from each other that we could not see the connections they saw (Clarke, 2003; Davis et al., 1992).

The approach I have outlined here acknowledges the reality of the daily grind—you will do "what works" for you in any case—and it gives you credit for coming to your own conclusions about why particular activities are successful in your classroom. It provides a principled basis for connecting the work of acknowledged scholars with your daily practice. And, perhaps most important, it provides the basis for sustained professional conduct, not only in the classroom, but in the larger, more politicized arena of educational decision-making. By explicitly acknowledging your historical and scholarly roots, you are able to build on the work of others and connect with teachers who are similarly inclined.

## On Learning and (Therefore) Teaching

I want to conclude by returning to the questions with which I began the essay and by addressing explicitly the relationship between learning and teaching implied in the title. My argument is simple—to be effective teachers we need to be clear on what we are attempting to accomplish; that is, we need to understand learning, which is the anticipated outcome of our efforts.

❐ What is learning?

As human beings we cannot *not* learn—merely by living and participating in the daily activities of life we are learning. Therefore, our teaching, while a reflection of what we believe about learning, is also an example of our learning. We learn as we teach, and we adjust our understanding of learning and teaching by attending to what is going on around us all the time.

So I define learning as *change over time through engagement in activity*. Individuals arrive at an activity accustomed to behaving in particular ways and by entering into the activity and adjusting their behavior to conform to the constraints of the situation, they change. The changes range from the small, focused phonological or grammatical adjustments to more global reorientations of attitude and participation. As teachers we create the conditions for these changes by calculating how much change individuals can tolerate and then nudging them toward the goals we have set for the class.

In *The Mouse and the Motorcycle* lesson, the activity that Aimee orchestrated required the students to read and comprehend text, define vocabulary, and spell correctly, among other things—the usual stuff of English classes. But they also had to negotiate the interpersonal situation in ways that gradually nudged them toward competent participation in an American school.

❐ How do you know when someone (including yourself) has learned something?

To answer this question we have to pay attention to changes that occur over time. This is not as easy as it sounds. Very often the most important learnings are not easily identified by pencil-and-paper assessments, nor even by observation. We have to be clear on what we are paying attention to, and we have to be patient with our students and with ourselves.[5]

We have to notice what learners, including ourselves, are able to do at the beginning of an activity, and then assess the amount of change that occurs over the course of the activity. But it is not just the activity of a particular day that is important. We need to attend to the pattern of learning as we engage in the same *categories* of activities day in, day out. We need to be aware of where we started out at the beginning of the year or semester, and we need to be clear on the kinds of learning required by the activities that we have organized and orchestrated. Very often evidence of learning proves elusive, peripheral to the curriculum focus during a lesson. We sometimes only gradually become aware of learning or discover something has been learned when we thought the lesson a bust.

Aimee's students produced written records of their understanding of *The Mouse and the Motorcycle*, and these helped her gauge the effectiveness of her teaching and organize her lessons for succeeding days. If we had not had the written answers to the questions, the dispute over the preposition in the phrase, "Ralph made faces *at* the dog," would have left us wondering whether the girls knew the correct answer. But we cannot be certain that they continued to use the preposition correctly, given the evidence we have. We only know that they succeeded in the task of the moment.

In other words, because we cannot *not* learn, and because learning is a constant feature of human activity, we cannot know precisely and definitively when something has been learned. We need to be able to tolerate the uncertainty at the same time that we develop measures that permit us to assess the progress our students are making.

❏ What is the relationship between your teaching and what your students are learning?

The response here is shaped by an understanding of the argument I have just made concerning how we know learning has occurred. Because *everyone*—students and teachers—involved in an activity is learning, the relationship between teaching and learning is cyclical and reciprocal. The teacher initiates the learning and then learns from the students how it is going. She learns from the students how the lesson is going and adjusts her behavior to improve the learning. As the teacher, you do the planning and launch activities, but once things are rolling, you are adapting and changing as much as the learners. In fact, if this is not the case, then you are likely to find yourself pushing on through a lesson and leaving the learners behind. You have to discipline yourself to attend to your own learning as much as to the learning of the students.

This means that assessment of the activity and of your participation in the activity is as important as assessment of student learning. Notes-to-self jotted in the margins of lesson plans, textbooks, and handouts can help you keep track of student responses and classroom choreography. The process is ongoing and emergent. That is, you need to be aware that a particular activity might seem to be more successful on one day than on another, so that you don't fall into the trap of thinking that, for example, comprehension questions are the key to success.

Aimee's lesson flowed like a conversation even though it was structured around the comprehension questions she had written down and passed out to the students. The *feel* of the lesson was accomplished by her response to the students and her ability to nudge them toward her goals. A less experienced teacher or a teacher who did not know the students well might have thought that the point was to finish the list of questions rather than orchestrate conversational interaction using the questions as a scaffold.

❐ How do your lessons reflect what your students are ready to learn?

The ideal lesson is one that is easy enough for students to experience some success but difficult enough to nudge them toward your learning goals. This means that your lessons must be based on your ongoing efforts at learning where the students are and what kinds of activities will be required to move them forward. You need to cultivate a regular rhythm of reflecting and adjusting your teaching to accommodate their learning. And, of course, you need to be aware that there are as many lessons occurring as there are students participating. That is, of course, the rationale behind "differentiated instruction" or "individualized teaching."

Aimee has divided her class in half and is working with a group of seven. This decision was based on multiple factors and included the availability of an assistant who worked with the rest of the students. Within the group of seven there were at least two distinct groups of learners if we attend to English language proficiency, and Eduardo was among the students who struggled the most with the language. All seven students participated, but Aimee orchestrated Eduardo's efforts closely, guiding his attention with gestures and questions directed only at him. She nursed his answers along and prompted him when he had difficulty, even as she was orchestrating the contributions of the other students.

❏ How do your lessons reflect what is expected of you by the curriculum?

This question evokes larger questions of institutional policy, procedure, and politics, and it touches on important philosophical issues that highlight an important feature of an ecological perspective of *curriculum* and *lesson*. The curriculum is a guideline, a document that serves learning in much the same way that a trellis serves the rose bush. A lesson is an instance in time, an event, a living phenomenon whose contribution to student learning is ambiguous at best.

The usual interpretation of such questions is that the curriculum lays out the content of the lesson and implies (perhaps even identifies) the nature of the event. The problem is that we do not know what is learned until after the event and, even then, as I have pointed out, we do not know for sure. This may seem like semantic or philosophical hair-splitting, but in fact it goes to the heart of a major problem we all face with the increase of accountability measures.

Aimee may have been working from a curriculum that stated, "read book and demonstrate comprehension," "write grammatically correct sentences," "interact effectively using appropriate language," in which case she would be able to answer confidently that the lesson reflected the curriculum. But any more detail in the curriculum runs the risk of hindering effective instruction rather than helping it.

We cannot identify in advance what will be learned over the course of a semester or a year; the best we can do is identify the broad outlines of knowledge, skills, and attitudes we want to move students toward and then keep these in mind as we work. At any moment, upon reflection, we should be able to talk about the learning of our students and the alignment of that learning to the curriculum. And, of course, by attending to the curriculum as we prepare and conduct our lessons, we engage in an iterative process that shapes both as we go.

## REFERENCES

Argyris, C., & Schon, D. A. (1978). *Organizational learning: A theory of action perspective.* Reading, MA: Addison-Wesley.

Ausubel, D. P. (2000). *The acquisition and retention of knowledge.* Dordrecht, The Netherlands: Kluwer Academic Publishing.

Bateson, G. (1979). *Mind and nature: A necessary unity*. New York: Dutton.

Bateson, M. C. (1994). *Peripheral visions: Learning along the way*. New York: HarperCollins.

———. (2000). *Full circles, overlapping lives: Culture and generation in transition*. New York: Random House.

———. (2004). *Willing to learn: Passages of personal discovery*. Hanover, NH: Steerforth Press.

Berger, P., Berger, B., & Kellner, H. (1973). *The homeless mind: Modernization and consciousness*. New York: Vintage Books.

Berger, P., & Luckmann, T. (1966). *The social construction of reality*. Garden City, NJ: Doubleday.

Bloom, B. S. (1969). *Taxonomy of educational objectives: The classification of educational goals*. London: Longman.

Bronfenbrenner, U. (1979). *The ecology of human development: Experiments by nature and design*. Cambridge, MA: Harvard University Press.

Bruner, J. (1966). *Toward a theory of instruction*. Cambridge, MA: Harvard University Press.

———. (1986). *Actual minds, possible worlds*. Cambridge, MA: Harvard University Press.

Clarke, M. A. (1994). Stepping softly: What constitutes "teaching" in communicative classrooms? In D. A. Hill (Ed.), *Changing contexts in English language teaching* (pp. 32–37). Milan, Italy: British Council.

———. (2003). *A place to stand: Essays for educators in troubled times*. Ann Arbor: University of Michigan Press.

Cleary, B. (2000). *The mouse and the motorcycle*. New York: Harper.

Cole, M. (1996). *Cultural psychology: A once and future discipline*. Cambridge, MA: Harvard University Press.

Cole, M., & Cole, S. R. (1996). *The development of children*. New York: Scientific American Books.

Davis, W. A., Clarke, M. A., Rhodes, L. K., Nathenson-Mejia, S., et al. (1992). *Colorado literacy study: Using multiple indicators to identify effective classroom practices for minority children in reading and writing*. Denver: University of Colorado at Denver.

Gagne, R. (1985). *The conditions of learning*. New York: Holt, Rinehart and Winston.

Goffman, E. (1974). *Frame analysis*. New York: Harper & Row.

———. (1981). *Forms of talk*. Cambridge, MA: Harvard University Press.

Holland, D., Lachicotte, W. J., Skinner, D., & Cain, C. (1998). *Identity and agency in cultural worlds*. Cambridge, MA: Harvard University Press.

Kegan, R. (1982). *The evolving self: Problem and process in human development*. Cambridge, MA: Harvard University Press.

———. (1994). *In over our heads: The mental demands of modern life*. Cambridge, MA: Harvard University Press.

Kegan, R., & Lahey, L. L. (2001). *How the way we talk can change the way we work: Seven languages for transformation*. San Francisco: Jossey-Bass.

Kramsch, C. (Ed.). (2002). *Language acquisition and language socialization: Ecological perspectives*. New York: Continuum.

Lave, J., & Wenger, E. (1991). *Situated learning: Legitimate peripheral participation.* Cambridge: Cambridge University Press.

Leather, J., & van Dam, J. (Eds.). (2003). *Ecology of language acquisition.* Dordrecht, The Netherlands: Kluwer Academic Publishers.

Leonard, D. C. (2002). *Learning theories from A to Z.* Westport, CT: Greenwood Press.

Maslow, A. (1970). *Motivation and personality* (2nd ed.). New York: Harper & Row.

———. (1993). *The farther reaches of human nature.* New York: Arkana.

Miller, G. A. (1969). *The psychology of communication.* Baltimore, MD: Penguin.

Parsons, T. (1962). *The structure of social action.* New York: The Free Press.

Piaget, J. (1998). *Jean Piaget's selected writings (9 Volumes).* New York: Routledge.

Rogers, C. (1951). *Client-centered therapy.* Boston: Houghton-Mifflin.

———. (1983). *Freedom to learn for the eighties.* Columbus, OH: Merrill.

Rogoff, B. (2003). *The cultural nature of human development.* New York: Oxford University Press.

Senge, P. (2000). *Schools that learn.* New York: Doubleday.

Shannon, C. E. (1958). A mathematical theory of communication. *The Bell System Technical Journal, 27,* 379–423, 623–656.

Skinner, B. F. (1976). *Walden two.* New York: Prentice Hall.

———. (2002). *Beyond freedom and dignity.* Indianapolis, IN: Hackett Publishing Co.

Stevick, E. W. (1996). *Memory, meaning, and method.* New York: Heinle and Heinle.

———. (1998). *Working with teaching methods: What's at stake?* New York: Heinle and Heinle.

Ulich, R. (1954). *Three thousand years of educational wisdom* (2nd ed.). Cambridge, MA: Harvard University Press.

Vygotsky, L. (1962). *Thought and language.* Cambridge: MIT Press.

———. (1978). *Mind in society: The development of higher psychological processes.* Cambridge, MA: Harvard University Press.

Wenger, E. (1998). *Communities of practice: Learning, meaning, and identity.* New York: Cambridge University Press.

Wertsch, J. V. (1998). *Mind as action.* New York: Oxford University Press.

## NOTES

1. The initial analysis of this lesson served as the basis for a plenary talk at the 1993 TESOL Convention in Atlanta, Georgia. Thanks to my co-presenter, Earl W. Stevick, for conversations that yielded many of these insights, and to Mary Lou McCloskey for the use of the hall. A subsequent version of the paper appeared in a collection of proceedings from a conference on English language teaching in Sorrento, Italy, edited by David A. Hill (Clarke, 1994).

2. A larger issue might arise: A skeptic could well ask, "How do we know that Aimee is a good teacher? What evidence could you present to confirm your analysis?" These are reasonable questions. To the first I would mention all the awards and testimonials she has won over the years. To the second I assert that the primary confirmation I require is your agreement that the case I have presented is reasonable. My purpose here is to present a particular approach to defining learning and to organizing teaching; if you find it helpful, that is sufficient.

3. I don't mean to imply that this is an either/or situation. You might well be interested in grand theory as well as a personal theory, but my guess is that it is the latter that concerns you most as you go about your business.

4. This perspective rests on a long and respectable intellectual tradition, phenomenology, which asserts that there is no knowing without a knower, and what matters in philosophical discussions such as these is the perspective of the individual involved in the activity, which would be you. If you are interested in this line of reasoning, consult work by the philosophers Edmund Husserl and Alfred Schutz and individuals influenced by them such as the sociologists Erving Goffman and Thomas Berger (Berger, Berger, & Kellner, 1973), Berger and Luckmann (1966), and Goffman (1974, 1981).

5. Mary Catherine Bateson (2000, 2004), linguist and anthropologist and sharp observer of learning, has helped me think through this issue. She uses autobiographical accounts in her teaching to help individuals discover how they learned to be who they are.

# ❸ Teaching as Learning, Learning as Life

## On Learning and (Therefore) Teaching, Continued....

People adjust to circumstances or events, and if the adjustment is maintained, we call it learning.

In the previous essay we saw that the seven children in Aimee Trechock's class adjusted their understanding of English vocabulary, grammar, and pronunciation as well as their awareness of reading strategies and norms of interaction, all the while totally engaged in the wondrous world of mice and motorcycles.

They were delighted by the bravado of the mouse making faces at the dog. They understood the significance of the mouse's behavior; as Mark put it, "Ralph made the face." And when Aimee asked him what about his tongue, he said, "He push it out."

They all continued talking about this event, and Aimee nudged them toward English competence by correcting Mark ever so slightly—"He pushed it out," she says, rather than "He stuck it out," which is probably what a native speaker would say. Later, as the children are attempting to get their answers correct on the sheet, Aimee says, "Ralph made faces at the dog," giving the children the correct verb—*made* not *do*—and preposition—*at* not *to*. If these fine points stick with the children, we can say that they learned a lot that morning. They changed their verbal representation of the world by acquiring the correct bits of vocabulary and grammar required to express these ideas in English. We call this *language acquisition*.

They also picked up subtle skills in interpersonal interaction. They learned how to participate effectively in the classroom in ways that will serve them well both in school and out of school. We call this *socialization*.[1]

The fact that we tend to notice acquisition more than socialization, and that we develop tests to measure the former but not the latter, should not obscure the fact that the two phenomena are examples of the same thing—learning—nor should it prevent us from seeing that both are changes that occur over time through engagement in activity. In fact, it is this insight that provides us with an important lens for our work as teachers. Once we tumble to the fact that our primary job is to create activities for our students and to observe them carefully to identify the changes that occur as a result of their involvement, we have a clear view of how to approach the school day.

At the risk of over-simplifying things, our work, boiled down to essentials, is devising activities that permit students to become engaged and that promote change.

Goals for lessons are most helpful when they are stated in broad terms that indicate the direction of learning. The curriculum needs to be little more than skeletal outlines of activities that nudge students toward those goals, and tests are most effective when they permit us to see what students have learned and point us toward the next set of activities we need to engage them in.

This is a highly simplified picture of teaching and learning, but it has the virtue of providing a rationale and a framework for teaching. It is my goal in this essay to elaborate on the approach that emerges from this perspective. In the previous essay I argued that classroom teachers should think of themselves as theorists. Here I argue that you should think of yourself as an observer of human behavior and action researcher who works for changes in the classroom and the school to promote learning. The questions I address are:

❒ How do you organize your time with students? What information do you use to make teaching decisions?

❒ How do you adjust what you do tomorrow based on what you did today? How do you reflect on your daily practice so that it goes beyond thoughtful pondering in the shower or on the commute to work?

❒ How does one make decisions now that still seem like good ideas weeks and months from now?

❒ What are the adjustments required of you and others (colleagues, administrators, community members, for example) to improve the environment for learning?

These questions encourage us to focus on the essentials of teaching—the observable effects of our lessons and the adjustments we need to make to improve student learning. They lead us away from the distractions of what might be called the "Best Practices Red Herring" or the "Methods and Materials Myopia"—an approach to teaching that focuses more on the trappings of teaching than on the actual learning of the students—and toward a thoughtful and reflective approach that is, in fact, the essence of research.

But we are tiptoeing into contested territory here because in the reciprocal snobbery of teachers and researchers, the former claim the high ground with regard to action and the latter see research as their territory. You may have heard the sarcastic question reputedly uttered by a skeptical teacher, "Oh, yes, it works in practice, but will it work in theory?" And it wasn't too many years ago that I attended a conference presentation where a university professor chided a teacher for attempting to do research in her own classroom. "You should leave that to the experts," he said.

And this line of argument will require you to adjust your sense of self; the roles and responsibilities of teachers are central to the issue here.

There are nuances and sore points to explore, so I have devised a brief self-assessment to provide focus. For each of the assertions on pages 64 and 65, indicate the extent to which you agree. A 1 indicates total disagreement and a 4 indicates total agreement. Scratch notes to yourself in the margins, and discuss the assumptions and issues behind them with a colleague.

There are no "right answers." Or rather, the answer will depend on your experiences and your teaching situation.

Disagree  Agree

| | | | | | |
|---|---|---|---|---|---|
| 1. | 1 | 2 | 3 | 4 | I am in teaching because I want to contribute to the greater good, to help students achieve their true potential, and to make a difference in the world. |
| 2. | 1 | 2 | 3 | 4 | Teaching is largely a matter of classroom management; once you control the situation, the students will learn. |
| 3. | 1 | 2 | 3 | 4 | Effective teaching is primarily a matter of closing the door and getting on with your work. |

4.  1  2  3  4    My goal as a teacher is to teach content; I don't expect to spend a lot of time on students who aren't interested in learning.

5.  1  2  3  4    Each class seems to have a personality of its own; some classes "click" and others don't. You have to adjust your teaching accordingly.

6.  1  2  3  4    I have a lot on my plate right now. I don't have time to do research. I'll become a reflective practitioner when the dust settles.

7.  1  2  3  4    I am interested in research only if it can tell me unambiguously what I should do in the classroom to be effective.

8.  1  2  3  4    Teachers teach; professors do research. The two activities are mutually exclusive.

9.  1  2  3  4    Politics are for politicians and administrators; my job is teaching, and I do not have time to get involved in school or community disputes.

10. 1  2  3  4    Cultural difference is a significant source of conflict in learning, but there is nothing teachers can do to ameliorate the tensions; we just have to teach the material and help students become better at succeeding in school.

As you have noticed, these assertions revolve around assumptions about the roles and responsibilities of a wide range of professionals involved in education: teachers, administrators, policy-makers, and researchers. I believe it is in teachers' best interests to expand their vision of themselves and to claim some of the territory usually seen as the province of others. Let me address each of the assertions to see if I can convince you.

**❶ I am in teaching because I want to contribute to the greater good, to help students achieve their true potential, and to make a difference in the world.**

As with all life decisions, yours in becoming a teacher probably didn't happen for a single reason, but I'm pretty confident that you didn't get into the profession for the money or the prestige. If you circled #1, it was probably due to a misplaced sense of humility. The fact is that teachers are by far the most important professionals in the world; beyond family and friends, teachers are the individuals who are in the best position to shape learners' attitudes and actions, and we can only hope that the effect of your efforts is to contribute to a better world.

This is an abstract and ambitious (some might say wildly pretentious and self-aggrandizing) way of characterizing the teacher's role in the grand scheme of things. However, anything less trivializes the work. It is important, of course, that students master the material. But we cannot escape the fact that, whatever else is being learned in our classes, the students are also learning who they are and what they can become. Learning—all learning, but especially the formal learning in schools—always impacts the identity of the learners, and teachers cannot ignore their role in helping students develop a healthy sense-of-self-in-the-world.

True, in the hurly-burly of the typical day, it is difficult to stay focused on these more altruistic aims, but keeping them in mind can get you through a rocky day or week. The grander your goals and the more distant your horizons, the more you are in need of broad strategies for organizing your efforts. And, given the enormity of the task and the complexity of the world, this needs to be seen as a long-term project requiring diligent effort, steady contemplation, and a routine of reflection and action.

**❷ Teaching is largely a matter of classroom management; once you control the situation, the students will learn.**

It is true that learning requires a sense of order and common purpose, and "classroom management" is one way of thinking about how to create the predictability of life that permits people to learn. After all, if learning is change over time through engagement in activity, then one of our responsibilities as teachers is to manage the environment in such a way that students are able to engage productively in the activities we have organized for them.

On the other hand, "classroom management" by itself is an inadequate way of thinking about the skillful orchestration of events that result in effective teaching. The problem is in the way this item is stated; it implies that control is possible and that teaching is largely a matter of applying the right techniques of control. And, the statement seems to separate classroom management from teaching—first get control, then teach.

Two points are pertinent here: First, human beings cannot be controlled except in the most superficial sense; the most effective management technique is, therefore, a lesson that grabs students' attention and in which they want to participate. Second, while there are certainly many management systems out there to choose from, classroom order is negotiated between teachers and students and will always be highly situational. That is, your classroom will reveal your personality and your negotiations with a particular group of students around particular activities, even if you are using the same management program as other teachers in the building.

In any case, the most effective management technique is to create lessons that students find engaging and that they participate in willingly and enthusiastically, making your job of managing them an easy one. And very often what you need to do to accomplish this is not immediately obvious or susceptible to formulaic approaches. That is, you need to create your own solutions to the problems you encounter, which means that you will need a system for approaching the task that is based on observation, reflection, and strategic action.

**❸ Effective teaching is primarily a matter of closing the door and getting on with your work.**

This has long been popular refrain in my circle of colleagues. There is something self-congratulatory about the stance—teacher as independent thinker and iconoclast, holding the line against a threatening but vague "power-out-there," the ubiquitous "them" that people blame for their problems.

And, the statement conveys a gratifying image of the teacher as a practical, hard-working, "roll-up-the-sleeves-and-get-the-job-done" sort of person.

But the stance carries another assumption—that teachers' work is contained in the classroom, that you can effectively close yourself off from what is going on in the school, in the community, or in students' lives. This leads to the common but mistaken notion that teaching is a matter of following a routine that is uncomplicated by the realities that students face when they are not with you.

It would be pleasant if life were that simple. But I argue that the teacher's job is to create authentic relationships with students and to nurture their learning so that they do well in school and succeed in life. This stance requires a reassessment of teachers' involvement in the community, the school, and students' personal lives.

If we see our teaching as rooted in authentic relationships with students, then we need to acknowledge that students' lives will need to be taken into consideration as we plan our lessons. To be sure, it is important to maintain a professional stance with regard to these relationships and to accurately assess the extent to which we can or should be involved in their lives. But we cannot escape the fact that the world outside the classroom enters every day as students stream into class, and it cannot be ignored.

Furthermore, we will not be able to ignore the politics and policies of the school and community in which we teach, which means that our effectiveness in the classroom depends to a certain extent on our ability to shape the policies of the school and our participation in or, at least, communication with, the larger community. And if we are going to be effective in this sort of effort, we will need an approach that goes beyond mere lesson planning.

**❹ My goal as a teacher is to teach content; I don't expect to spend a lot of time on students who aren't interested in learning.**

It is certainly the case that enthusiasm for subject matter and a love of content are important factors in effective teaching. And, of course, all of us want to convey a sense of wonder and excitement to students as they discover the mysteries that have attracted us to our subjects.

But we have to be careful in our approach to this issue. It is all too easy to blame a failed lesson on students' lack of interest or stubborn resistance. This gets us off the hook, but it may not explain what went wrong. Perhaps we miscalculated how much could be covered or misjudged the pacing of the lesson. Maybe we did not have an effective way of hooking them in.

And, we need to learn to avoid taking their dis-or-un-interest too personally. School, for most students, is a mandatory environment. They may be in our class for reasons that are totally beyond their control, and their rejection of our lessons may have more to do with their resistance to larger forces than with their opinion of us or the subject matter.

But for me the point is that the best teaching comes from individuals who understand that they are teachers of learners first and of subject matter second.

We need to work to know our students and to help them develop the interests and skills needed to master the lessons we provide. As Earl Stevick might put it, "We learn the students and the students learn the material" (Stevick, 1998).[2]

What this means is that effective teaching hinges on careful observation and conscientious adaptation in response to problems. Good teachers prepare lessons that clearly present the information and skills students need to learn, but their success comes from the adjustments they make as they see how students react.

❺ **Each class seems to have a personality of its own; some classes "click," and others don't. You have to adjust your teaching accordingly.**

While it is true that each group of students is different than the sum of its parts, and a fact of life that different people and different situations require adjustments, what I would like to focus on here is the apparent assumption that teachers are the passive recipients of class lists. That is, I want to challenge the common practice of administrators, following institutionalized routines based on test scores or other demographic formulas, determining the size and composition of the classes you teach.

Class personality is a function of the range of skills, abilities, and personal characteristics of the students, and teachers are the best sources of insight into what combination of factors will constitute a healthy mix for a good personality. Teachers need to participate in the decisions that lead to assignment of students to classes and the range of factors taken into account in this sort of decision-making should be based on a wide variety of factors—academic achievement (in English and native language), home culture/language, previous school experience, etc.

❻ **I have a lot on my plate right now. I don't have time to do research. I'll become a reflective practitioner when the dust settles.**

This is a handy refrain for busy people. I use it a lot when I want to avoid an unpleasant task, and I have been known to postpone requests from my dean with similar laments about my busy and productive life.

But I suspect this is just another example of the specious dichotomy between thought and action or theory and practice that is prevalent in our society. Or it may be nothing more than a variation on strategies for procrastination or responsibility-avoidance. If I don't have time to be reflective about my practice, then my practice is going to be haphazard and ineffective. I am reminded of the bumper sticker—"Life is what was happening while you were making plans." No matter how hectic life seems and no matter how pressed for time I am, I have to develop habits of work that permit me to gather information about what I am doing and how it is going, and to make adjustments to improve my teaching as I go.

Another point that figures in here is the assumption that thoughtful teaching does not reach the level of reflective practice if it does not result in published articles or elegant program documents or memos to colleagues. For me the solution has been to recognize that on some days I am able to be more reflective than on others, and my notes-to-self on those days are longer and result in more lasting adjustments in my teaching. But my routines of preparation and assessment remain the same regardless of how much time I have and are always available for scrutiny when I decide to return to them. It is the habit that contributes to the quality of reflection on action.

**❼ I am interested in research only if it can tell me unambiguously what I should do in the classroom to be effective.**

There are at least two problems here. One has to do with the common definition of "research" as published articles. I think teachers can be forgiven for developing a skeptical attitude about this. As farmer/philosopher/novelist Wendell Berry says, the publish-or-perish ethic in the academy assures that most of what is "publishable" will not be readable (Berry, 2000). Of course, what he means is that many research articles are written with other researchers—not classroom teachers—in mind as the audience. Most teachers do not look to such research when searching for effective techniques to use in the classroom. They are more likely to take the advice of an experienced colleague or to adopt an appealing activity presented at a conference.

The other problem is the assumption that some "expert" who has written an article can tell you without qualification what you should be doing in your classroom. This is unlikely; there are no prescriptions for success and, alas, no guarantees that following a particular routine will make you a good teacher.

But what if you think of "research" as the careful attention you give to your daily routines, the information you collect on your students, or the time you devote to preparing your lessons? Or, what about the data you collect that permits you to argue for changes in curriculum, testing, or the school schedule? Or a different way of assigning students to classes? All of these are examples of research that could make a significant impact on the quality of your daily life.

**❽ Teachers teach; professors do research. The two activities are mutually exclusive.**

This is another example of the dysfunctional labeling of roles and responsibilities, coupled with the usual difficulties of semantics. It is true that professors have to do research (or at least, they have to publish) in order to keep their jobs, whereas teachers are generally required to spend most of their time teaching. But thoughtful, successful teaching requires collecting and analyzing data on your lessons, your students, and your own conduct, and that should be called research.

Of course, merely calling this kind of activity "research" does not make it so, especially in a school where there is no forum for exchanging ideas about teaching. It becomes necessary to think about implications for school change and adjustments in expectations for teachers. If teaching is understood to be the thoughtful conduct of creating environments for learning, then the activity that contributes to its success will be seen as research. And it will follow that time is required for teachers to do the research and to report back to their colleagues on what they have learned.

**❾ Politics are for politicians and administrators; my job is teaching, and I do not have time to get involved in school or community disputes.**

Good teaching is more an institutional accomplishment than a personal tour de force. A good school can lift a mediocre teacher, and a bad school can drag a good one down. What this means is that teachers must participate in school-wide decision-making.

So, whether we like it or not, we need to see teaching as essentially a political activity. You have to pay attention to the power differentials that influence your daily routines. Decisions are being made all the time in the schools and in society at large that have direct consequences for your teaching, and you ignore them at your own peril. This does not mean that you have to run for office, but you do need to be involved in the politics of decision-making if you want to be an effective teacher. You may have to volunteer for a committee or two, and you may have to lobby your colleagues and administrators from time to time to influence decisions and events.

⑩ **Cultural difference is a significant source of conflict in learning, but there is nothing teachers can do to ameliorate the tensions; we just have to teach the material and help students become better at succeeding in school.**

*Culture* is a big and complex topic, and it is easy to feel overwhelmed by it. It is undeniable that cultural differences *are* a source of conflict in society in general and in schools in particular. But teachers must resist becoming paralyzed by the complexity. If we approach our work as amateur anthropologists attempting to understand the traditions that students bring with them to school, we will begin to discover insights that can contribute to our teaching.

For example, one way of characterizing culture is as "patterns of behavior" (Rogoff, 2003); students enter the classroom accustomed to the particular rhythms and routines acquired at home. If we discover what those are and use our understanding of them as the basis for decision-making, we improve the chances that our lessons will build on, rather than clash with, the assumptions and expectations of the students.

In any case, merely teaching the material is rarely going to be a successful strategy, regardless of the cultural backgrounds of your students. Good teachers are always attentive to the responses of students to lessons and thoughtfully focused on the possible causes of resistance. There are not going to be any easy solutions to the problems that confront them every day. Teachers need policies, procedures, and resources that make it possible to work with diverse groups of students and to reduce misunderstandings. But more than this, teachers need to participate in the development of those policies and procedures, and in the identification and procurement of resources that will support quality teaching in multicultural situations.

## Teacher as Action Researcher

In the remainder of the essay I hope to persuade you to adopt the attitude of an anthropologist and to develop the skills of an action researcher as you think about your work as a teacher.

The title of this essay contains the argument in a nutshell, but it takes some time to unravel it. It goes something like this: Teaching is merely helping others grow in a particular direction—toward an understanding of a complex issue, or mastery of math concepts or language skills, or insights into politics, history, geography, or science, for example. Good teaching is a matter of fostering authentic relationships with learners and moving them toward our goals. We have to start where the learner is, which means that our primary job is learning the learner. We learn the learner; the learner learns, among other things, the material.[3]

Similarly, learning is a deceptively uncomplicated phenomenon—it is change over time through engagement in activity. It is the most natural thing we humans do. In fact, we have been doing it since we were born (perhaps even before, but to pursue that argument would take us down a long detour), and it is something we cannot *not* do. We are always learning. If you are alive, you are learning. Learning *is* life.

Hence the title, *Teaching as learning, learning as life.*

This assertion is at odds with most perspectives on education in which school is seen as distinct from the rest of experience. Teaching is often viewed as the implementation of methods and materials. School learning is viewed as qualitatively different from learning outside of school.

But this is wrong. The contexts may change, but the nature of learning remains the same. Humans are adaptable, and our behavior is certainly shaped by the environment. And there is no denying that schools are organized differently from home and community or that our experiences there contrast, sometimes dramatically, with experiences in other situations. However, it does not follow that the nature of learning, the fundamental process of change in response to experience, changes with the demands of context.

In fact, it defies the logic of the species. Human infants are born with the innate predisposition to learn, to adapt in response to experience, to connect and communicate with others in their immediate surroundings. In fact, it is not an exaggeration to say that from birth the individual is engaged in a struggle to define himself or herself in relationship to others. An early example is sucking, followed closely by other coordinated responses with the mother. The number of participants grows as the child matures, and the process of acculturation is an extension of early propensities to notice and adapt to differences in the environment. The appearance of language is one of the most noticeable adjustments to other human beings, but close observation of infants reveals that all of their responses to others have communicational importance. They attend to their mothers' faces and body movements, and the cooing and cuddling characteristic of adult/infant interaction is recognizable as the precursor of more sophisticated social interaction. It is illogical to assert that this natural process of learning changes merely because the child goes off to school.[4]

What is different, of course, is the institutionalization of the experience. The child at the mother's knee is the apprenticeship model, a time-honored tradition of teaching and learning that is appropriate for transparently authentic tasks and small groups in intimate settings. Modern schooling, with large classes, mandated curricula, and standardized tests, presents a very different experience. So, what is different is the environment; learners respond differently to school according to their experience at home, but the basic processes of learning are the same. The role of teachers is to adapt the environment in ways that will engage learners.

Of course, this constitutes an attitude, a philosophical perspective on teaching and learning, not a teaching method. But it does have significant implications for how we approach the process of teaching and learning.

1. It requires me to attend closely to how students are responding to school and to my instruction, and it means that the content of my instruction may be less important than the relationships I form with the students and the example of curiosity and excitement for learning that I model for students.

2. It means that teaching is not so much a matter of adopting a method as it is finding an approach to working with learners that suits me and my style. I work to define my own personal approach to teaching. This requires me to define my values and commitments and to examine potential methods and materials against them.

3. Because my students are always learning—cannot *not* learn, in fact—my responsibility is to create an environment that will engage their attention and make them want to learn what I want them to learn.

4. This is *not* a search for best practices or the perfect set of methods and materials. There is no one best way of teaching out there to be discovered and acquired. Teaching is not a matter of implementation of formula or procedures, so there can be no claim about the value of a technique independent of the situation in which it occurs or the learning that results.

5. In fact, an understanding of context is essential if I am to understand why a particular practice seems to work or fail. And context extends far beyond the immediate surroundings. *Context* is a collective term for all the information an individual uses to decide from among which *set* of alternatives to make the next move (adapted from Bateson, 1999, p. 289). All individuals at all times bring their own experience to bear as they make decisions about the events and circumstances that face them. This means that a particular situation will have as many contexts as there are participants.

6. As I adapt teaching procedures to my own classroom, my success will depend on my understanding of my students and their home situations, coupled with my negotiation of school policies. This means that I need to be aware of multiple levels of context as I work.

7. And this requires that I adopt the stance of action research as I develop my teaching philosophy and practice.

I suspect that the majority of the voting public, most policy-makers, and a significant portion of the educational community would disagree with the argument developed here. Let me start with the conclusion and work backward.

## Why "Action Research"?

Teachers need to become leaders in their schools. Teaching in today's political and institutional climate requires thoughtful approaches to complex problems of practice; there are no pat answers to the problems we face, and we do not have the luxury of focusing exclusively on the classroom and our students. We need to take an active role in shaping the school environment so that we can teach effectively in our classrooms. This means that we often need to teach others—colleagues, administrators, parents, or sponsors—how they can participate effectively in our change efforts. Action research is the approach that works best in this endeavor, and a bit of background is required to understand why.

Action research has a long and distinguished history, dating back to the early years of the century and traceable to the American philosopher and educator John Dewey and the corporate activist Kurt Lewin (Dewey, 1916, 1933, 1975; Lewin, 1946). There have been numerous developments over the years, and recently it has become the focus of considerable scrutiny by education scholars (Elliot, 1991; Adelman, 1993; Edge, 2001; Reason & Bradbury, 2001), but it is not necessary to describe the approach in all its complexity. I'll take the phrase at face value: action informed by research and research for the purpose of action.

But why "research" you may wonder: "Isn't that a bit pretentious? Aren't we merely required to thoughtfully attend to a situation and then develop a plan? Isn't this the responsibility of teachers?"

Yes, this would be the case if all that were required was the solving of mundane teaching problems in your classroom. But significant problems require more than that. Let me provide an example to make my point here.[5]

### MARIA'S DILEMMA

Maria, whom you have considered a serious and sincere student, has recently begun missing class or arriving late, and when you attempt to discuss the problem with her, she becomes quiet and defiant. School policy is straightforward: mandatory referral for multiple infractions followed by suspension. You hesitate, however, because of her previous record, and because you suspect that punishment is not likely to improve the situation. You do a bit of poking around, and you discover that her mother is ill and Maria is often required to take care of her siblings. You're not sure why she didn't just tell you this when you asked, but it is clear that she is carrying a significant burden and that support is what she requires, not the additional worries of school retribution. You ask around and discover that a number of girls have similar responsibilities at home. In fact, a rough cross-check of attendance records indicates that more than half of the referrals for tardiness and absences during the past month were for girls with child care responsibilities at home. You talk to the principal about what you have found, and the two of you decide to write a proposal for district support of emergency child care. You gather a group of colleagues and community health workers and come up with a structure for coordinating school resources with community facilities. The proposal is revised during a series of meetings, and by the start of the new school year the school has an innovative program in place for helping families and improving school attendance.

This is not an extraordinary case, especially for learners from immigrant families. The process you used to address the issue is action research. Let's examine the sequence of events a bit more closely.

❒ First there is the fact that you have been *observant*—you have developed a sense of what is normal with regard to Maria's behavior.

❒ Then, you notice a problem and you ask yourself a number of questions that frame your *search for a solution*—"What's going on here with Maria? Why has she suddenly changed from conscientious to resistant? How can I improve the situation?"

❒ You poke around a bit, a process that researchers call *collecting data;* the goal is to answer the questions you have generated.

❒ You discover a pattern that accounts for the problem. This is called *analysis* in research circles.

❐ You *take action*, which in this case means collecting allies and drafting a proposal to district personnel asking for funds to provide child care for families
who need it so that students will not miss class.

❐ Of course, the story continues beyond this point, and the *process of inquiry* and
the requirement for *continued action* never stop.

❐ Funds are always tight, and the program you propose will compete with other
worthy projects for support; there is undoubtedly a long struggle associated
with *providing support* for Maria and other students in her situation.

❐ You and your colleagues set up an *evaluation plan* that shows the program is
achieving its intended results, and you discover that you need to constantly
defend the program to administrators, colleagues, and others in order to keep
it going.

This is *action research, an ongoing cyclical process of observing, asking questions, collecting information, analyzing, and responding to problems that impact you and your students.*
But it goes beyond the response of the moment and extends to efforts at influencing policy and practice in the larger environment. If Maria is to succeed in
school, budgetary and administrative decisions will have to be made to change
the way the schools operate, and this will not happen unless arguments supported by data are presented to support the changes.

Action research therefore becomes the approach for the everyday professional activity of being a teacher. And, given the demands on your time, it pays
to approach the process deliberately. Helping you do that is the goal of the rest
of this essay.[6]

## Action Research Procedures

The focus of action research is always on the researcher—working systematically to understand and improve his or her own practice. The basic routine of
action research is a recursive cycle of six steps: observe, reflect, describe, analyze (and act), write it up, assess, and start again.

### 1. Observe

The kind of observation you practice goes beyond the conventional meaning of the word. It is a focused, structured effort at seeing what is happening
and understanding what events mean for the participants. It requires you to
get beyond your prejudices and preconceived notions, or at least to factor them
into your efforts at understanding what you are seeing. You need to make the

familiar strange (Erickson, 1992), to come to each situation as if for the first time. Above all, you work to see the world from the perspectives of the people you are observing.

I have had to learn to take field notes so that I can reconstruct what I have experienced, and in situations where it is not possible to take notes, I have had to learn to attend to what is going on so that I can jot down items of interest as soon as I am free. You have to develop your own techniques to suit your habits and style, but here are some pointers that I have found helpful:

❒ I use a split-page format with a margin on the right where I can go back and annotate my observations.

❒ I make maps of the room with seating charts so that I can reconstruct who was where.

❒ I learn everyone's name in a hurry, and I work at remembering key facts about individuals so that I can begin developing expectations about how they think and act.

❒ I note the time at the top of every page, and at every juncture in the activity I am observing.

❒ I have learned to take verbatim quotes and note who said what to whom.

In the example of Maria, the observations might have taken the form of attendance records and notes written after school in which you noted her absences and her reactions to your inquiries. Interviews of other teachers, notes taken after telephone calls, and descriptions of other girls' attendance records would be important sources of data as well.

## 2. Reflect

The stance of the anthropologist is one of respectful curiosity. You observe and make notes and ask yourself, "What do the natives think they are doing? Why are they responding the way they are? What rules are they following that would lead them to behave in the way they do?"

It is important to suspend judgment, assuming that, however strange and unpredictable the situation and events seem to be, they must appear normal and predictable from the perspective of the participants. Things are the way they are *not* by accident. Specific events and recurring situations may not have been planned to occur exactly the way they do, but constraints, structures, and procedures converge to produce what you see happening.

And so, you reflect. And you ask questions. And make notes. And reflect some more. Here are some guidelines to facilitate the process:

❑ As soon as possible after an event, sit down and review your notes, adding elaborations and questions in the margins to help further your understanding of what you have seen.

■ I use a different color ink or pencil for this so that I can distinguish between notes taken on-site and notes taken later.

■ Focus your attention on questions that *you* have, items that you think will help you understand and act.

❑ As soon as possible write up the notes. Focus on describing what you have seen and on recording reactions and questions to follow up on.

❑ Generate questions that will help you focus your observations for the next encounter. There is no predicting what you will see, and the sorts of questions you will have are prompted by your own experience and interests. But here are some possibilities:

■ Who sits next to whom? What are the apparent friendship/antagonism patterns among people?

■ Who talks and who is silent?

■ What are people doing while something else is going on? For example, during a demonstration or lecture, who is attending and who is doing something else?

■ Who is absent? Late? Who has the homework and who doesn't?

■ What are the quiet students doing? Very often our attention is focused on the talkative students, and we forget to notice the quiet ones.

In the case of Maria, after each encounter with her, your questions would become more focused on number of people who might provide you with more information. Each step in the investigation of the patterns of absences would be characterized by more clearly focused questions. You might decide you should have talked to friends of hers to discover why she was absent, for example—a simple note-to-self, "Check with Tina..." would be sufficient.

## 3. Describe

As you observe and reflect on your notes, you begin to arrive at an understanding of what you have seen. The descriptions vary in length and detail, but they are always attempts to capture events and situations as objectively as possible.

Descriptions take several forms. One might be nothing more than a brief note-to-self after a lesson. Another might be a summary of a week's worth of lessons or of a unit that just completed. This is an important discipline to establish because it helps you consolidate your memories and clarify your understanding. Or, as you begin to focus on situations that you want to understand better, you might draw on several days' worth of notes to compile a description of a focal event.

In the example of Maria's attendance and attitude problems, your descriptions of her behavior would have taken several forms, from brief paragraphs to one-page summaries of your attempts to understand what was going on. You would have noted her comments, gestures, facial expressions, along with counts of absences and notes about the circumstances as far as you knew them.

## 4. Analyze (and Act)

Analysis is a matter of finding patterns, of identifying the sequence of events that seem to characterize the situation you are interested in. It is also your effort at going beyond description to attempt to account for the reasons why things occur as they do. This is easier said than done, but it is an essential step if you hope to identify appropriate action.

When I say "patterns," I am referring to cycles of events because we are interested in patterns over time. Life comes in cycles—conception, gestation, birth, growth, death; spring, summer, autumn, winter; MTWThF; etc.—and our efforts at improving conditions for learning must be crafted within the same rhythms. It would be futile, for example, to talk to Maria about arriving late when she enters the room; at that moment she is distraught and flustered and the best use of your time is to help her settle down and get to work. However, later in day you might discuss with her strategies for communicating with you when she learns about her mother's impending doctor visit and for attempting to make the best use of her time so that her school work does not suffer.

The key to effective action is to select the point in the cycle that is most likely to produce the effects you want to accomplish. And this raises the issue of scale—deciding the level on which you are going to act. You want to help Maria directly, so you work with her to find strategies to improve her efforts. At the same time, you recognize that there are larger issues involved, and you focus on collecting the data and influencing school and district policy concerning tardiness, support for families, etc. Cultural values, family practices, the specific situations of Maria's family and of the community all figure in to your thinking. This is part of the rationale focusing on at least three levels of scale as you work.

John Dewey used the phrase *take intelligent action,* by which I think he meant that we need to always be aware of the possibility that what we are doing is a tentative effort at improving a situation based on what we know at the moment, and that we may have to step back and reassess our efforts and modify our approach.

### 5. Write It Up

At each stage in the process, you write. It is an unpleasant fact of life that the majority of time you have to (re)present what you have learned in order to convince others to change their opinions about what is required. The audience determines to a large extent how you write it up. For colleagues and an administrator you know well, a brief bulleted outline or email might be sufficient. For more distant powers, formal reports and PowerPoint presentations become more effective. If you are teaching in a language institute, your audience might be the owners of the school. If you are teaching in a non–English speaking culture, there will be other considerations for you to take into account.

### 6. Assess

At each stage of the process you ask yourself, "Do I have it right? Are things moving in the right direction?" Researchers refer to this as "validity" and "reliability," or "warranted assertability." Teachers practice ongoing assessment of their decisions in their daily work, punctuated by formal evaluation in the form of teacher-produced and standardized tests. If you are just embarking on a teaching career, you will bring your experiences as a student to this question. There is no ultimate, authoritative judge of this. It is a process of approximation, of assessing where you are and then reentering the fray.

## Caveats and Qualifications

Written out like this, in straightforward and descriptive fashion, these admonitions take on a surreal quality, as if all you have to worry about is keeping track of what you are doing so that you can analyze it and write it up, when, in fact, the intensity of the teaching day and the myriad demands of being a teacher make all of this seem impossibly quixotic.

So, let's approach the task from the other end and say, given the realities of the typical day in the life of a teacher and given the importance of developing a system for thinking about what you are doing so that you can learn from the experience, how might you start?

Well, for starters, I have found that a three-ring notebook with dividers and pockets is helpful, coupled with a commitment to myself to keeping every scrap of paper in some sort of order so that I can find it when I want to refer to it. Examples include such things as lesson plans and notes on things you would like to do next time, memos and minutes from meetings, notes on conversations, to-do lists that serve as a reminder of what you had hoped you would be able to do if you had not run out of time, etc. Having such a notebook and systematically putting stuff in it at least carries with it the possibility that you will be able to find the data when you want to take a look at it.

A second indispensable feature of reflective practice is a file drawer with folders for each of the students—a place where you can neatly file things as you are working with an individual, or where you can throw things at the end of the day so they will be there when you find time to return to it.

And third, take a look at your calendar and carve out time for regular contemplation of what you are doing. This is the hardest requirement, but if you do not schedule time for thinking, you won't find time to think. Sounds harsh, but what gets done reveals what is important, and if you discover, at the end of the week, that you spent every minute of the week dashing from pillar to post, reacting in a frenzy to everyone else's agendas and not actively shaping events so that you can claim some authorship of your own life, you will have to concede that someone else is dictating how you live.

It seems like a relatively simple decision to be the author of your own life, rather than a player in someone else's drama.

## REFERENCES

Adelman, C. (1993). Kurt Lewin and the origins of action research. *Educational Action Research, 1,* 7–24.

Bateson, G. (1999). *Steps to an ecology of mind.* Chicago: University of Chicago Press.

Berry, W. (2000). *Life is a miracle: An essay against modern superstition.* Washington, DC: Counterpoint.

Clarke, M. A. (2003). *A place to stand: Essays for educators in troubled times.* Ann Arbor: University of Michigan Press.

Dewey, J. (1916). *Democracy and education: An introduction to the philosophy of education.* New York: The Free Press.

———. (1933). *How we think: A restatement of the relation of reflective thinking to the educative process.* Boston: D.C. Heath.

———. (1975). *Experience and education.* New York: Collier Macmillan.

Edge, J. (2001). *Action research: Case studies in TESOL practice.* Alexandria, VA: TESOL.

Elliot, J. (1991). *Action research for educational change.* Milton Keynes, UK: Open University Press.

Erickson, F. (1992). Ethnographic microanalysis of interaction. In M. D. LeCompte, W. L. Millroy, J. Preissle (Eds.), *The handbook of qualitative research in education* (pp. 201–225). New York: Academic Press.

Gattegno, C. (1976). *The common sense of teaching foreign languages.* New York: Educational Solutions.

Kegan, R. (1982). *The evolving self: Problem and process in human development.* Cambridge, MA: Harvard University Press.

———. (1994). *In over our heads: The mental demands of modern life.* Cambridge, MA: Harvard University Press.

Kramsch, C. (Ed.) (2002). *Language acquisition and language socialization: Ecological perspectives.* New York: Continuum.

Leather, J., & van Dam, J. (Eds.) (2003). *Ecology of language acquisition.* Dordrecht, The Netherlands: Kluwer Academic Publishers.

Lewin, K. (1946). Action research and minority problems. *Journal of Social Issues, 2,* 34–46.

Reason, P., & Bradbury, H. (Eds.) (2001). *Handbook of action research.* Thousand Oaks, CA: Sage Publications.

Rogoff, B. (2003). *The cultural nature of human development.* New York: Oxford University Press.

Stevick, E. W. (1998). *Working with teaching methods: What's at stake?* New York: Heinle and Heinle.

## NOTES

1. The distinction between *acquisition* and *socialization* is not a minor one, but it would be too great a detour to pursue it here. Briefly, some scholars argue that we need to use the latter word in thinking about second language learning in order to underscore the complex and subtle physical, mental, and social changes that occur when one becomes a competent participant in another culture: See Kramsch (2002) and Leather and van Dam (2003).

2. Stevick credits Caleb Gattegno, the creator of the *Silent Way,* with this insight, but because my understanding of the concept of learning the learner comes from reading about and discussing lessons with Stevick, I cite him here and elsewhere when I mention it. But for the full story, refer to Gattegno 1976 and Stevick 1998.

3. I apologize for the cumbersome repetition of *learner* when I might have been expected to use *student* or *individual* or a variety of synonyms. I believe we should think of ourselves as teachers all the time, even (or perhaps especially) when we are engaged in negotiations with colleagues and administrators.

4. Harvard psychologist and teacher educator Robert Kegan provides an extended argument for this perspective in *The Evolving Self: Problem and Process in Human Development* (1982) and *In Over Our Heads: The Mental Demands of Modern Life* (1994).

5. This is a fictionalized version of a true story. Thanks to my CU Denver colleague Alan Davis for this story from his days in the San Luis Valley of southern Colorado.

6. In the remainder of the essay I will make assertions about the nature of teaching and learning and school and community that are developed in greater detail in *A Place to Stand* (Clarke, 2003).

# ❹ Philosophy as Autobiography

$M$y purpose here is to examine the philosophy you have had to develop as part of your professional preparation program and that you dust off from time to time for prospective employers and school accreditation committees. It is probably the case that teachers have always been expected to have philosophies, but in today's climate of politically charged accountability, the need to be clear on what you are doing and why has become increasingly important. The question is, "Can you make it work for you?" Can you make your philosophy into a tool that improves your quality of life, your teaching, and your dealings with administration and community?

Here are some other questions I have been wrestling with:

❐ What is a philosophy of teaching? Of what use is it and to whom? Who dictates what constitutes an adequate philosophy?

❐ Who are the authorities whose teachings guide my decision-making?

❐ How do I integrate my classroom experience into my philosophy?

❐ And a number of tactical questions: What should one include? What options are available for organizing it? How to maintain it, keep it fresh and relevant?

I define philosophy as a document that sets out an approach to life and work. I see it as a tool that guides my decision-making on a day-to-day basis, and that I use to shape my participation in larger curricular and political arenas. It comprises three distinct components:

1. **Core Values**—my important commitments in life and work, the principles by which I conduct myself.

2. **Authority**—the source of those values and the basis on which I justify my beliefs and actions.

3. **Practices**—strategies, tactics, methods, and materials that I use to put my core values into action.

I believe that all humans operate according to philosophies that conform roughly to this outline and that they use to make and rationalize decisions. Most people would not dignify their daily rumination by calling it a philosophy, but at the same time, we all believe our behavior to be consistent and we can defend our actions with reasons that fall into these three categories. Teachers, of course, are required to produce formal documents that are called philosophies, but even so, most of us are reluctant to present ourselves as philosophers. The problem, as I see it, is that the word has acquired rarified connotations associated with Plato, Socrates, and Dewey, on the one hand, and negative associations that come from its use as a tool of accountability, on the other.

What I argue here is that we need to claim philosophy as our territory, and work from within a philosophical framework to improve our teaching and to influence the conditions under which we work. I also argue that the teaching philosophy should be thought of as a personal document derived as much from an understanding of one's life experiences and predilections as from an examination of the scholarly canon.

## Claiming Philosophy as Teacher Territory

You may not put much stock in philosophy, or you may see philosophies as the tools of professors and administrators, distant from the concerns of classroom teaching. Or, perhaps you are happy with your philosophy, but you have not seen it as autobiographical. Maybe you do not see the two genres as connected. And besides, you do not have time to work on your philosophy or your autobiography because you have a stack of papers to grade, dishes to wash, a meeting to chair, or a chair to upholster, or…or…or….

Exactly! Life just keeps coming at you, and you do not have time to stop and get organized because the onslaught is so irritatingly insistent!

I sympathize. But the way I see it, we have only two choices—comply with the demands of modern life by following someone else's rules or create our own definitions of reality and play the game according to rules we believe to be important.[1] It is in this spirit that I have commandeered the teaching philosophy and organized my thinking so that it accomplishes goals important to me while it satisfies the requirements of the significant powers in my life. Here is my reasoning:

1. All human beings have a theory of how the world works and a philosophy on how they conduct themselves in it. And this is not a luxury for teachers, who increasingly must be prepared to present and defend their theory of learning and philosophy of teaching.

2. Teaching is a function of relationship.

   a. The quality of the teaching is a function of the quality of the relationship.

   b. The quality of the relationship depends in part on the quality of self-awareness of the individuals in the relationship (and, obviously, you can't increase the self-awareness of others, but you can work on your own).

3. "Self-awareness" is, in part, a matter of listening to the stories one tells about oneself.

   a. You may not see yourself as an autobiographer, but I'm pretty sure you regularly characterize yourself to others (and yourself) as "… the sort of person who…," which reveals how you see your approach to life.

   b. As with all stories, the audience is a crucial part of the telling. What you choose to tell and how you tell it will be influenced by your perception of what the audience will find interesting or compelling.

   c. I call these stories "autobiography."

Let me elaborate a bit on these points.

It is a widely held position that humans construct mental models of the world they live in. "Reality" is not an objective entity out there to be discovered; it is not the same for each of us, but rather, a construction that varies according to individual experience.[2] For most people this constructed reality is not articulated in an explicit statement of belief so much as a collection of "rules of thumb" that are articulated when they are faced with a troubling decision or forced to give a rationale for their behavior in an argument with a loved one or a boss. When these views are formalized and written down, they are typically referred to as theory and philosophy. And increasingly, the philosophy has become a formal expectation of teachers.

The nature and use of philosophy, however, requires some attention. The dictionary definition of *philosophy* is "the rational investigation of the truths and principles of being." Ludwig Wittgenstein, the renowned Austrian philosopher and rural math teacher, would have agreed: "Philosophy aims at the logical clarification of thoughts. Philosophy is not a body of doctrine but an activity. A philosophical work consists essentially of elucidations" (Wittgenstein, 1961, 4.112).

This means that a philosophy constitutes an ongoing effort of clarifying our roles and responsibilities in the world of teaching. Anthropologist and systems theorist Gregory Bateson articulated the idea of the "pincer maneuver," which gives us a method for doing this work:

> I try to teach students…that in scientific research you start from *two* beginnings, each of which has its own kind of authority: the observations cannot be denied, and the fundamentals must be fitted. You must achieve a sort of pincers maneuver. (Bateson, 1999, p. xxviii)

If we substitute "teaching" for "scientific research" in his definition, we arrive at an understanding of life in which both worlds—the world of experience, the daily life of classrooms and sandboxes—and the world of fundamentals, the philosophical and theoretical assertions about the way the world should be and the way the world works—need to be balanced in an ongoing effort of negotiated understanding. Or, to put it more plainly: We get up in the morning with expectations of justice and fair play and how we might expect to see them in our classrooms, the school, and the world at large. And as the day unfolds we bring this understanding to bear on the events and circumstances we encounter. If our expectations are not met or if we encounter injustice or foul play, we either have to revise our view of the world or we need to search for examples that confirm our world view. The fundamentals and our observations have to be fitted.

This is something we all do every day. In fact, you could argue that mental health requires some level of congruence between what we *believe* to be the nature of reality and our day-to-day *experience* of it.

But in order to improve our teaching, we need to set aside time for thinking about it, not merely in the usual way of reflecting on how things went last time we tried an activity as we tweak the lesson plan we are working on. All teachers do this sort of thinking about their teaching. I am advocating a more formal commitment, one that is scheduled into the week just as are class time and faculty meetings, time where we record our efforts, describe how lessons went, pose questions and articulate problems, *and most important,* time where we attempt to connect these sorts of mundane details to the core values that drive our teaching.

But I need to be clear that I use the word *philosophy* to mean something rough and ready, a handy tool for thinking and planning and working out life's problems, large and small. Something akin to the Swiss Army Knife—lots of parts that serve different purposes, portable, flexible, ingenious, and constantly evolving, a tool that comes in different sizes depending on what I need to accomplish.

The analogy of the Swiss knife is strained a bit when I think of another important aspect of this type of philosophy—the fact that a personal philosophy creates itself as we work on it.

We are only partially aware of what we believe; how we think and act is constantly evolving because of our experiences, and the act of writing it down actually causes it to become more real. We can step back and consider what we have written, decide to try it out, then come back and revise it. It begins to take on a useful role in our lives.

And when I use the word *autobiography,* I do not mean a thick tome that records every event in your life and gathers dust in your grandchildren's attics. My idea is more of a messy combination of photo album and diary, bulging with notes and clippings and scribbles that you leave lying about so you can revise it all the time. Perhaps it is a loose-leaf notebook in a canvas bag, which you take along on vacations and car trips. You remove a page or two every once in a while and use it, folded length-wise, as a book mark in the novel you are reading so that you can capture ideas that you find interesting.

You've heard the advertising jingle, "You are what you eat." Well, they've got that right, but they didn't go far enough. A more accurate adage would be, "You are what you do." What we do on a day-to-day basis—how we behave when we are alone and with others, how we react to crises, and how we conduct ourselves in the mundane business of getting through ordinary days—all this influences who we are. As teachers we need to be clear on the connections between the values we espouse, on the one hand, and the decisions we make and the actions we take day in and day out, on the other. The two are inextricably connected—how we spend the minutes and hours of our days simultaneously shape who we are *and* reveal our values. I don't need lofty proclamations or erudite citations of research to know what people value. All I need is access to their calendars and checkbooks to figure out what is important. If they spend their time volunteering in soup kitchens and homeless shelters or if they donate a considerable portion of their income to such causes, I can surmise what their commitments are.

So the place to begin building a philosophy is not in the library; it is a careful scrutiny of your life.

As to my claim that personal philosophical pondering will energize your work, consider an important fact: We tend to work hardest on the things that we enjoy and are important to us. Teaching will be easier and more satisfying if we can align it to our life commitments. There is a less-honorable rationale, one that appeals to your vanity: Who, truthfully, do you find more interesting than yourself? And what could be more fascinating than discovering how your own identity and history, your tastes and preferences, your pet peeves and projects might be integrated into your work?

I also need to issue a caution: This is potentially disturbing work. If you take seriously my admonition to plumb the depths of your own history to arrive at an understanding of why you teach the way you do, you may discover things about yourself that you were avoiding and that require serious effort and adjustment. I didn't say it would be easy; I merely claim that it is important.

It is important because increasingly we are working in environments over which we have dwindling influence. Because of economic and political pressures, decisions that were once left to teachers are now matters of policy and procedure, and whereas we used to take our spheres of influence for granted, we now have to construct arguments and rationales that make sense to individuals who may not share our values or priorities. In such cases, the justification for a position very often rests on what might be called philosophical or theoretical tenets.

But, I repeat myself.

To continue with the three-point rationale for philosophy as autobiography: In the previous essay I dwelt at length on the assertion in #2, that teaching is a function of relationship. What needs to be underscored here is the importance of self-awareness in the development of the relationship. I hope you'll forgive me for trotting out Shakespeare in support of this assertion: "This above all: to thine own self be true, And it must follow, as the night the day, Thou canst not then be false to any man" (Polonius, to his son, in *Hamlet*, Act 1, Scene 3). It may be trite, but that does not make it less true.

The third point, concerning the importance of paying attention to the stories we tell about ourselves, begins to move us closer to the connection I want to make between autobiography and philosophy. The fact is, we are who we are, but there are at least two significant aspects to this truism. The first is the action—the motion, engagement, activity of our daily lives. How we spend our days influences who we are and how we see the world. We become identified, both to others and to ourselves, with our customary activities, our preferred ways of spending time. Think about the things you do when you unexpectedly find yourself with some free time—do you head to the tennis courts, go shopping, dig in the garden, hide in a bookstore with a latte, or go to a matinee?

Our rhythms and routines come to define us to a great extent, and we find ourselves saying, "I'm the kind of person who..." followed perhaps by one of those defining activities, which brings me to the second point—how we represent these rhythms and routines to the world and to ourselves. The stories we tell about ourselves, whether out loud to others or silently in our own minds, shape the way we think about our lives and the way that others perceive us.

Two of my colleagues have very full and busy lives—jobs, families, school and community commitments, recreational activities, etc.—and regularly arrive late for meetings amidst apologies and bags bulging with books, notes, calendars, and granola bars. One tells stories of flat tires, missed connections with child-care providers, messy entries on calendars that led to double booking, etc. The other apologizes and frames the late arrival as too many important commitments and the need to get better organized. Same situation, similar set of problems, but one person's story conveys a picture of confusion while the other implies urgent coping with the demands of a busy life.

The same thing is true in the more formal narratives that we use to shape people's impressions of us—entries in resumes or the brief biographical statements that are contained in reports, or even the excerpts in the school directory or on the bulletin board in the hallway. So, it behooves us as teachers to attend to how we develop our stories.

This may strike you as an odd way of thinking about who you are, about personal identity: "Isn't my personality pretty much determined at conception?" you might be asking yourself. My answer is, "No, at least, not entirely."[3] I do not discount the importance of genetics; it seems reasonable to assume that certain features of personality are set at birth, just as, for example, eye and hair color and basic physical frame. Studies of twins who have been separated at birth would seem to bear this out.

However, the case I am arguing is that we develop rhythms and routines in our daily lives that significantly shape who we are and how we think about ourselves, and that this is an important area of personal discretion that we should pay attention to.

I do not want to get mired in an investigation of personality theory. What I want to do is develop an approach to philosophy that is consistent with the view of learning and teaching I am developing in this book. I believe that it is important for teachers to develop an understanding of learning that keeps daily realities in focus and permits them to adjust their teaching practices in principled ways. I have great respect for learned scholarship based on neuro-psychological research, but I do not know what to do, as a teacher, with information about biochemical cortical functioning, the role of the amygdala in affective aspects of language learning, or studies of motivation that require an understanding of an individual's childhood.

I want a theory of language learning that permits me to make informed decisions on a daily basis.

I am following a respectable strand of scholarship (Kegan, 1982, 1994; Holland, Lachicotte, Skinner, & Cain, 1998a; Norton, 2000b; Rogoff, 2003) in asserting that your identity is an ongoing negotiated accomplishment, even though you have to be content with the cards you were dealt at conception. And I believe that the place to start is with autobiography. Perhaps it would be useful to consider an example of what I mean. I'll offer my own story as a starting point.

## EMERGING INSIGHTS

Mine was a happy childhood spent in the shadow of the Rocky Mountains with all the benefits that accrue to being a white anglo-saxon protestant heterosexual baby boomer male raised in the post-WWII era and narrowly missing the Vietnam draft by virtue of a weak knee (a wrestling injury) and alternative service at the American University in Cairo.

From my father I acquired a love of reading and a philosophical acceptance of human foible, including my own. From my mother I inherited a high tolerance for routine and the ability to focus on work. I spent a lot of time with my grandparents on their fruit farm in Paonia, Colorado, and although I never seriously considered becoming a farmer, I identify strongly with rural settings, small town life, and folk wisdom passed down from generation to generation.

If I were to identify pivotal events in my life I would nominate travel—to Mexico and Costa Rica, to Egypt and North Africa, to Europe and Japan—and sequestered immersion in ideas at the University of Colorado, the University of Costa Rica, the American University in Cairo, and the University of Michigan. Even more important than these professional events is the nurturing of an extended Bomer/ Clarke/Barr clan and lucky decisions in love that have provided enduring sources of security and satisfaction.

I believe that in the past of all teachers lurk formative experiences as learners. I have fond memories of many teachers, but almost every day I thank Mrs. Binkleman, my ninth grade English teacher, for requiring us to memorize Chaucer, Shakespeare, and Donne, and for modeling a single-minded focus on English language and literature in spite of the hooliganism of her irreverent students. I learned a great deal about English and language teaching from her.

I also benefited from my years of studying Spanish. As a junior high school student I enjoyed the drills and dialogues orchestrated by Señor Benevidez, and the class was certainly different from anything I expected. It was conducted entirely in Spanish; we memorized mountains of dialogues, and we were expected to discern grammatical and lexical meaning without the benefit of English explanations—without even a textbook. In fact, we saw no written Spanish at all until halfway through the first year. When I got to high school two years later, I was confronted with the request by the teacher to "conjugate the verb *estar.*" I was struck dumb; I had never heard the word *conjugate,* and I was not prepared for instruction, conducted principally in English, on Spanish grammar. I did not enjoy these classes much, and it is probably instructive that I cannot remember the teacher's name, but I did learn how to analyze sentence structure.

Later in that same year the grammar teacher retired, and the ebullient Señorita Burrow ("Soy Burrow, no burro.") crashed into our lives with infectious enthusiasm and interactive language learning activities. She did not use drills or require us to memorize dialogues, nor did we talk about Spanish in English. Her classroom was the scene of riotous conversation and improvisation, in Spanish, and we students did most of the talking. In subsequent years at the University of Colorado, I had a wide range of Spanish teachers, each of whom approached teaching in different ways.

These experiences as a language learner later proved to be instructive. I do not think I was particularly reflective about the teaching I experienced as a schoolboy, but like all learners I had definite preferences for particular teachers, activities, and materials. Without knowing it, I had developed an awareness of differing approaches to language teaching. In my studies at the University of Colorado, the American University in Cairo, and the University of Michigan, I learned that those three teachers— Señor Benevidez, Señora Anonima, Señorita Burrow—were representatives of the "audiolingual method," "grammar translation," and "communicative competence" paradigms, respectively.

Thus began my attempts to understand language teaching and learning. I took language teaching methods classes as an undergraduate in Boulder and as a graduate student in Cairo and Ann Arbor. I came of age as a teacher in the era of "designer methods" (Brown, 2000; Kumaravidevalu, 2003), when everyone was convinced that the secret to good teaching was the skillful implementation of teaching techniques, proceeding from a coherent foundation of method and theory (Anthony, 1963).

Early on, my search was narrowly instructional; I was looking for teaching methods that would motivate students and provide effective mechanisms for mastering content and skills. I learned a lot from my fellow students and teaching colleagues in graduate school at the American University in Cairo and the University of Michigan; the exchange of tips and teaching techniques in the carrels where we all hung out between classes was intense, borne by the pressures of time and the expectations of our students. These were hothouses for teacher development in which we unembarrassedly admitted ignorance and sought counsel, questioned the application of the theory we were reading in graduate courses, took advice on particular students, commiserated on failed lessons, and rejoiced together on successes.

We also benefited from the lectures and workshops of itinerant experts who passed through. The most influential of these for me was Earl W. Stevick, who worked for many years at the Foreign Service Institute in Washington, DC, and whose thoughtful analysis of the details of classroom life coupled with a commitment to humane approaches to students provided me with model and guide in my search for a professional identity (Stevick, 1980, 1982, 1996, 1998b).

Although I brought an anthropological perspective to my work as a teacher, it took me several years to understand that classrooms are situated in complex relationships with schools, community, and culture, and to understand how that understanding might be utilized in my teaching. I found the work of several social scientists helpful as I sought to forge connections between the classroom and "the world out there," but it was Gregory Bateson, with his analysis of systems and system change, who provided me with the theoretical perspective of human interaction and learning that frames all of my work. Pete Becker, a friend of Bateson's and a professor of linguistics at the University of Michigan, was the person who suggested I read *Steps to an Ecology of Mind* not long after it came out in 1972. I have been reading it ever since.

Over the years, as I moved in and out of different countries and classrooms, as I adjusted my focus to include teaching teachers as well as teaching language learners, and as I attempted to see the patterns that connect border wars with report cards, I gradually moved systems theory, as developed by Bateson and scholars influenced by him, to the center of my vision (Watzlawick, Beavin, & Jackson, 1967; Wilden, 1987; Bateson, 1994, 1999; Harries-Jones, 1995).

More recently, I began to explore the work of developmental constructivists (Kegan, 1982, 1994) and sociocultural theorists (Holland et al., 1998b; Toulmin, 2001; Rogoff, 2003), who attempt to connect the broad sweep of history with current events and with individuals' sense of self.

The result, which I should probably have foreseen but which came as a bit of a surprise, has been that my vision has expanded. Everything seems to be an example of everything else, and this is reflected in the recursive nature of the arguments developed in these essays; this book can be seen as an example of *philosophy as autobiography.*

The details of my life are of minimal interest to you, except by extension. That is, if you were to write a similar narrative, what would you discover? How might it affect your approach to teaching? Would it cause you to stop and think about your convictions and comfortable assumptions? Would you discover gaps in your rationale for your professional conduct—instances, perhaps, where you have difficulty explaining your reasons for using a favorite technique or set of materials?

For me, the accusations implied by these questions strike some tender nerves. The exercise proved more difficult than I thought it would, and as I returned to each draft I was amazed to discover omissions or pretensions, conveniently forgotten contributions of friends or family, posturing that close colleagues or former students would call me on if they read it—that sort of thing. But what began to emerge was a clearer view of what I valued as a teacher and the classroom activities that I favored. Occasionally I would have to admit that I didn't understand why I think a particular activity "worked," or even that I had no clear criteria for determining if, in fact, a lesson could be called a success.

In the process, it became clear to me that this was not a narcissistic exercise—that gaining a clearer understanding of who I am and what I value as a teacher provides the tools for getting through the day.

Which brings me to the reason why all this effort is worthwhile. The quest for some degree of control over the conditions of life and work involves a continuing struggle toward *coherence*—toward the alignment of vision and action, toward an aesthetic consistency between what you think and how you act.

Understanding who you are and how you came to be that way is an important step in the process. As I contemplate my autobiographical vignette, I am able to identify the features of my upbringing, teaching experience, and education that predispose me toward particular teaching activities and professional commitments. This awareness constitutes a foundation and framework for working toward coherence.

## Getting Down to Basics

If the following constitute the basis on which we make our decisions daily

1. core commitments
2. the authority on which these rest
3. representative activities that reflect Numbers 1 and 2

... and if we desire our behavior to be consistent over time and in different settings, and if we hope to learn from our mistakes and successes, and if we aspire to keep up with the professional literature—then it behooves us to develop ways of thinking through how this is to be accomplished.

Pause a minute. Ponder the connections between Numbers 1 and 3 and core commitments and favorite teaching activities. What do you believe, and how does it show up every day in your classroom? If, for example, you believe in a democratic classroom where students have a voice in what goes on, can you point to particular activities that impartial observers would agree confirm that conviction? And can you explain particular activities in terms of this conviction?

Run it the other direction, your favorite activities and how they reveal your core values: Would an observer be able to infer your philosophy of life merely by watching you teach? What would your students report to be your favorite activities, and would you agree with them? Would they agree that you are dedicated to the values you identify as important for you?

Or, from yet another point of view: What would you say to your administrator who happened past your classroom just as your efforts at orchestrating student participation in classroom decision-making erupted into an unseemly argument between students with different political commitments, passion for their points of view, and eloquent but profane epithets? How would you justify the risks taken with such activities? How would you defend your teaching practices in the face of clear evidence that they don't always work?

Now, let's examine Number 2—who do you think of when you attempt to make the connections between 1 and 3? Who authorizes your choices? Who comes to mind as the authority for your behavior, and what difference does it make when the audience for your presentation changes? My grandfather, for example, looms large in my understanding of how to treat fellow human beings, but then so does teacher and author Earl Stevick. Which authority I cite depends on whom I am addressing and what I hope to accomplish. I am more inclined to cite my grandfather when discussing teaching decisions with students or colleagues who share my respect for ancestors. When discussing teaching with administrators or other authorities, I am more likely to cite scholars such as Stevick.

It is instructive to examine your philosophical convictions and classroom activities from this perspective, but the important thing is to remain loose while you do it. That is, in order to learn from the activity, you need to take a playful, even irreverent approach; the goal is to surprise yourself with insights that typically are unavailable for inspection, and it is difficult to do this if you approach the task as if you are being graded on it by a superior or a judgmental colleague. Play with the following exercises to see what emerges for you.

In each case, however, your awareness of the assumptions and expectations of your audience shapes the presentation. Your director or principal might be interested in your grasp of theory, but your colleagues will not sit still for lofty lectures and your students have no interest at all in why you teach the way you do. What is required is that you arrive at a clear understanding *for yourself* of your philosophy and the uses to which it might be profitably put.

Here is my recommendation for accomplishing that.

1. Sketch the key events and activities that have shaped you as a learner and a teacher. For starters you might consider:
   a. What activities do you remember enjoying as you grew up?
   b. What types of classroom activities do you enjoy as a learner?
   c. What experiences with other languages and cultures do you think of as formative in your decision to become a teacher?
   d. What events and situations come to mind as you think about your own classroom learning?

2. Identify broad tendencies in your approach to teaching and learning. I've arrayed a number of continua for you to consider. For each one, think of particular events or situations and mark a spot on the line that indicates your tendency. If your preference has changed over the years, indicate

the differences with a *P* (for *Past*) and an *N* (for *Now*). If your preference changes depending on whether you are evaluating an item as student or teacher, indicate both. Jot notes in the spaces to remind yourself of those vignettes.

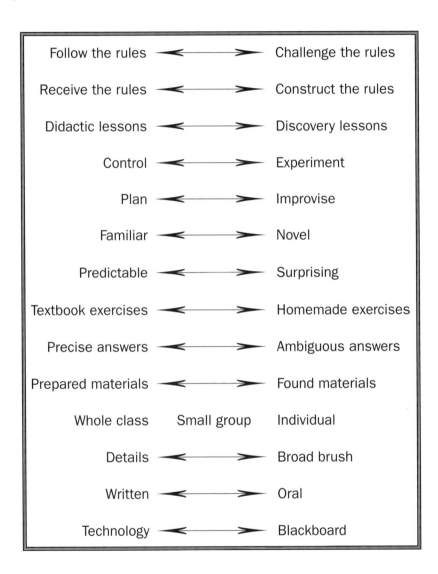

| | |
|---|---|
| Follow the rules | Challenge the rules |
| Receive the rules | Construct the rules |
| Didactic lessons | Discovery lessons |
| Control | Experiment |
| Plan | Improvise |
| Familiar | Novel |
| Predictable | Surprising |
| Textbook exercises | Homemade exercises |
| Precise answers | Ambiguous answers |
| Prepared materials | Found materials |
| Whole class    Small group | Individual |
| Details | Broad brush |
| Written | Oral |
| Technology | Blackboard |

3. Connecting values, authority, and practice.

Work from daily experience; jot notes-to-self that identify techniques and materials you use, and offer the justification (i.e., the authorities you would cite) for different audiences (for example, your students, the director of your program, a reporter or member of the school's governing board). Identify the audience for each column.

| Favorite Activity | Core Value | Authority for Audience 1 | Authority for Audience 2 | Authority for Audience 3 |
|---|---|---|---|---|
|  |  |  |  |  |
|  |  |  |  |  |
|  |  |  |  |  |

Now, come at it from the other direction, citing different activities:

| Core Value | Representative Activity | Authority for Audience 1 | Authority for Audience 2 | Authority for Audience 3 |
|---|---|---|---|---|
|  |  |  |  |  |
|  |  |  |  |  |
|  |  |  |  |  |

This is such a transparent activity that you, in fact, did not even do it—you just skipped on down to this sentence, am I right?

What if I told you that I believe that such an exercise, completed faithfully and diligently, will reveal that you, like most teachers, select activities based primarily on personality, habit, and convenience, and only secondarily on theoretical grounds? Would that pique your pride or curiosity sufficiently to induce you to return and complete the activities?

What if I were to present the task as one of self-defense—based on the assertion that teachers today cannot count on the goodwill and support of their administration or the public and that it behooves us to be prepared with a sound rationale for everything we do?

I admit that may sound just a tad paranoid, but recently I had a teacher in a methods class proclaim that she taught "at the will" of administrators and that she dared not deviate from mandated behavior until she was able to discern just how serious they were going to follow up on administrative mandates. This same teacher was, in general, an independent thinker and a critical consumer of ideas and teaching methods, but this outburst revealed the pressures she was under in her school. I do not think that hers is an isolated case. So, go back and fill in the charts so we can continue the conversation. Here's a sampling of my own to give you a start.

| Favorite Activity | Core Value | Authority for Audience 1 (fellow professionals) | Authority for Audience 2 (students) | Authority for Audience 3 (parents, lay persons) |
|---|---|---|---|---|
| Reading comprehension questions that have no single correct answer. | Students must become independent learners and depend on themselves. Confusion in manageable doses is a healthy thing. | Constructivist views of learning: (Vygotsky, 1978; Cole, 1996; Stevick, 1996) | "Life—there are no answer keys out there, so why would you expect them in this class?" | Two reasons: "Life..." and "Research shows..." sorts of statements; establishes my credentials as a professional. |
| Focused language and literacy work in which students work alone on exercises, followed by small group, followed by class discussion (rather than, say, didactic presentation of material by me). | Teaching "good citizenship" is part of my responsibility; students must learn to arrive at their own conclusions and to defend their positions and to compromise as they work together. | Sociocultural views of teaching: (Dewey, 1938a; Freire & Macedo, 1987a; Norton, 2000a; Kramsch, 2002) | "Your parents or sponsoring organizations sent you here to learn how to use language and literacy skills to communicate effectively." | "John Dewey and other progressive educators..." argue that students learn best by doing, not by sitting in rows and being talked to. |

Approaching it from the other direction, and citing different activities:

| Core Value | Representative Activity | Authority for Audience 1 (fellow professionals) | Authority for Audience 2 (students) | Authority for Audience 3 (parents, lay persons) |
|---|---|---|---|---|
| Language is central to an individual's sense of identity. | Authentic activities that bring real-world phenomena into the classroom for students to work with; language drills that use facts from students' lives. | Critical views of language teaching: (Holland, et al. 1998b; Stevick, 1998a; Norton, 2000a) | "School prepares you for life. Here you get to practice without fear of ridicule or censure." | Same as for students, but in addition, pointing out that whatever we do is aligned with professional standards and the school curriculum. |
| Teaching is a function of relationships; it is my job to learn the students. | Frequent use of individual and small group conferences and requests for "scribble sheets"— informal assessments at the end of class that permit students to anonymously evaluate me and the activity. | Earl Stevick, who argues that we must pay attention to what goes on "inside and between" people. Dewey—we must start where the learner is. Adult educators, who know that students will walk away if lessons are not relevant. (Dewey, 1938a; Stevick, 1998a; Drago-Severson, 2004) | Common sense: You need to tell me your honest opinion of the class so I can adjust it to your needs. | "Best pedagogical practices" require frequent authentic assessment. |

There are many things to be learned from this sort of activity, especially if you orchestrate conversations around it with friends and colleagues. You may discover, for example, that colleagues also like a particular activity but have different rationales or cite different authorities in support of it. Or, just as likely, they might doubt that the way you conduct the activity would be acceptable to the scholar you cite in support of it. And, it is entirely likely that you and your colleagues would not be able to agree that particular activities actually reveal your adherence to the identified core values.

The point is, there are no ultimate "right answers;" it is not the purpose of the effort to discover "best practices." Rather, the goal is to become clearer on your own rationale for how you teach and to develop the means for defending your actions as required.

Another important point is the one I have previously alluded to—regardless of the scholarly citations we muster to support our teaching, we will always tend toward activities that we find personally agreeable. These, in turn, can be traced to life-long habits and preferences, family traditions, and comfortable daily activities. Art and music lovers will be inclined to import art and music into their classes, and amateur astronomers will figure out a way to bring heaven to earth. This is natural and it is healthy, with three qualifications.

First, we need to leaven our preferences with insights from current scholarship and adjustments to the professional and political realities within which we work. There really is nothing new under the sun, so teachers do not have to fear that their favorite teaching techniques will be discredited, but wily veterans also know that they need to justify what they do in the vocabulary of the day. That is, our favorite activity may be one that we picked up years ago when different gurus were in vogue and the rhetoric that is now considered politically incorrect was used to describe acceptable teaching, but it is safe to say that, if the technique works, you can justify it according to the current pedagogical wisdom. It may take some work, but it is prudent to make the effort.

Second, we need to work to assure that students who do not share our enthusiasms are not left on the margins of activities. This requires a relentless empiricism, an unflinching eye on *all* of our students, not just the ones who seem to enjoy our teaching.

And third, we need to expand our awareness of the personal trajectory that brought us to where we are as teachers. Hence, the importance of autobiography.

4. Discovering omissions and blind spots.

The danger with this approach is that it might lead to unreflective acceptance of personal preference as the sole basis for teaching decisions. The three caveats are intended as antidote to this problem, and the following are advocated as exercises in the service of greater clarity of motivation.

a. Think back on the last time you used one of the activities nominated in the boxes. Fill in the boxes with the names of students depending on their level of engagement.

| Activity | Engaged | Compliant | Resistant |
|---|---|---|---|
| | | | |

b. For each of the "compliant" and "resistant" students, list their favorite activities, their preferences for learning, their favorite subjects.

c. For each of these students, list the things *you* did or did not do that prevented them from becoming engaged.

The point of this exercise is to distribute responsibility equally for failed lessons. If it is my responsibility to create an environment that engages students, and if my teaching reveals my personal preferences and inclinations, then I need to develop habits of assessment that ensure that I do not blame students for failed lessons when in fact the problem is as much my fault as theirs.

It is human nature to pay attention to the students who seem engaged in the lesson. What this exercise requires is that you force yourself to attend to the students who are indifferent or openly hostile to your efforts. But rather than focusing on getting them to comply with your demands, Steps b and c require you to ponder ways *you* might change to increase their interest in the lesson. This is consistent with the argument I have been making throughout the book: the only person over whom I have any control is myself, and it is in line with the emphasis on autobiographical approaches to understanding teaching. That is, I know that the lessons I devise are comfortable ones *for me*, perhaps even ones that I picked up from favorite teachers during my years as a student. What I need to cultivate are strategies for expanding my vision beyond my comfort zone, and this activity is designed to do that.

Let me give you an example. Thinking back on the past couple of semesters, here are some students and their responses to my teaching. The names are psuedonyms.

a. Think back on the last time you used one of the activities nominated in the boxes. Fill in the boxes with the names students depending on their level of engagement.

| Activity | Engaged | Compliant | Resistant |
|---|---|---|---|
| Reading comprehension questions that have no single correct answer. | Felicity | Federico | Alicia |

b. For each of the "compliant" and "resistant" students, list their favorite activities, their preferences for learning, their favorite subjects. No need to talk here about Felicity, who seems to enjoy the ambiguity of exercises that have no single correct answer.

    i. Federico, however, is more comfortable in the assigned role of "student" and likes knowing that there are correct answers. He has an engineering background and is a good student, so he complies with these sorts of activities, but he would prefer work that has focused goals and clear guidelines.

    ii. Alicia, I suspect, feels betrayed by this sort of activity. She knows I made up the exercises and that I could just as easily provided activities where there are "real" answers. She views this sort of thing as game-playing. She enjoys puzzles and problem-solving, but she wants to know the rules and the correct answers. History and political science are her favorite subjects, but she has not yet considered the point of view that individuals with particular biases write the books she reads; she still tends to think if something appears in a book it must be correct.

c. For each of these students, list the things *you* did or did not do that prevented them from becoming engaged.

    i. I did not spend enough time individually coaching Federico on the merits of the activity. I pushed forward with the activity hoping that his general goodwill and the camaraderie of his group-mates would bring him along.

    ii. Alicia is hyper-sensitive to my comments and attention. I need to pay more explicit attention to her needy (my, perhaps unfair, characterization) approach to learning. I did not bolster her efforts with personalized commentary, nor did I ask if she understood the task, which often elicits lots of questions and concerns but also tends to help her get into the task.

| Activity | Engaged | Compliant | Resistant |
|---|---|---|---|
| Focused language and literacy work in which students work alone on exercises, followed by small group, followed by class discussion (rather than, say, didactic presentation of material by me). | Federico | Roberto | Hyun Kyung |

b. For each of the "compliant" and "resistant" students, list their favorite activities, their preferences for learning, their favorite subjects. The engaged individual is the same Federico who merely complies with my "ambiguous comprehension questions." He enjoys the small group work in general and likes defending his answers in conversation with his classmates.

    i. Roberto, however, is a respectful student who would just as soon have me earn my salary by actually teaching the class rather than organizing all these cheesy group discussions. He likes sports and does well in school in general, so I can usually coax him along with jock talk and by invoking my authority as teacher.

    ii. Hyun Kyung, however, is paying her own tuition and views this sort of thing as a waste of time and money. She is a civil servant who has her eye on the career ladder; she enjoys worksheets and written assignments, and she thrives on lectures and explicit instruction.

c. For each of these students, list the things *you* did or did not do that prevented them from becoming engaged.

    i. I did not appeal directly to Roberto as I handed out the worksheets and got the students into small groups. I might have spoken directly to him about how he could help the group. I could have kidded him about his recent sports enthusiasms and established some male camaraderie around common interests.

    ii. I find Hyung Kyung's personal reserve and quiet resistance off-putting, and I have not gotten to know her well. She is not a trouble-maker and she does get her work in eventually, so I have permitted her to bounce along in the group work; I suspect that she is coasting on others' efforts. I need to be more solicitous and attentive to her needs, I suspect.

As I said, these are real people and real situations; without being too hard on myself, I am able to see how particular exercises and activities might be improved by holding myself to the ideals I have been invoking in these essays, by taking myself to task. I tend toward brash and competitive participation in group work, even (or especially, perhaps) if I am not particularly confident, so I am drawn to students who exhibit the same tendencies. I have to be careful to not dismiss the anxieties of timid or fearful students. I also need to guard against over-reaction to blustery males.

5. List the things that you dislike most or fear happening in class. What do you do to avoid the occurrence of these events?

You've read my autobiography and seen my responses to these exercises. What would you conclude are my greatest fears as a teacher? How would you imagine my avoiding them? Well, I forgive you for not spending much time analyzing me, but what are your fears? What extremes will you go to avoid them occurring in your classroom?

I hope you will take the time to work out the answers, but ready or not, here are a few things I have learned about myself as a result of this sort of exercise, and which I offer in the spirit of collegiality and support.

❒ I dislike too much chaos and confusion.

❒ I fear rejection by my students and dismissal of my lessons.

❒ I fear the committed cynic, the accomplished sneerer, the literate gadfly who has no loyalties and defies all authority.

My contention is that you could have guessed these sorts of things from the information I have provided in this chapter and elsewhere in the book. But in any case, here is my elaboration on these three points.

I think most first-born males raised by doting mothers in our male-centric society are accustomed to being the center of attention and in control of things, but whether that is true of others, it is true for me. I revel in other people's confusion, and I want to nurture *their* creative attempts at solving problems, but when it gets really wild, I tend to back off. I like to have a sense of order and control, and I am a list-maker who likes to check things off as I accomplish them. So I usually have my lesson plan pretty well laid out, and I want to be in control of activities. I want to define the limits of chaos and confusion in my classroom, and I try to end every class period with answers to the question, "What have we learned today?"

I have experienced a lifetime of support and appreciation, and it has conditioned me to expect both, especially from my students. I work hard on my lesson planning, and if they don't recognize that, I am not above pointing it out. I regularly challenge students to work hard, and the one thing that drives me up the wall are the blasé underachievers who are unimpressed by school, the importance of learning, and my contribution to their own achievement.

I am also an easy target for the cynic, especially the learned one, because I am convinced about the importance of teachers and teaching, and I am inclined to take myself too seriously. I tend to be pompous and self-righteous in these matters, and I am easily made to look foolish by the Oscar Wildes of the world.

So what's the value of such self-disclosure? Well, as Robert Burns said,

> Oh, wad some Power the giftie gie us
> to see oursels as others see us!
> It wad frae monie a blunder free us,
> An' foolish notion.[4]

It goes back to the idea that good teaching is a function of relationship and that good relationships are founded on self-understanding. I won't belabor the point, given that this is probably the tenth time I've said it, but I will comment that the three insights I have just divulged have, indeed, kept me from making more of a fool myself than I might otherwise have done if I hadn't made the effort.

## Summarizing the Effort

I hasten to assure you that even though this is my official stance toward self and teaching and that I am committed to the approach, not a semester goes by without my violating my own resolutions. That is, I don't want you to get the impression that I am so accomplished in this that my flaws only accentuate my perfections. This is intended to be a real—as in realistic—effort at self-disclosure, not a hero narrative from a modest but accomplished award-winning teacher. Rest assured, I have some bitter experiences and failed lessons that I could regale you with and that serve as the stalkers of my memories as I craft these examples.

Which brings me to an important point that I hope is becoming clearer— we are always part of the problems we are trying to solve. Harvard psychologist

Robert Kegan has developed a theory of adult development in a complex world that helps us here (Kegan, 1982, 1994; Kegan & Lahey, 2001). He observes that our tendency is to focus on what we want to accomplish rather than attempting to understand all the subtle and ingrained habits of mind and behavior that continually hinder our efforts at personal change. Rather than taking the New Year's resolution approach to change that usually ends in failure, he argues that we need to understand that we not only have commitments but *counter-commitments*, and that they provide perfectly reasonable explanations for why we often fail to achieve the goals we set for ourselves.

For example, among my major commitments as a teacher are:

❐ authentic classrooms that foster personal growth

❐ intense learning activities that promote cognitive and emotional health

At the same time, I also have the following counter-commitments, which often prevent me from following through on my primary commitments:

❐ a desire to have things work out the way I envision them (control issues)

❐ the belief that my own worth is reflected in others' opinions of me

This means that it is not unusual for me to spend hours developing activities that engage learners in real-life tasks, only to mess things up by intervening when the going gets rough or backing down from a requirement when students express skepticism of the activity. As I have attempted to show, these insights can be gleaned from an examination of my personal history.

All of this may have left you wondering if we are still discussing philosophy. You may be ready to concede that a critical scrutiny of your life is beneficial in general and helpful in improving your teaching, but you are not convinced that it constitutes philosophical work. For this, you might argue, we need to examine the work of, say, John Dewey or Paolo Freire, two important figures in educational philosophy, for insights into the philosophical bases for teaching.

The approaches are not mutually exclusive. I have, for example, been influenced by Dewey (1929, 1938b), Wenger (1998), Freire (1970), and Freire & Macedo (1987b), especially their convictions about the importance of democratic schooling and the value of starting with what the individual learner brings to the situation. I like Dewey's critique of school as an institution where the teachers' habits and routines have assumed greater importance than students' needs and interests. I am drawn to Freire's insistence that learners need to be posing problems rather than solving problems posed to them by teachers. And I am especially sympathetic to the view that education in general should open up worlds and create attitudes of curiosity and critique, rather than promote a uniform understanding of the world and obedience to authority.

But I resist the implication that seems to arise when philosophies are discussed as part of teachers' responsibilities—that the most important source of inspiration for and justification of our work should be philosophers of this stature. Their contributions are important, but our own personal experience is equally compelling.

I think this is the sort of work teachers must be engaged in if we are to maintain any trace of control over the work of schools. With mandated curricula, high-stakes testing, and increased attention to compliance, educational exchanges require thoughtful, articulate participation by the individuals who are most knowledgeable of students and most directly impacted by decisions.

In a very important sense, the questions are, "Who commands? Where is the locus of authority?" Is it to be individuals removed from the daily lives of learners, or can we shift it toward teachers, who in spite of all they have to do, are the best qualified and most reasonable source of wisdom?

It may be that this is work for professional organizations and political parties, but I am confident that if individual teachers do not come to grips with the sorts of issues I raise here, even sympathetic reforms will prove inimical to our work.

What do you think?

## REFERENCES

Anthony, E. M. (1963). Approach, method, and technique. *English Language Teaching Journal,* *17,* 63–67.

Bateson, G. (1999). *Steps to an ecology of mind.* Chicago: University of Chicago Press.

Bateson, M. C. (1994). *Peripheral visions: Learning along the way.* New York: HarperCollins.

Berger, P., Berger, B., & Kellner, H. (1974). *The homeless mind: Modernization and consciousness.* New York: Vintage Books.

Berger, P., & Luckmann, T. (1966). *The social construction of reality.* Garden City, NJ: Doubleday.

Brown, H. D. (2007). *Principles of language learning and teaching* (5th ed.). New York: Longman.

Cole, M. (1996). *Cultural psychology: A once and future discipline.* Cambridge, MA: Harvard University Press.

Dewey, J. (1929). *The quest for certainty.* New York: Minton, Balch, and Co.

———. (1938a). Criteria of experience. In *Experience and education* (pp. 33–50). New York: Collier-Macmillan.

————. (1938b). *Experience and education*. New York: Collier-Macmillan.

————. (1938c). The need of a theory of experience. In *Experience and education* (pp. 25–32). New York: Collier-Macmillan.

Drago-Severson, E. (2004). *Becoming adult learners: Principles and practices for effective development*. New York: Teachers College Press.

Freire, P. (1970). *Pedagogy of the oppressed*. New York: Seabury Press.

Freire, P., & Macedo, D. (1987). Literacy and cultural pedagogy. In *Literacy: Reading the Word and the World* (pp. 141–159). South Hadley, MA: Bergin and Garvey.

————. (1987). *Literacy: Reading the word and the world*. South Hadley, MA: Bergin and Garvey Publishers.

Geertz, C. (1973). *The interpretation of cultures*. New York: Basic Books.

————. (1983). *Local knowledge: Further essays in interpretive anthropology*. New York: Basic Books.

————. (1995). *After the fact: Two countries, four decades, one anthropologist*. Cambridge, MA: Harvard University Press.

Goffman, E. (1974). *Frame analysis*. New York: Harper Colophon Books.

Harries-Jones, P. (1995). *A recursive vision: Ecological understanding and Gregory Bateson*. Toronto: University of Toronto Press.

Holland, D., Lachicotte, W. J., Skinner, D., & Cain, C. (1998a). *Identity and agency in cultural worlds*. Cambridge, MA: Harvard University Press.

————. (1998b). A practice theory of self and identity. In *Identity and agency in cultural worlds* (pp. 19–48). Cambridge, MA: Harvard University Press.

Kegan, R. (1982). *The evolving self: Problem and process in human development*. Cambridge: MA, Harvard University Press.

————. (1994). *In over our heads: The mental demands of modern life*. Cambridge, MA: Harvard University Press.

Kegan, R., & Lahey, L. L. (2001). *How the way we talk can change the way we work: Seven languages for transformation*. San Francisco: Jossey-Bass.

Kramsch, C. (Ed). (2002). *Language acquisition and language socialization: Ecological perspectives*. New York: Continuum.

Kumaravidevalu, B. (2003). *Beyond methods: Macrostrategies for language teaching*. New Haven, CT: Yale University Press.

Mead, G. H. (1934). *Mind, self, and society*. Chicago: University of Chicago Press.

Norton, B. (2000a). Claiming the right to speak in classrooms and communities. In *Identity and language learning: Gender, ethnicity, and educational change* (pp. 133–154). New York: Longman.

————. (2000b). *Identity and language learning: Gender, ethnicity, and educational change*. New York: Longman.

Parsons, T. (1962). *The structure of social action*. New York: Free Press.

Rogoff, B. (2003). *The cultural nature of human development*. New York: Oxford University Press.

Stevick, E. W. (1980). *Teaching languages: A way and ways*. Rowley, MA: Newbury House.

———. (1982). *Teaching and learning languages*. New York: Cambridge University Press.

———. (1996). *Memory, meaning, and method*. New York: Heinle and Heinle.

———. (1998a). Materials for the whole learner. In *Working with teaching methods: What's at stake?* (pp. 48–67). Albany, NY: Heinle and Heinle.

———. (1998b). *Working with teaching methods: What's at stake?* Albany, NY: Heinle and Heinle.

Toulmin, S. (2001). *Return to reason*. Cambridge, MA: Harvard University Press.

Vygotsky, L. (1978). Interaction between learning and development. In *Mind in society* (pp. 79–91). Cambridge, MA: Harvard University Press.

Watzlawick, P. J., Beavin, J. B., & Jackson, D. D. (1967). *Pragmatics of human communication: A study of interactional patterns, pathologies, and paradoxes*. New York: W.W. Norton.

Wenger, E. (1998). *Communities of practice: Learning, meaning, and identity*. New York: Cambridge University Press.

Wilden, A. (1987). *The rules are no game: The strategy of communication*. New York: Routledge & Kegan Paul.

Wittgenstein, L. (1961). *Tractatus Logico-Philosophicus*. New York: Routledge & Kegan Paul.

## NOTES

1. Hmmm…. As I write this I wonder if perhaps there is a third choice—ignore the demands of others and proceed on our own, but I can't see this sort of ostrich behavior as a healthy way to live. Also, I suspect it is merely a dangerous variation on the second choice, one that will lead to some sort of inevitable blind-side collision with reality.

2. This assertion serves as a cornerstone for most social scientists. My thinking on it has been influenced by Gregory Bateson (2000), Peter Berger (1966, 1973), Clifford Geertz (1973, 1983, 1995), Erving Goffman (1974), Robert Kegan (1982, 1984), and Talcott Parsons (1962).

3. The scholars I find most compelling on this topic are Robert Kegan (1982, 1994), Talcott Parsons (1962), and George Herbert Mead (1934).

4. Excerpt from *To a Louse* by Robert Burns. Roughly translated, "Oh, would the Lord give us the ability to see ourselves as others see us. It would save us from blunders and pretensions."

# ❺ Authenticity in Language Teaching: Working Out the Bugs[1]

$M$y intent in this chapter is to craft an approach to instruction that achieves both my goals and students' goals. I want to orchestrate lessons that students find engaging and relevant and that I believe make significant contributions to their command of English and their mastery of life skills.

This is no easy feat. School—as a societal institution and as a lived experience—has assumed such daunting significance that it has taken on its own reality. Rather than activities organized to help learners function effectively outside the classroom, lessons often become coercive struggles of will where both teachers and students believe they have accomplished something if they emerge unscathed. Completing an activity is often viewed as significant by both, even if it has no obvious value beyond the classroom.

However, I believe that most teachers enter the profession to make significant contributions to the greater good through inspired teaching and that most students genuinely want to learn. It is in that spirit that this essay is offered. The questions that have helped me focus are these:

❐ How can we harness the curiosity and enthusiasm that learners bring with them so that they master the knowledge and skills required by society?

❐ What can we do to create meaningful, authentic activities within the constraints of the required curriculum?

❐ What can we do to mitigate the pressures of school that often provoke resistance from students?

Here is the argument in brief.

*Authenticity,* broadly defined as the attempt to engage learners by orchestrating lessons that connect in meaningful ways with their experiences, needs, and aspirations, is an important goal for all teachers, but especially so for teachers of English language learners. In addition to the pressures that all students experience to succeed in school, second language learners struggle with personal and cultural identity issues that we need to attend to.

Although long recognized as an important characteristic of language teaching, authenticity has proved elusive primarily because we have been too ambitious in our approach to the issue. What is required is not the production of elaborate life-like tableaus in the classroom but, rather, principled adjustments to everyday lessons that give students opportunities to exercise some degree of autonomy and choice in the activities.

To anchor the discussion I examine a lesson in which I used a story from a daily newspaper to teach language and literacy skills. The primary tension I had to negotiate was how to create the informal conversational atmosphere appropriate to newspaper discussions while at the same time bearing down on the grammar, vocabulary, and discourse skills required by the curriculum.

Ecology provides the theoretical and philosophical framework for the approach; by attempting to craft instruction that honors natural processes of learning, I work to provide flexible scaffolding for lessons that permits me to nudge learners toward my goals.

On a practical level, seven principles of lesson preparation and orchestration emerge as key elements in achieving a lesson that captures student interest while meeting curricular goals.

I conclude with reflections on the bugaboos that often prevent us from teaching authentic lessons. I argue that very often the greatest impediment to this sort of teaching is the inhibitions we have developed that prevent us from responding honestly and openly to students. It is in this sense that I am using the word *bugaboos.*

## Why Authenticity?

Most teachers would agree that school is one thing and real life another, and that one of the important purposes of school is to prepare people for the world outside the classroom. The relationship between school and "the real world" is a complicated one, subject to contentious discussions in some circles, but the pressures on schools today make the debate a moot point—when you put 20 to 30 people in a room and require them to attend to the same things at the same time and then test them to see how well they have done, you have pretty much eliminated any possibility that they would confound what is going on in the classroom with their lives outside those walls. In fact, it is precisely the differences between school and life-otherwise that provoke much of the alienation and resistance that characterize schooling in contemporary life.

The issue for English language teachers is doubly compelling because the subject of study is also an instrument of communication and an important aspect of one's identity. The languages we speak become important indicators and shapers of our sense of self; success and failure in school often carry more weight for English language learners than in other classes, especially if the learners are immigrants or refugees for whom the outcome of their studies has direct impact on their circumstances in life.

No wonder, then, that the issue of authenticity becomes important—we seek to make our classroom activities compelling for learners so that they will participate enthusiastically and derive maximum benefit from our efforts. It behooves us, then, to develop an understanding of what *authenticity* is and to craft strategies for achieving it. I have prepared the exercises that follow to help focus the endeavor. Ponder and respond according to your experience:

---

**Authenticity**

---

1. How do you think of authenticity in relation to your teaching? Which definition seems most relevant for you as a teacher?

   a. "…real, genuine, life-like, not fake…"
   b. "…relevant, current…"
   c. "…personally meaningful, connected to one's life concerns…"
   d. "…engaging, compelling, interesting, piquing one's curiosity…"

   Other: _____

2. In general, what do you consider to be the relative importance of the following lesson characteristics for achieving authenticity in your teaching (1 = not important; 4 = important)?

1 2 3 4   Topical currency, relating to events and people in the news

1 2 3 4   Personal importance, relating to students' experiences and aspirations

1 2 3 4   Action-oriented, getting students out of their chairs and interacting

1 2 3 4   Curricular effectiveness, achieving course objectives

1 2 3 4   Project-based, producing a product or outcome relevant to students' needs

1 2 3 4   Entertainment value, appealing to students' sense of humor and enjoyment

Other: _____

3. Ponder the following activities and indicate the extent to which you think they would lend themselves to authentic learning activities (1 = not easily; 4 = easily orchestrated as authentic activities)

1 2 3 4   Autobiographical writing exercise

1 2 3 4   Role-playing dialogue activity

1 2 3 4   Text-based grammar exercise

1 2 3 4   Vocabulary learning exercises

1 2 3 4   Field trip excursion

1 2 3 4   Reading comprehension exercises

1 2 3 4   Writers workshop, peer-feedback activities

Other: _____

From the perspective I'm developing here, all four of the definitions offered under #1 are reasonable departure points in thinking about authentic lessons. That is, although the emphasis is different in each of the definitions, what unites them is the individual learner as reference point. A key consideration in working toward authentic lessons is the need to organize lessons with the students' past experiences, current needs, and future aspirations in mind, and at the same time working to make the activity vibrant and engaging. Notice that the emphasis is on the student's perspective; *authenticity* will always be a slippery concept in education, but the ultimate arbiter is the learner—if a lesson does not feel authentic to the students, it is not authentic.

Similarly, the lesson characteristics listed in #2 are all important aspects of authentic teaching from this point of view. I put "curricular effectiveness" in the middle of the list because I think it represents the most problematic aspect of authentic teaching; the other items in the list more easily lend themselves to adaptation to student interest and inclination. Because *authenticity* assumes student centeredness, and the curriculum represents an institutional abstraction of student need, the task of the teacher is to constantly balance the needs of the real students in the class against those of "typical" students for whose needs the curriculum was developed. Our ability to craft authentic lessons will always be a negotiation of this tension between institutional goals and individual goals.

As for the items in #3, I generated them off the top of my head, a list of common activities that I have used and that I imagine are familiar for most teachers. The purpose was to provide a specific touchstone for the argument, but I think you could add all the classroom activities you have ever used and we could discover ways of making them authentic.

So, you may be wondering, if all the variety represented in these lists can be seen as viable foundations for authentic teaching, what distinguishes authentic lessons from all other, nonremarkable instances of teaching?

And my answer is: Authenticity is in the conduct of the lesson. Specifically, it is the result of the focused, sensitive response of the teacher to the efforts of the students. It is the nuanced interaction between teacher and student and among students that permits the individuals involved to experience the activity as having value in and of itself, apart from whatever significance it may have for the lesson.

In other words, this is not a search for methods and materials or best practices. Humans are too variable and the conditions under which languages are learned too complex for there to be a single solution or simple formula that will apply to all teaching conundrums. But we can adopt strategies that permit us to make the lessons we teach more personally meaningful for us and our students, to make them more authentic. Let me show you what I mean.

## The Lesson: Bugs!

Ecology, which is the framework I am using to develop these ideas, does not provide prescriptions for teaching. Rather, it offers a framework for understanding how students respond to our lessons. These responses, considered patterns of adjustments to events, provide us with the basis for making our own adjustments as we plan subsequent lessons. Teaching becomes, therefore, *negotiation*. And the negotiations will go more smoothly if we remember certain "facts of life," from an ecological perspective:

First and most important, you cannot make students learn what you want them to learn. Or, more precisely, you can only create opportunities for them to adjust their thinking and behavior in response to activities you have orchestrated. The best we can do as teachers is construct environments for learners and negotiate activities that nudge them to behave in ways we want them to behave. You cannot prevent students from learning, but you have a limited range of possibilities for getting them to learn what you want them to learn.

As a result, lesson plans become rough outlines of prospective activities—lists of materials needed and notes-to-self that help you maintain your balance and keep your eyes on your goals as the lesson proceeds.

This means you cannot stipulate in advance what someone will learn; the best you can do is identify the learnings as they emerge from the activity and adjust your teaching to nurture more learning.

And this requires us to understand that teaching is not so much a matter of mapping out in advance precise expectations for a lesson as it is identifying some broad goals for class time, sketching an outline of the activity that you would like to occur. In an important sense what we do is launch the lesson and hope that we're prepared for what happens.

And, once launched, our primary responsibility is to respond to the students' energy and initiative by nudging them toward things that we want them to learn—new vocabulary, grammatical structures, discourse features, etc. Let me illustrate these points by walking you through a lesson I taught a few years ago at Spring International Language Center in Denver.

I had an intermediate-level group of learners from around the world, thirteen individuals: seven Japanese, six women and one man, average age about twenty; two Colombians, both male, about seventeen; one Russian physician, female, about forty; one Korean male, about twenty; one Austrian male and one Swiss male, both about nineteen.

We met Monday through Thursday for an hour in a large room that permitted flexible grouping—around a large conference table, in small groups around tables, in pairs with chairs together, etc. Sometimes we used all of these groupings in one class session. It was a lively group composed of individuals who had many reasons for being in the United States—to improve their English, to study at American universities, to find political freedom and economic opportunity, to relax and enjoy themselves before returning to school in their own countries. It was not always clear to me which motivation had priority, but

I tried to respond to them in ways that conveyed the legitimacy of their reasons for learning English.

I saw my responsibility as focusing the energy without stifling it. At the time I was working on a textbook, *Choice Readings*, with former graduate student comrades and continuing co-authors Sandra Silberstein and Barbara Dobson; many of the lessons provided opportunities for classroom testing readings and exercises from the book (Clarke, Dobson, & Silberstein, 1996). I also made extensive use of the *Denver Post*, one of two major Denver daily newspapers. I concocted exercises to be done in class and for homework, and I orchestrated group reading and discussion sessions based on what the students and I found of interest on a particular day. We worked on language and literacy skills, and I spent considerable time urging them to be conscious of their strategies. They were to keep a journal in which they recorded their efforts at accomplishing this and in which they kept class notes, new vocabulary, etc. We regularly spent class time discussing their approaches to learning and using English.

I wanted class sessions to provide opportunities for authentic use of the language so I worked to reduce the hierarchical roles of "teacher" and "student," striving to create a flow of activity that resembled conversation at a cafe or in a living room.

One lesson, which I have come to think of as the "Bugs Lesson," involved an article about the noisy invasion of cicadas in the Midwestern United States that summer. Here is a version of the lesson plan—bullet points that helped me stay on track once the lesson got going.

**LESSON PLAN**

1. Wait until someone notices the story, then do skim/scan and discussion.

2. Skim/Scan:
   - ❏ What does the picture show?
   - ❏ What are bugs? Which bug is causing the problem?
   - ❏ What *is* the problem?

3. Vocabulary from context (orally):
   - ❏ What is the meaning of: *shriek* (Paragraph 3), *hot line* (Paragraph 9), *nuisance* (Paragraph 15)?
   - ❏ What word means *silent* in Paragraph 8?

4. Comprehension:
   - ❏ Hand out comprehension questions to get them focused.
   - ❏ Individual/Pair/Class: Respond to Qs, exchange ideas

These were notes-to-self in case the session lagged; the overall goal was to promote conversational exchanges around the reading punctuated by focused didactic spurts in which I bore down on vocabulary, grammar, punctuation, etc., all in the service of reading comprehension and critical thinking. I had these notes to guide me, but generally I was aiming for an atmosphere of friendly contentiousness sprinkled with didactic moments. Here's how the lesson unfolded. (You might want to read the article on page 146 before you continue.)

## THE BUGS LESSON

The students pick up their newspapers as they enter and begin looking through them. This is the usual routine—my effort at promoting relaxed and interest-driven class sessions. I take the roll and hand back some papers as they settle into their favorite sections of the paper.

I give them some time to read. After a few minutes I see Juan, one of the Colombians, pause as he examines the photo of three-year-old Robby Graves contemplating a cicada emerging from its shell.

"Hey, that's interesting. What's that all about?" I ask as I point to the picture.

Several students notice the photo and turn to the same page in the *Post*. I prod others gently, hoping to spark some interest in the story without putting Juan on the spot.

When I have most of the students focused on the story I ask some skimming questions of the group, pausing as they answer, responding conversationally to their guesses, etc. These were some of the questions that came up.

❏ What does the picture show?
❏ What are "bugs"?
❏ Which bug is causing the problem?
❏ What *is* the problem?

Different students chime in with answers as they focus on the picture and the text. The exchanges still have the feel of a coffee shop conversation rather than a classroom exercise, as some students are not quite paying attention to the story.

But the ones who have shifted to the story now take a few minutes to read to see what is going on in Illinois with all these bugs. Meanwhile, I am leaning forward in anticipation of their answers, hoping to increase their focus a bit. The discussion of the article is speculative and somewhat tentative. People are variously engaged; some have opinions and defend them using portions of the text, while others seem merely amused by the problems caused by the bugs.

Most of the class has now joined the group. I structure the exchanges with the questions I devised. The conversation becomes fast paced and more focused. My idea is to get them to behave in ways that are typical for newspaper readers—looking quickly at headlines and pictures, asking questions of oneself and reading to answer them, talking among friends about the news of the day.

By now everyone is working on the article. I ask them to focus on some vocabulary items that I suspect they will not understand on their own:

❏ What is the meaning of: *shriek* (Paragraph 3), *hot line* (Paragraph 9), *nuisance* (Paragraph 15)?
❏ What word means *silent* in Paragraph 8?

I help them revise their guesses as I write brief definitions on the board for them to refer to, and I handle other vocabulary questions in the same way.

I notice that we have about thirty minutes left in the class, so I move into a more directive mode. I read the story aloud while they follow along. This forces them to read more quickly than might be comfortable, emphasizing the psycholinguistic principle that good readers are not word-by-word readers but rather, predictors—skimmers and scanners who can tolerate ambiguity and partial understanding.

When I have finished I pause for a moment to give them time to reread and ponder as necessary.

I pass out the questions I have prepared and tell them to work for a few minutes on their own. (See the *Bugs!* Worksheet that follows.)

After most students have had a chance to answer the questions, I tell them to get in small groups or pairs to compare answers. They know that they are to refer to the article to confirm or modify their answers. I do not state a time limit at this point but give them about ten minutes to work as I move among them monitoring their exchanges, helping them with vocabulary, exchanging opinions about the relative virtues of spraying or eating invading insects.

***Bugs!* Worksheet**

Name:_____ Date:_____

**1.** Where is this happening?

**2.** What is the problem?

**3.** How often does it occur? Why?

**4.** Would you eat a cicada? According to the story some people in Illinois have eaten them. Why?

**5.** Write a letter to friend summarizing the story.

We have only a few minutes left, but we start in on the questions, with individuals taking turns reading items aloud and giving answers. In the case of disagreement I ask students to read the portions of text that support their answers. I try to maintain the conversational feel of the exchanges even as we delve into grammatical complexity or details of dictionary definitions.

The class time ends. I ask them to save the article for our continuing work with it. The homework is to finish writing answers to the questions. I call their attention to the last question, which asks them to write a paragraph as if it were part of a letter to a friend. I tell them to think of this as a first draft of a writing assignment because we will work on it the next day and it will be the homework for the following day.

I bid them good day and they leave for their next class.

From my point of view the lesson was a success. I was able to balance the light-hearted conversation with focused work on reading comprehension, critical discussion, and focused language work. Everyone participated, and the hour passed quickly. Everyone seemed reasonably focused on the next day's work.

And I believe the lesson met the students' expectations. They appeared engaged throughout the lesson, and the focused scribbling of notes and verbal exchanges as we worked on the vocabulary and discussed the ideas indicated that they were getting "serious" work accomplished.

However, I do not want to make more of this lesson than is merited. In fact, it was in many ways an *unremarkable* session. But that is actually what is required if this discussion of authenticity is to contribute to our teaching without creating unrealistic expectations. Good teaching hinges on the extent to which we can string together many such mundane lessons—learning occurring all the time within the natural unfolding of events. And as we orchestrate events we cultivate relationships—relationships that are authentic to the extent that everyone involved believes that the exchanges are sincere efforts at communicating about something important.

The basic strategy is to establish a routine that everyone finds reasonably comfortable, and then to stretch those comfort zones by creating small disturbances that require students to adjust their behavior slightly in the direction of the goals for the lesson.

## Principles of Lesson Preparation and Choreography

The principles that emerge from this approach are few and universally applicable. That is, they do not require adherence to a particular teaching method or program; they can be used with equal facility by teachers working within any instructional tradition. Let me elaborate on each of them with illustrations from the Bugs! lesson.

*Be clear on what you are trying to accomplish.*
It is easy to get so caught up in the details of a specific lesson or the mandates of the curriculum that we forget the larger goals for the lesson—such things as proficiency in the language, critical thinking, conversational expertise, etc. Steven Covey, the guru of personal competence and leadership, refers to this as "beginning with the end in mind" (1994, p. xx). Basically, this principle helps us remember the larger picture. As I organized my teaching the summer of

the Bugs! lesson, I had to constantly keep reminding myself that as long as everyone was using English we were making progress toward my goals. I kept a running record of the vocabulary and grammatical structures that arose in our lessons, I regularly touched bases with the students to get a sense of their opinion of the class, and I tried to vary the content and dynamics of the lesson in ways that would prevent us from getting in ruts. Balance in the service of English language learning was my goal.

---

**Working toward Authenticity:**
**Seven Principles of Lesson Preparation and Choreography**

---

1. **Core Values:** Be clear on what you are trying to accomplish.

2. **Rhythm and Routine:** Establish a predictable pattern of activity.

3. **Strong, Transparent, Light:** Modify the routine with improvisations that strengthen engagement.

4. **Head and Heart:** Create activities that make students think and appeal to their emotions.

5. **Interaction:** Provide opportunities for structured collaboration in pairs or small groups.

6. **Self-Authorizing Choices:** Give students chances to make decisions that *they* believe important.

7. **Feedback:** Respond throughout the lesson so that students know how they are doing.

---

*Establish a basic rhythm and routine.*

Class sessions consisted of three broad sections—review of material covered the day before and introduction to the day's lesson, new material, and assignment for the following day. I would often put the lesson plan on the board to remind the students of this structure and to serve as a reference point for myself. My goal here was to create a sense of security and predictability, both necessary elements for relaxed learning.

*Modify the routine with improvisations that maintain patterns of light, transparent, and strong activities.*

As important as routines are in learning, so too are "disturbances" that jar students out of their complacency. But the disturbances are not random harassments; rather, they revolve around three criteria that could be thought of as anchors of authenticity. As events unfold and as we contemplate adjustments, we ask ourselves the following kinds of questions (Stevick, 1971, 1998):

*Strong...............Weak*

Does the activity accomplish important goals? Do students emerge with knowledge, skills, and attitudes that contribute to their immediate academic success and long-term life chances?

*Transparent.........Opaque*

Can the students see why we are asking them to engage in the activity? Do the goals of the lesson align with their understanding of the world, their current realities, their future goals? Called "relevance" in some circles, the main point to focus on is the students' perception of the situation; it doesn't matter if we believe the activity to be important if they do not agree. Our ability to convey the importance of the lesson directly influences their engagement and motivation to learn.

Light.............Heavy

Does the session go trippingly? Do people enjoy themselves? Does time fly? Or do students lose interest or forget why we are doing it?

In general, the newspaper work we did that summer could be described as light and transparent. Students enjoyed the relaxed approach and the fact that they could choose what they read. And they all were interested in learning about the United States in general and Denver in particular. However, it was not always clear how strong the newspaper activities were. The more serious students were suspicious of any use of class time that did not obviously connect with their goals of passing exams and getting into the college of their choice.

In order to ensure the strength of lessons (and to appease the serious students), I created vocabulary lists from the stories we read and concocted exercises and quizzes to heighten the academic validity of the newspaper reading. In addition, I orchestrated grammar work, usually in the form of sentence-focused comprehension questions and writing exercises where students had to maneuver concepts we had been reading about and use the vocabulary and grammatical structures to express their own ideas. And I tied in the newspaper content with subjects that came up in the other textbooks we were using.

But my attention to the three continua was not limited to overall planning and general objectives of the class work. I would also attend to these criteria as I conducted the lessons, orchestrating impromptu interrogations around vocabulary or grammar, pushing students to express themselves concisely, to explain concepts identified in the readings, etc. For example, at one point an exchange with Akihiro erupted into a prolonged discussion of food and food preparation:

**EATING CICADAS**

*M:* Akihiro, would you read Number 4 and give us your answer, please?

*A:* (He reads: "Would you eat a cicada? According to the story some people in Illinois have eaten them. Why?" And he makes a face.)

*M:* So, what do you think?

*A:* I think I do not eat it.

*M:* You would not eat it?

*A:* No.

*M:* Complete sentence please.

*A:* I would not eat it.

*M:* Eat what?

*A:* The cicada.

*M:* Why do you think the people in Illinois are eating them.

*A:* I don't know.

*M:* What does the story say?

*A:* (Turns to the story in search of the relevant text. Begins to read silently.)

*M:* Read aloud, please.

*A:* (Reads) "Michael Kendall, a Chicago attorney, tested one of the recipes with some cicadas he found Monday night in his brother's suburban back yard. 'We parboiled them and then sautéed them in butter and garlic and ate them like shrimp,' Kendall said. 'They taste sort of like a starchy potato. They had a sort of scallop-like consistency.' "

*M:* So, what do you think?

> *A:* I don't know. What means *parboiled?*
>
> *M:* Anyone? (An exchange occurs and we settle for "a way to cook." Similar prompting results in adequate definitions of *sautéed* and *starchy.*)
>
> *A:* I still don't eat.
>
> *M:* Why not?
>
> Etc.

Akihiro was not able immediately to explain why he would not try the cicadas, so I asked the rest of the class what they thought about the dish. There followed a spirited discussion of things edible but not appetizing, and it was discovered that just about everyone was able to cause someone else to grimace in disbelief as they mentioned foods they had eaten or, at least, claimed to know to have been eaten by someone they knew. As the conversation continued I filled the board with exotic dishes and words pertaining to food preparation. The activity also generated a list of descriptive adjectives that ranged on a continuum from *delicious* to *disgusting.*

As the discussion wound down, I conducted a brief drill by pointing at the words on the board and eliciting pronunciations, definitions, and sample sentences. I mentioned that these would all be candidates for the weekly vocabulary quiz.

This little segment lasted only about ten minutes, but it illustrates how an exchange around a small point in the lesson can yield a variety of benefits. In my view, the session qualifies as "light," and the focused vocabulary work and brief drill at the end permit the designation of "strong" and "transparent."

The virtue of the triad *strong-light-transparent* is that it provides a principled way of responding to students' interests and energies with a balance of attention to factors that matter differently to the people involved.

*Create activities that provide a balance for head and heart—something to make students think and something to appeal to their emotions.*

For the head this lesson offered focused attention to the English language and a serious debate about culinary and gustatory customs in different cultures. Yes, the latter had a light-hearted air to it and was played by all as a chance for exaggerated reactions to differences of opinion, but the activity itself was familiar to the students as a time when they had to offer examples to support their contentions and when they were expected to use the text as the basis for their opinions. The banter and repartee changed abruptly to serious, thoughtful debate as we explored the invasion of the cicadas and its effects on people living in the affected part of the country.

*Provide chances for interaction.*
Virtually every class session included the expectation that students would work with each other in pairs or small groups. I usually structured activities with questions or bulleted discussion points, and they knew that this was the time when they were expected to improve their command of English.

*Give students chances for self-authorizing choices.*
The students also knew that they were expected to decide matters for themselves and to defend their choices. It is this point more than any other that touches on the essence of authenticity in the classroom. Classroom activities will be experienced as authentic to the extent that students believe that their participation is "real," based on their interests and commitments and motivated by their goals and objectives. This is true whether people are discussing their civil liberties or the difference between salty and sweet.

*Provide feedback throughout the lesson so that students know how they are doing.*
The feedback also needs to be attuned to both head and heart. I try to be encouraging of all attempts to use the language but at the same time give people feedback on the accuracy of their choices. At times I chose to focus on the spirit of their efforts by deferring linguistic correction until later, but there were days when we spent most of our time on grammar, vocabulary, and stylistic details. An important part of students' sense of security and predictability required for uninhibited use of the language is confidence that they will be listened to—that both what they say and how they say it will receive attention from the teacher.

## Authenticity: Working Out the Bugs (and Bugaboos)

The obstacles to authentic teaching are many, and the pressures of mandated curricula and tests loom as the most prevalent. However, the primary constraint is psychological—our own inhibitions and assumptions. In other words, what keeps us from interacting authentically are *bugaboos* of interpersonal interaction and instructional reticence. I found this definition on MSN Encarta®:

> **source of fear or annoyance:** *something that causes fear, annoyance, or trouble, especially an imagined threat or problem [Mid-18th Century]*

Let's face it—teaching is a solitary profession. We spend most of our time alone with students. If we believe that our lessons lack authenticity, it is not because anyone is standing over us and threatening us with a stick if we do not conduct the lesson in a particular way. It is because we have internalized the stick and used it as the excuse for responding to students in role rather than authentically. With that thought in mind, I would like to return to the questions with which I began the essay.

❑ How can we harness the curiosity and enthusiasm that learners bring with them so that they master the knowledge and skills required by society?

My response to this question is deceptively simple: By getting to know our students and by learning what it is that piques their curiosity and prompts their enthusiastic response. I realize that this sounds Pollyannaish in an era of large classes and mandated curricula, but the apparent impossibility of the goal should not deter us from pursuing it. Any effort at learning our students will result in improved choices on our part, even if what we know falls dramatically short of the ideal. At the very least, an awareness of the importance of this tenet will encourage us to listen and observe, to shift our stance from the conventional role of "teacher as knower" to "teacher as learner." And this will be a step in the right direction.

❑ What can we do to create meaningful, authentic activities within the constraints of the required curriculum?

The problem with this question is that it evokes images of grand excursions into the community or of dramatic and intricately choreographed reality-show activities. But it is possible to achieve meaningfulness and authenticity in small and unpretentious ways merely by attending to ourselves and our students as *persons* rather than as *personas*, as individuals attempting to make sense of a particular situation rather than as role-players. Schools, like all societal institutions (hospitals, courts, companies), tend to elicit formulaic responses to situations rather than honest, unique responses. This is particularly true in language classes where your efforts to help students acquire the form of the language often overrides communicative considerations—when you ask students to tell you the time, for example, even though you are wearing a watch. The key here is to create a rhythm and routine that permit you step back from your role and engage the learners in the reality of the moment.

❑ What can we do to mitigate the pressures of school that often provoke resistance from students?

Once we have begun to move toward teaching-as-relationship rather than teaching-as-method, we can adjust our approach to classroom management and evaluation, two areas in which teachers and students are often cast as adversaries rather than collaborators. What we desire is an atmosphere characterized by public agreement rather than by compliance to rules and policies. So much of what is experienced in schools as coercion and compliance can be avoided if we work with students to identify the norms we would like to govern our interaction and if we can come to an understanding of the responsibilities that we all have in maintaining those norms.[2]

## REFERENCES

Clarke, M. A. (1999). Gregory Bateson, communication and context: An ecological perspective of language teaching. In D. J. Mendelsohn (Ed.), *Expanding our vision: Insights for language teachers* (pp. 155–172). Toronto: Oxford University Press.

Clarke, M. A., Dobson, B. K., & Silberstein, S. (1996). *Choice readings*. Ann Arbor: University of Michigan Press.

Covey, S. R. (1994). *The 7 habits of highly effective people*. New York: Fireside.

Harries-Jones, P. (1995). *A recursive vision: Ecological understanding and Gregory Bateson*. Toronto: University of Toronto Press.

Kegan, R., Lahey, L. L. (2001). *How the way we talk can change the way we work: Seven languages for transformation*. San Francisco: Jossey-Bass.

Stevick, E. W. (1971). *Adapting and writing language lessons*. Washington, DC: Foreign Service Institute.

———. (1998). Materials for the whole learner. In *Working with teaching methods: What's at stake?* (pp. 48–67). Albany, NY: Heinle and Heinle.

## NOTES

1. I first worked on these ideas for a book in which all the contributors—language teachers and teacher educators—examined the influence of individuals from outside the language teaching profession. My chapter focused on the work of Gregory Bateson. It was my attempt to show how systems theory can be used as a lens for understanding classroom teaching. It was also an example of how the ideas of one scholar have influenced the work of another. The version presented here has been adapted considerably from the one I presented in the book, and I have removed most of the text related to Bateson's life and work. If you are interested in learning more about Bateson, see my essay (Clarke, 1999) and the book by Peter Harries-Jones (1995).

2. Strategies for accomplishing this atmosphere are explored by Robert Kegan and Lisa Laskow (Kegan & Lahey, 2001).

# ❻ Authenticity Revisited:

# Rhythm and Routine in Classroom Interactions

The previous essay always raises red flags with teachers, and I often get responses that reflect the pressures they are under. The questions most frequently asked are:

- ❏ How do I find the time to create authentic lessons as I cope with all the pressures of the day?
- ❏ How can I make lessons authentic when I am teaching with mandated curricula, textbook, and materials?
- ❏ How do I know if a lesson is authentic?

The goal of this essay is to address those questions.

The first two questions are addressed by the same response: Because I am defining authenticity as an interactional accomplishment, what is required is the appropriate attitude, not extensive reservoirs of time nor specially crafted materials. This is not to deny the value of time and materials in effective teaching. But it is important to underscore the assertion that good teaching is a function of relationship, and whether you are teaching one group of small children all day long or successive waves of adolescents and adults in fifty-minute classes, the key element of authentic instruction rests with the quality of your response to the learners as you orchestrate activities.

The answer to the third question is a bit more complicated: You cannot know if an activity was authentic until after it has occurred, and then all you can do is reflect on the students' responses to you and the activity and make an educated guess as to how it went. If they appear to have enjoyed the lesson, and if their responses seemed to come from an unrehearsed appreciation of your efforts, you can reasonably claim that it was authentic. In fact, a lesson does not have to go the way you planned it, nor do students have to enjoy themselves for it to be considered authentic; the defining criterion of authenticity is that it evoke responses from students that they consider "real" and "meaningful" in some way.

But permit me to approach the questions from an oblique angle, by taking another look at the Bugs! lesson, this time as it appears in a textbook.

## The Bugs! Lesson from an Ecological Perspective

Ecologists encourage us to view all life with the same lens, using the same principles for understanding rain forests and tide pools, ants, tadpoles, hippos, and humans. Individuals are always considered in relationship to their environments, and both the individuals and the environments are understood as open systems, living entities.

Applied to education, this approach situates teachers and learners in classrooms, which in turn are seen as functioning within the systems of school and community. Among the most salient features of an ecological perspective of teaching are the following:

1. Individuals and groups of individuals function according to their natural rhythms of being and behaving.

2. Learning occurs in spurts and cycles, prompted by a combination of internal and external responses to situations and events.

3. Because of these two points, learning is seen

   a. as an interactive phenomenon involving the environment and the individual.

   b. as a negotiated phenomenon that must be understood in context.

4. All of which, taken together, means that learning is best understood as an emergent phenomenon that cannot be precisely controlled or predicted.

5. And teaching is viewed as creating environments for learning rather than as delivering instruction.

The argument yields a deceptively simple corollary: Who we are as teachers and how we behave in the classroom is just one variation of who we are as humans and how we behave in general. The roles of "teacher" and "student" are institutional labels that may or may not help us achieve our goals, but in any case need to be kept in perspective lest we become more committed to maintaining our authority as teachers than to promoting learning. The quest to become a good teacher is not primarily a search for the newest and best techniques and materials. It is more a matter of establishing authentic relationships with students and nudging them toward instructional goals through rhythmic adjustments of the daily routine.

This is not to deny the importance of finding attractive materials and creative techniques; it is, however, to flip the order of importance—to establish an attitude toward teaching that will inform our quest for scintillating classroom devices. As we search for new activities, we need to be aware that they are not ends in themselves but, rather, tools of authentic relationships. My goal here is not so much to critique methods-and-materials approaches to teaching as it is to gain a perspective on the endeavor that will lead to more effective teaching and healthier learning.

My routine that summer was to put things in motion by presenting the newspaper as the focus of attention and orchestrating events as they got rolling. But the direction of the session and the content covered depended to a large extent on the students. Their interests provided the energy for the class. On a number of occasions, news stories that had not attracted my attention drew prolonged debate among students, and I would scrap exercises that I had prepared in order to go with the flow of interest in the class. The daily routine gradually emerged, and we developed a general rhythm that characterized all of our sessions.

Ecological theorists characterize this tendency in more technical language, talking about groups functioning toward stability (Bateson, 1999; Capra, 2002), but the essential point is to recognize that people and groups of people develop patterns of behavior that "feel comfortable" and that resist change. Students enter our classrooms with expectations developed from their previous educational experiences, but they soon develop individual and group norms for functioning in response to the routines we use in our teaching.

English language learners have to attend to a number of differences from their previous educational experiences, among the most likely of which are:

❐ differences between their language and English—sound system, grammar, and general discourse conventions, for example

❐ differences between cultural features of communication, including modes of politeness and formality, physical distance in conversation, body language, and group behavior

❐ differences between the customs and conventions of schools and classrooms

In the Bugs! lesson I wanted the students to see the language the way I saw it, to pay attention to the sorts of details that English speakers notice. Because they were all academically proficient students in their own countries, I did not have to teach them about basic conventions of print or remind them that English is read from left to right as I would have if they had been emergent readers. But they were still working on understanding subtle factors of newspapers in the United States, such as the differences between news stories and editorials, for example. I was also helping them recognize the conversational signals used to indicate turn-taking, questioning, confusion, disagreement, etc. And they needed to learn that the class sessions were indeed lessons—lest they think we were just sitting around having a pleasant chat.

We had established rhythms in the class, predictable cycles of activity within which small variations of language use, encounters with new words, and examination of grammatical structures all provided opportunities for learning. By the time the Bugs! lesson occurred, we conducted most class sessions the same way, which included a preliminary time for greetings, followed by focused reading and discussion punctuated by grammar and vocabulary work, and ending up with assignments for the next day.

We had developed habitual ways of responding to events. As a group, we collaborated in maintaining the routine, with different individuals contributing to variation on different occasions. The younger males, for example, tended to interject comedy and gossip if we veered too far toward "serious" linguistic work, and Svetlana, the Russian physician who was studying toward her citizenship exams, lobbied for more worksheets and focused study of language structure.

By the time of this lesson the students were fairly relaxed about classroom procedures and activities. I had worked to create an informal atmosphere in which I exercised control through friendly pressure rather than strong authoritative measures. That is, I tried to frame classroom tasks as conversations and opportunities to discover interesting facts about English and the English-speaking world. I gave assignments and I graded papers, but I worked for a collegial as opposed to the hierarchical relationship that typically characterizes classrooms. I was only moderately happy with the results, because Juan, Carlos, and Akihiro were serious party animals who tended to influence the class in ways I viewed as frivolous. I would have liked them to be more serious in their approach to activities, but I would have had to abandon the informal approach to accomplish it, and I was reluctant to do this. This is consistent with the view that the only way to change people is to create an environment for them to change themselves, and although more coercive measures might have resulted in their conforming to my expectations for a short period, I think the changes in attitude and study habits would have been short lived.

The Bugs! lesson also reflects my conviction that improvements in language learning attitudes and strategies can only occur when students are given opportunities for authentic language experiences—opportunities to seek information and ideas that they are interested in, and to read for one's own purposes. By reading the newspaper and talking in a conversational manner, I modeled the behavior I wanted them to adopt. I tried to maintain a low profile as teacher during this time. However, I also believe that English language learners need focused input—in this case language activity that was transparently organized to improve their literacy skills. With these points in mind I got up regularly at the crack of dawn to read through the paper in search of appropriate material for class work. I prepared the questions with students' abilities and interests in mind, and with an awareness of language and reading skills I wanted to develop.

This tension between teacher-organized and student-initiated activities is an example of the difficulties faced by all teachers who want their classes to have an aura of authenticity. It illustrates the ecological feature of distributed control and emergent learning (Johnson, 2001).

*Distributed control* refers to the fact that there is no single source of control over people, even in a classroom. The teacher is not in control so much as orchestrating events. The responsibility for the conduct of the class is distributed across all participants by virtue of the fact that all decisions and all actions are negotiated.

The phrase *emergent learning* is used to emphasize the fact that learning is apparent only after the fact; we may launch an activity intended to teach subject-verb agreement, but until the lesson is over and we can assess what actually happened, we will have no idea what was learned. Because learning was occurring all the time, and because each learner brought his or her own experiences to bear on each situation, I did not try to control what was being learned. In this lesson, there were some items that I believe everyone was learning—vocabulary pertinent to the situation with the cicadas, for example.

But there were other, more subtle learnings that were occurring as well. For example, I suspect that for most of the students a fairly significant insight acquired that summer came as they learned about me and my approach to teaching. They gradually became aware that, in spite of my informal demeanor, I had high expectations for their time and energy; this realization came as I quietly but insistently pushed them to answer questions, waited while they struggled, and followed up with additional homework or individualized assignments when I discovered gaps in their understanding.

As a result of this experience they may have also concluded that school in the United States differs significantly from school in their countries—not because I specifically taught them this, but as a result of apperceptive learning. This is learning that occurs on the periphery of consciousness as a result of day-in-day-out participation in the rhythms and routines of the classroom. I organized lessons so that students would acquire not only English, but also the values of what might be called democratic interaction—respect for others, freedom of choice, opportunities to fail or succeed on one's own terms. These are not lessons that can be learned from didactic teaching—no lectures on how to work independently—they have to be experienced so that the insights and understandings seep in around the edges of consciousness and become habits of mind. This is the sort of learning that approaches the process we usually refer to as *socialization.*

And this may be a defining characteristic of an "authentic" lesson—the extent to which the didactic element is mediated by "normal" conversational or interactional dynamics. However, we need to develop strategies for accomplishing this.

## Strategies for Authentic Interaction

The principles described in the previous essay provide rules of thumb for lesson preparation and orchestration that increase the chances for authentic activities, but it is the quality of the interaction that shapes a student's opinion of the activity. This means that the tension between authenticity and inauthenticity must be constantly negotiated. The teacher's responsibility in this negotiation is to keep the interaction fresh, to make it real by alternating between didactic moments and conversational episodes. We cannot escape the fact that good teaching is relentlessly interpersonal; teaching methods and materials, curricula and tests, programs and textbooks—all these are the scaffolding on which we build personal relationships with students.

An important aspect of the effort is to constantly reframe the activity so that students respond, not as objects of your lessons but as agents of their own interests. You have to move in close to the students, both physically and psychologically; your proximity encourages concentration and focused attention on the lesson elements you want them to master. The language occupies a central position in the lesson because, ultimately, it is the scaffolding of the curriculum you are teaching toward. As the lesson unfolds you check students' comprehension, pushing them to be precise and making sure you understand what they understand of the lesson. As you clarify for yourself what they understand about the material, you push them to articulate their own opinions, to probe perspectives and explore insights as you extend their comprehension beyond their initial understandings. In the process, you shift perspective so that you are able to see the lesson and the world from their point of view. To the extent you achieve this you are better able to leverage the sort of learning that you want from them.

The points I have just made can be presented as a list (see box) and numbered for convenience sake, but it is important to emphasize that these are not sequential steps toward authenticity. Rather, they are points of reference in the cyclical development of activities as you negotiate the lesson. What is required at any moment will depend on many factors and on your understanding of what is required to keep the lesson moving in the direction you want it to go.

---

### Strategies for Authentic Interaction

1. Constantly reframe the activity.

2. Move close to the students.

3. Check comprehension; examine and clarify details.

4. Extend comprehension; explore insights and probe perspectives.

5. Shift perspective.

---

I will illustrate what I mean by annotating the Bugs! lesson and by commenting on the same lesson as it appears in *Choice Readings* (Clarke, Dobson, & Silberstein, 1996). In order for this to go well, you need to have worked the textbook exercises (pp. 145–148) as if you were a student. I know this feels like an obnoxious imposition, but it represents an important step in shifting perspective from teacher to student. The goal, stated somewhat simplistically, is to experience the activity as the students will experience it, and to attend to your strategies as you read the story and answer the questions. Make notes to yourself to remind you of what you did, and use them to evaluate the strategies your students employ. Use your insights as the basis for checking and extending conversation, working on language points, and moving close to students.

## 1. Constantly reframe the activity.

"Reframing" is an approach to understanding situations and events that is taken from the sociological research of Erving Goffman (1974) and the applications of Lee Bolman and Terrance Deal (2003) to organizational change. It consists of attempting to step back from the moment and see yourself and others from different perspectives, to put yourself in the position of spectator or observer, rather than actor. What you want to accomplish in this instance is to get people to participate, not as students, but as readers and critical thinkers, to engage in the activity as thinking/feeling human beings, rather than as characters in the drama we call "school."

I am working for this in Bugs! in the beginning when I encourage students to peruse the newspaper in search of articles they find interesting; my hope is that they will be able to participate in the activity as newspaper readers and forget for the moment that we are in an English class. My exchange with Akihiro about whether or not he would eat cicadas (p. 124–125) is intended to accomplish a reframing for him. For the moment, I am hoping, he is responding to me, not as a student but as a somewhat finicky eater.

If I were teaching the *Choice Reading* exercise, I would use the Overview questions in an effort to get students to think about what we are doing as newspaper readers.

---

### Overview

In most cases, when you read a newspaper article, you do not need to comprehend everything in order to understand what the story is about. Look at the headline, the subtitle, and the photograph on page 154 to answer the following questions.

1. What do you guess the article will be about?

2. What does "Midwest" refer to?

Now read "Bugs Make Skin Crawl in Midwest" quickly, without stopping to look up unfamiliar words. Then answer the Comprehension questions.

---

Also, as we work through the exercises, my efforts at getting at their personal opinions would be examples of reframing. In general, I would keep the following points in mind as I prepare for lessons and as activities proceed.

❏ The reading determines what I do with it—different genres encourage different approaches and different activities.

❏ Work with students to step back from assignments and ask:

■ Why are we reading this?

■ Who wrote it?

■ What is the purpose of this reading?

■ What questions do I have about it?

■ How do I approach it?

❏ Remember that "chapter in a textbook" is a type of reading and help students take a critical approach to the texts they are required to use.

❏ In the case of the *Choice Readings* exercise, I work to make what I know about newspaper stories available to students:

■ use of pictures to support stories, entice readers, increase interest

■ by-lines to give credit to reporters

■ city of origin of a story or the news service (such as the Associated Press or United Press International.)

### 2. Move close to the students.

Because authenticity is an interpersonal accomplishment I want each student to feel that I am communicating directly with him or her, so that he or she is less likely to try to hide behind the role of student, scrunching down in the desk at the back or taking refuge in staring intently at the book to avoid being called on. I am therefore using the phrase *moving close* in its literal as well as figurative senses. This means moving in among students as they work on activities, but it can also mean calling on a student from across the room, or referring to a student's known preferences and inclinations as the lesson proceeds.

In the Bugs! lesson, I move about the room as the students read the newspaper and respond to my questions, and this is characteristic of all my teaching. The following options also have the effect of increasing my direct contact with students and are especially important if I am using a textbook, which tends to evoke student-as-student role playing in people:

❏ Keeping teacher talk to a minimum with the primary purpose of orchestrating student talk.

❏ Prompting student participation in a variety of ways and with a variety of immediate goals:

■ Calling on students randomly, jumping around the room in ways that keeps everyone on their toes.

- Proceeding in fixed order so that people have the chance to mentally prepare their answers.

- Asking questions designed to bring out the expertise of individuals.

- Abruptly asking students to confer with a neighbor to discuss the answer to a question; this shifts the conversational dynamic from teacher/student to peer pressure.

- Shifting from individual to group so that the class can help an individual with the answer, thereby provoking a sense of relief.

- Or, shifting from the group to the individual in ways that encourage more focused attention to the matters at hand.

- Using silence and "wait time" to give students a chance to think, but also to keep the focus of attention on the individual to answer.

❐ Organizing activities that put responsibility on the individual:

- Moving desks and chairs often to put students close to the board.

- Using the overhead projector to make it possible for the whole class to see the text or questions, and asking individuals to come to the front to record their responses or the responses of others.

- Giving students roles such as "time keeper" or "recorder of answers," thereby subtly shifting responsibilities among the participants.

- Asking questions of the group but providing time and silence for individual work before calling on individuals.

### 3. Check comprehension; examine and clarify details.

### 4. Extend comprehension; explore insights and probe perspectives.

Although all of the strategies I'm examining here are inextricably intertwined with each other, these two need to be considered in the same breath because I find it almost impossible to separate them in the flow of the classroom as I work for authentic interactions with my students. At all junctures of the lesson, I toggle back and forth between confirming that they understand the language and the ideas we are working on and pushing them further, helping them to understand the implications of a particular point or to articulate their personal feelings and opinions.

For example, in the Bugs! lesson, my initial questions revolve around the facts of the story. The students need to know that cicadas are insects—large buzzing whirring noisy obnoxious crunchy creatures that come swarming into communities like an invading army, filling the air with noise and threatening trees and sanity with their escapades. But "bug knowledge" is not going to strike receptive chords with most students; the story, however interesting it might be for me, is likely to seem like just another teacher-generated assault on their consciousness, not unlike the noisy invasion of cicadas. So I have to shift quickly to personally meaningful connections between cicadas and the students, which I do with questions that encourage them to put themselves in Elmhurst, Illinois, and consider what it might be like to be there during the mating season.

In working with textbook exercises, which may or may not have been written with an eye toward authentic interactions, I find that I am constantly working to shift attention from the details of the language—vocabulary, grammar, discourse features, etc.—to facts, concepts, and potentially emotion-charged perspectives of the material we are working on. Here are some points I keep in mind as I work the room.

❏ Move between comprehension of basic vocabulary, grammar, concepts and student opinion, experience, attitude.

❏ Move between group consensus and individual opinion. Everyone can agree on the definition of a word—*shriek*—for example, but individuals are likely to differ in their tolerance for "high-pitched noise." Ask questions that get at the differences.

❏ Move between thorough comprehension and critical reading:

■ "So, what are the newspapers reporting here?" "Why do you think this is news in the U.S.?" "Would this be news in your country?"

■ "What is *parboiled*?" "Would you eat shrimp? Bugs?"

❏ Attend to the larger issues of democratic participation in discussions. What do I want students to understand as a result of the activities?

■ Attitude of independence: deciding for themselves how to read something, how to negotiate texts, conversations.

■ Skills for different purposes:

▪ skim/scan for quick take on a piece of text

▪ thorough comprehension

▪ enjoyment

▪ critique

■ Critical stance toward language and communication: Questioning the author's agenda, purpose, knowledge, credentials.

The basic element underlying these strategies is my own curiosity about what students know and think. I approach each interaction, each episode in the class, as an opportunity to get to know individuals better and to use that knowledge to nudge them toward my goals.

## 5. Shift perspective.

The result of this approach to teaching is that I will gradually adopt an alignment to students, methods and materials, teaching and learning that permits me to appreciate the emergent nature of human relationships—the fact that we create the relationships as we interact. Stated like this, it might appear that I have moved beyond the mere teaching of languages into some ethereal realm of altered states of consciousness, and Robert Kegan, the Harvard psychologist on whose work I have constructed this approach, would agree (Kegan, 1982, 1994; Kegan & Lahey, 2001). I encourage you to pursue these ideas by reading his work.

However, I believe it is possible to make the adjustments I am advocating without a profound understanding of the theories behind them, and I believe that the rationale for approaching teaching can be appreciated merely by attending to the argument I am making, which is this:

a. The overriding goal of teaching is to entice students into our world, at least insofar as our command of the language and the curriculum constitute a "world."

b. This includes, at the very least, mastering the language skills necessary to read and comprehend texts in English and to negotiate conversations in the language.

c. We have to enter their worlds; we have to begin where the learner is and create activities that move them toward our world.

The work of the student is usually clear, either explicitly spelled out in the curriculum and materials or implicitly understood by the sorts of lessons and assignments we prepare for them.

Our work is essentially to understand where they are in their journey toward our goals (assuming we have managed to get them on board). And this involves our shifting our perspective so that we truly understand who they are, what they think, and what matters to them. All of the tactics outlined in

Strategies 1–4 contribute to this goal, and the chances of our succeeding in orchestrating authentic lessons rests largely on the extent to which we can accomplish #5.

In the Bugs! lesson, for example, my understanding of the varying experiences, needs, and aspirations of my students contributed to my decisions as I orchestrated activities. I knew that the younger students were not particularly motivated by grades or other trappings of school, and that they would rather be somewhere else practicing English with people their own age. I had to appeal to the "amusement factor" of lessons if I was to succeed in getting them to work. For the older students, however, the lessons needed to have academic merit and obvious pay-off if they were to reach their goals of obtaining citizenship, studying at the university, or securing employment.

In working with a textbook, I need to view the exercises as scaffolding for my questions, rather than accept the goals of the textbook authors, which are typically focused primarily on language points. I am interested in moving students toward mastery of the language, of course, but my focus is on shifting the footing of my relationship with students. My goal is to move from the tensions that characterize the interactions-in-role of teacher-student, where the pressing of the former is met with resistance by the latter, toward a more collaborative stance based on understanding in which the teacher probes the students' responses in order to discover how they view the world.

Robert Kegan characterizes this as "moving from the language of constructive criticism to the language of deconstructive criticism" (Kegan & Lahey, 2001, pp. 121–145). He is addressing the interactions that occur at work, where an individual approaches a colleague hoping to change the way he or she thinks or works. Typically, such interactions are characterized by polite exchanges in which each participant articulates his or her position, merely waiting for the turn in the conversation rather than attempting to understand each other. Kegan argues that this dynamic only appears to be communication, and in reality merely permits the speakers to dig themselves deeper into their own positions. He believes that we need to deconstruct the situation under consideration by unpacking the other person's understanding of the situation.

In the language classroom, the effect is to move from the language of didactic intention to the language of sincere curiosity. The effect often appears counterproductive. For example, in the exercise items #6 and #9, ask students to check all the answers they think are correct. From the teacher's point of view, all answers have merit in promoting conversation, even though strictly speaking some answers are definitely wrong.

6. What is the problem? Check (✓) all answers that you think are correct. Be prepared to defend your choices.

— a. They are noisy.

— b. They bite.

— c. They harm young trees.

— d. They eat clothing.

— e. They make you itch.

— f. They get in your food, especially shrimp dishes.

9. What is the effect of the newspaper and television stories? Check (✓) all answers that you think are correct. Be prepared to defend your choices.

— a. They are helping people deal with a serious problem.

— b. They provide entertainment.

— c. They are causing problems.

— d. They provide important information.

— e. They make money for themselves by selling newspapers and attracting viewers.

— f. They will help scientists in efforts to get rid of the problem.

The teacher's goal for the interaction is not to get the correct answer and move on but rather to probe the position of the student, encouraging exchanges between students, orchestrating conversation and increasing one's understanding of the thinking of the students.

Also, consider the value of T/F items. Item #7, for example, has a correct answer according to the story, but that is not necessarily what we want; if students are inclined to argue, we want to encourage the argument.

7. T / F   The best way to solve the problem is to spray insecticide on them.

Opinion questions, such as #10, provide the archetype of this approach, in which the student cannot be wrong—he or she is the expert on his or her own feelings.

10. If Michael Kendall invites you to dinner soon, will you go? _____
_____

And language-focused scaffolding that moves students toward their own opinions: Item #11, for example, helps people build toward their own stance on the topic.

---

11. In the headline: What is the meaning of *make skin crawl?* Check (✓) all answers that you think are correct. Be prepared to defend your choices.

___ a. cause your skin to itch

___ b. horrify

___ c. make nervous

___ d. make curious

___ e. cause hunger

Does your skin crawl at the thought of bugs like this? _____

---

## Conclusions and Conundrums

So, the answers to the questions posed at the beginning of the essay can be succinctly summarized:

❐ How do I find the time to create authentic lessons as I cope with all the pressures of the day?

No time is required in preparing for authentic instruction apart from adopting the stance of a sincerely curious conversation partner. It is a matter of attitude adjustment, not schedule or work adjustment.

❐ How can I make lessons authentic when I am teaching with mandated curricula, textbook, and materials (that I may have had no say in choosing?)

The key to authenticity with mandated materials lies in establishing independence from the text, in developing your own criteria for use of the exercises. By using the exercises as departure points rather than destinations, you are able to craft interactions that have a chance of feeling real to students while moving them toward your goals.

❐ How do I know if a lesson is authentic?

The brutal truth is that you can never know for sure how students have experienced your teaching. What matters is sustained effort and patient attention to the details of relationships with students.

The challenge of this approach to authenticity in teaching is that it assumes the teacher is willing to move out of role, to come out from behind the desk and meet students on the common ground of human relationship. And, the requirement is no less daunting for the students. Most students and most teachers do not want to take this risk. The sense of security that we derive from the predictability of the school routine permits the smooth functioning of the day, and as long as everyone cooperates, it may seem sufficient. But it also permits everyone to move through the day without having to do the real work, the difficult work, of actually getting to know each other. And this is what is required if we desire authentic lessons.

In order to negotiate the tender territory between predictable roles and routines, on the one hand, and the potentially intimidating unpredictability of improvisation that authentic interactions require, we need to develop patterns of activity in our classrooms that honor both human characteristics: the need for predictability and the desire for surprise. Within the routines of the day we want to nurture a rhythmic alteration of expected cadences, nudging students away from dependence on the comfortable toward appreciation of the pleasingly unexpected.

## REFERENCES

Bateson, G. (1999). *Steps to an ecology of mind*. Chicago: University of Chicago Press.

Bolman, L. G., & Deal, T. E. (2003). *Reframing organizations: Artistry, choice, and leadership*. San Francisco: Jossey-Bass.

Capra, F. (2002). *The hidden connections: Integrating the biological, cognitive, and social dimensions of life into a science of sustainability*. New York: Doubleday.

Clarke, M. A., Dobson, B. K., & Silberstein, S. (1996). *Choice readings*. Ann Arbor: University of Michigan Press.

Goffman, E. (1974). *Frame analysis*. New York: Harper Colophon Books.

Johnson, S. (2001). *Emergence: The connected lives of ants, brains, cities, and software*. New York: Scribner.

Kegan, R. (1982). *The evolving self: Problem and process in human development*. Cambridge, MA: Harvard University Press.

———. (1994). *In over our heads: The mental demands of modern life*. Cambridge, MA: Harvard University Press.

Kegan, R., & Lahey, L. L. (2001). *How the way we talk can change the way we work: Seven languages for transformation*. San Francisco: Jossey-Bass.

## Reading Selection 2
# Newspaper Article

In "Reading for Different Goals," in Unit 1, you learned that there are different reasons for reading and that for different reading tasks, you must use different strategies. This exercise is designed to show you that you can understand the main ideas in a reading selection without understanding every detail and without knowing the meaning of all of the vocabulary.

## *Overview*

In most cases, when you read a newspaper article, you do not need to comprehend everything in order to understand what the story is about. Look at the headline, the subtitle, and the photograph on page 154 to answer the following questions.

1. What do you guess the article will be about?

2. What does "Midwest" refer to?

Now read "Bugs Make Skin Crawl in Midwest" quickly, without stopping to look up unfamiliar words. Then answer the Comprehension questions.

## *Comprehension*

Answer the following questions using short answers. In some cases you can mark your answer on the story itself. True/False items are indicated by a T / F before a statement.

1. What is a cicada? _____

2. Where was the story written? _____ Will readers in Los Angeles and New York be having problems with cicadas?

   _____

3. T / F   The cicada is a yearly problem in the Midwest.

4. T / F   The cicadas arrive every 17 years from South America.

5. How long does the problem last? _____ Why do the cicadas come out of the ground?

   _____

# Bugs Make Skin Crawl in Midwest
## Region worked up about cicada invasion

By The Associated Press

1   CHICAGO — The Windy City is going bonkers over bugs.

2   There are nightly updates on the TV news, recipes in the newspaper, even a special hot line heralding not the coming of the apocalypse, but the emergence of inch-long critters called cicadas.

3   The noisy devils unearth themselves every 17 years to mate, shriek incessantly, and drive homeowners crazy.

4   Millions of the winged creatures are expected to emerge in parts of Illinois, Iowa, Indiana and Wisconsin during the next few days, covering backyards and forests with their brownish, crunchy bodies.

5   After mating and laying eggs that will remain underground for another 17 years, the cicadas will die. The orgy should be over by early July, and experts say the creatures are harmless.

6   But that hasn't calmed the hysteria.

7   "It's completely unfounded," said Field Museum entomologist Phil Parrillo. "People are going out and getting insecticide to spray on them, but they're only going to be here for a few weeks. Gee whiz, don't worry about it."

8   The males produce a large shrill sound; the females are mute.

9   "They may be a nuisance in terms of the sound that they make," he said yesterday. And they can damage young trees where they lay their eggs.

10   "Other than that, they're really not going to cause a problem," he said.

11   Midwesterners might get a different impression from reading the newspaper or watching the news lately.

12   "The cicadas have reached Elmhurst," a broadcaster announced in a teaser for a recent television newscast.

13   WLS-TV news has run five or six reports "saying that they're on their way, and also a story on what people

INVADER EMERGES: Robby Graves, 3, of Elmhurst, Ill., watches a cicada shed its shell yesterday.

can do to protect their young trees," said Jim Lichtenstein, assignment editor.

14   The cover of a recent Chicago Tribune Sunday magazine featured the warning: "Get Ready! The 17-year itch of the cicada is about to begin."

15   The Chicago Sun-Times last week set up a hot line, which has received at least 60 calls a day from curious or horrified homeowners with questions

about the bugs.

16   Michael Kendall, a Chicago attorney, tested one of the recipes with some cicadas he found Monday night in his brother's suburban backyard.

17   "We parboiled them and then sauteed them in butter and garlic and ate them sort of like shrimp," Kendall said. "They taste like sort of a starchy potato. They had a sort of scalloplike consistency."

Reprinted from the *Denver Post*, May 30, 1990, 2A.

**Unit 6**   Reading Selection 2   /   155

6. What is the problem? Check (✓) all answers that you think are correct. Be prepared to defend your choices.

___ a. They are noisy.

___ b. They bite.

___ c. They harm young trees.

___ d. They eat clothing.

___ e. They make you itch.

___ f. They get in your food, especially shrimp dishes.

7. T / F   The best way to solve the problem is to spray insecticide on them.

8. You should be able to guess the general meanings of the following words from the context of the story. The numbers in parentheses indicate the paragraph in which each word can be found.

a. (3) What is the meaning of *shriek?* _____

b. (8) Which word means *silent?* _____

c. (9) What is the meaning of *nuisance?* _____

d. (15) What is the meaning of *hot line?* _____

9. What is the effect of the newspaper and television stories? Check (✓) all answers that you think are correct. Be prepared to defend your choices.

___ a. They are helping people deal with a serious problem.

___ b. They provide entertainment.

___ c. They are causing problems.

___ d. They provide important information.

___ e. They make money for themselves by selling newspapers and attracting viewers.

___ f. They will help scientists in efforts to get rid of the problem.

10. If Michael Kendall invites you to dinner soon, will you go? _____

_____

**Unit 6**   Reading Selection 2   /   156

11. In the headline: What is the meaning of *make skin crawl?* Check (✓) all answers that you think are correct. Be prepared to defend your choices.

____ a. cause your skin to itch

____ b. horrify

____ c. make nervous

____ d. make curious

____ e. cause hunger

Does your skin crawl at the thought of bugs like this? _____

12. The following words are used to describe the cicada. The number in parentheses indicates the paragraph in which each word can be found. Using the descriptions, draw a picture that expresses your impression of the cicada.

   a. (1)  bugs
   b. (2)  inch-long critters
   c. (3)  noisy devils
   d. (4)  winged creatures
   e. (4)  brownish, crunchy bodies
   f. (9)  nuisance

# ❼ Teachers and Gurus

How do you cope with the external pressures of the profession? In the previous essay I was interested in how to achieve a balance between the demands of curricula on the one hand and students' interests and needs on the other. Here I focus on negotiating the implicit and explicit expectations fostered by the "best practices" view of instruction that characterizes education today—the notion that researchers and gurus possess the wisdom and insight needed to be a good teacher.

I begin with an examination of a composition lesson. I show how my teaching both reflects the influence of experts and departs from them, and I examine the dynamic between "gurus" and "classroom teachers." The questions I address are:

❒ How do we get students to take responsibility for their learning? How do we balance control and initiative in activities?

❒ How does one keep up with the scholarly work in the field? How do you integrate the advice of experts into your teaching?

❒ How does one respond to educational mandates from administrators and policy-makers?

The lesson I describe occurred at the University of Michigan and was first written up for the *TESOL Quarterly* (Clarke, 1984).[1] I use an activity called the blackboard composition, a group effort at writing in which a topic is selected and developed in a loosely controlled jam session. The teacher or one of the students writes sentences on the board as they are generated by the class. Each sentence is critiqued and refined as the work proceeds until a respectable composition results. This allows the teacher to focus on specific problems of vocabulary, grammar, and style while simultaneously demonstrating the process of composing a representative product, both of which—process and product—serve as models for students' writing.

My upper intermediate–level class is composed of sixteen young adults (nine men and seven women) between the ages of eighteen and twenty-three: four Japanese; three Venezuelans; two Mexicans; four Arabs (two from Egypt, one from Lebanon, and one from Saudi Arabia); and one student each from Turkey, Taiwan, and Nigeria. All are attending an intensive English program (four hours a day, five days a week) in preparation for university-level work in the United States. The particular class session described here takes place on Monday morning of the seventh week of a fifteen-week semester. Because we use the blackboard composition regularly to launch their writing, the students are familiar with the routines and rhythms of the activity.

## THE BLACKBOARD COMPOSITION

After the business of the class is taken care of, I remind them that we are going to write a blackboard composition on "Love and Marriage in the United States." For several weeks we have been reading, talking, and writing about the mores and morals of Americans. The topic has generated a great deal of interest. The students developed a questionnaire and conducted a survey of their English-speaking peers. As a result of the semester's efforts, everybody has accumulated a wealth of information, insight, and opinion on the topic.

I give the class a few minutes to get organized. This is time that the students use according to their own inclinations: Some seem to meditate, eyes half-closed, chins resting on palms, pencils tapping lightly; others scratch notes; one student rifles through her book bag in search of the questionnaire and a previous paper; two students talk quietly at the back of the room. Most seem gratifyingly engaged in the activity, although one student appears to be sleeping, and another arrives late and does not really get down to work.

I ask them to compare notes and discuss their musings in pairs and small groups. The object of their discussion is to produce a list of main ideas around which we can build an essay. I do not indicate a time limit but, rather, circulate among the groups, eavesdropping on the discussions and commenting on the growing lists of main ideas. After a few minutes, I call the class to order and ask them to pull their desks closer to the board; the students are now in productive disarray, clustered close and focused on the task.

A student raises his hand. His group believes that the title of the composition should be changed to "Love and Courtship in the United States." Marriage, they contend, is less interesting than courtship, and besides, the topic needs to be narrowed. There is a murmur of assent, and I substitute Courtship for Marriage on the board. Another student suggests that we narrow the topic even further by discussing love and courtship in Ann Arbor, since that was the area covered by the survey. After a brief discussion, this suggestion is withdrawn; the group does not want to limit itself to a discussion of Ann Arbor. Perhaps they are thinking of salacious examples from racier locales that they want to use.

I ask for a sampling of main ideas, writing them on the board as students call them out. As we fall into the familiar rhythm of the activity, a pleasant hum of banter and discussion develops, providing a backdrop for the energy that is focused on the task. The main ideas are jotted down, in sentence fragments, on the long board that covers one side of the classroom. We hit a lull and pause to study the selection, which includes:

| | |
|---|---|
| influence of leisure time | freedom |
| disintegration of family | feminism |
| changing values in society | role of parents |
| goals of young people | generation gap |
| sexual promiscuity | advertisements |
| the importance of sports | financial realities |

One student points out that the ideas are not all equal; some seem more important or more relevant than others. I move to the side of the board and lean against the wall, not speaking, but nodding in agreement. One of the students goes to the board, adds *the importance of religion* to the list, and sits down. Some of the students are copying down the main ideas, others are going through their notes; a few are scribbling in their copybooks. I walk to the board at the front of the room. "Shall we start?" I ask. "What'll be our first sentence?"

There is a momentary silence, then one of the scribblers offers, "Today the American have too much freedom." I write it on the board, correcting the grammar as I write and step away, looking at the sentence in a manner intended to convey thoughtful contemplation: "Today Americans have too much freedom."

"It seems kind of negative," one of the Japanese women quietly asserts. "How about, 'Today, American youth have much freedom'?"

"A great deal," says a voice from the back.

The Nigerian, who is sitting at the front, goes to the board and writes it out below the other sentence: "Today, American youth have a great deal of freedom."

"How do these relate to our title?" I ask. More murmurs and scribblings.

"Try this one," says one of the Venezuelans. "Today, because of too much freedom, American youth enjoy love and courtship."

". . but their parents don't," adds the Nigerian. Amid the chuckles of the class, he writes the new sentence on the board. We now have three sentences:

> Today, Americans have *too* much freedom.
> Today, American youth have a great deal of freedom.
> Today, because of too much freedom, American youth enjoy love and courtship, but their parents don't.

"What is the point we're trying to make?" I ask, and the discussion becomes a noisy exchange, developing into a debate in which one group of students maintains that Americans allow their children too much freedom, while the other group admits that there is a great deal of freedom in the United States but that this is not necessarily negative. After considerable give-and-take, during which we hear impassioned references to religious tenets and emphatic quoting of newspaper articles and survey results, we finally settle on an opening sentence:

> Today, because of the freedom enjoyed by American youth, love and courtship have become very complicated.

The group identifies two major points that can serve as the focus for the next sentence: "freedom" and "the complexity of love and courtship." They decide to produce a couple of sentences that elaborate on freedom before tackling the complexity issue. I put our topic sentence at the far end of the front blackboard, erase the trial sentences, and we begin the process again, building the first paragraph, sentence by sentence.

We are now in full swing. The board fills with sentences, each modified according to suggestions from me and from the students. An adjective or two are added to a noun phrase, two sentences are collapsed into one with a relative clause, and a nonfinite verb phrase is suggested to serve as a sentence opener. A few sentences are rejected because they are too vague, while another sentence is erased because it is too wordy. I walk to the back of the room and sit in a student desk during one debate between two students who differ on the need for examples as opposed to explanation. The group decides both can be used. At several points I am at the board asking how to vary the types of sentences we are using, asking for a closer link between two sentences in the paragraph, or for details that give the reader a clearer picture of our point of view. Grammar errors are generally caught by the students. From time to time, I correct spelling and punctuation errors without comment. Word choice and stylistic options are areas where I am usually needed to point out a problem or to suggest an alternative. Several times we get caught up in differences of opinion about the content, about what we want to say. There are sporadic attempts at coercion and, from time to time, bursts of Arabic, Japanese, and Spanish signal that commitment to the debate has over-taxed the English proficiency of the debaters. We work to find out exactly what the disagreement is, and we produce sentences that reflect the different opinions. The issue is then decided by a vote, but the other sentences are there to be copied down by the students who championed them. At several points I glance at the clock, wrestling with my frustration at the snail's pace of the essay; with most of the hour gone, we only have half a dozen sentences. Once or twice I cut the debate short, modify the sentence under consideration, explain why my changes are necessary, and urge the class to pick up the tempo. From time to time I stroll between the desks and position myself behind a student who appears only mar-ginally involved, hoping that my authoritarian proximity will spark a little energy.

Finally, with about ten minutes left in the hour, I call a halt and remind them that their compositions are due at the end of the week. They are to use the paragraph we have written as the beginning of a three-page essay with the same title.

They are to use their peer review groups to work on the essays. I will give them twenty minutes on Wednesday to work on the papers, but I predict that they will need to meet in their groups outside of class during the week. The peer review groups were established early in the semester. After I had seen a few writing sam-ples from everyone, I ranked the students from best to worst and then assigned them all to groups of three, being careful to put individuals of different abil-ity together: Group 1—Students #1, #16, #8; Group 2—Students #2, #15, #9; Group 3—#3, #14, #7, and so on. I tinkered with the membership of the groups until I had a mixture of languages and a male/female balance in each one. I also paid some attention to personality differences, hoping to avoid groupings that were obviously destined to fail because of conflicts. The groups were used as an extra source of feedback and support. Approximately one of every three writing assignments required the groups to convene in order to read and critique each other's papers. On such occasions, the grade of the poorest composition was given to each student in the group.

The students use the remaining minutes to copy down the main ideas that have not been used, to confer with group members, or to get organized for their next class. The bell rings, and they disappear into the corridor.

## Qualifications and Elaboration

A few comments are needed to put the lesson in perspective. First, it is important to be clear that I am not offering this activity as prescription; I needed a detailed description of my teaching to anchor an examination of the relationship between classroom decision-making and models of teaching—any lesson would do, even one that did not qualify as successful.

In the same spirit, I am not presenting this vignette as a "hero narrative." Although I am generally satisfied with my teaching, I have no difficulty admitting that I am not a master teacher. At the same time, the glimpse of this composition class is a reasonably accurate portrayal of an activity that I use regularly in my teaching. But the points I want to make here concern the importance of informed, confident decision-making, not virtuoso performance. In the typical week of lessons, there are going to be diamonds and stones, and a focused examination of any class could arguably provide sufficient data for productive reflection.

And finally, I do not claim that the scholars whose work I discuss represent the final word on composition teaching. Rather, they were the important authorities whose work I studied in graduate school and early in my career; their work remains important to me to this day. The argument I am making applies in general to this relationship between the classroom teacher and noted authorities.

## Acknowledging Intellectual Debts

All teachers stand on the shoulders of their teachers. What follows is a list, briefly annotated, of my mentors in the teaching of writing.

### Robert B. Kaplan

Although I have always been interested in writing, I had not given much thought to the problem of teaching writing to English language learners until I arrived at the American University in Cairo to work on my M.A. in Teaching English as a Foreign Language. Composition was taught there in the manner that it was taught in many intensive English centers—as an extension of the grammar class. I was struggling with sentence combining, substitution frames, and a variety of other "controlled composition" techniques, feeling free-floating frustration at my lack of success, when I read Kaplan's article, "Cultural Thought Patterns in Inter-Cultural Education." Kaplan argues that because rhetorical principles are culture specific, the teaching of writing must focus on discourse units larger than the sentence (Kaplan, 1968). From the moment I read the article, I began working on ways to teach "above the sentence." The basis for this instruction was the presentation, explanation, and analysis of model paragraphs and essays, combined with attempts to get students to recognize the rhetorical requirements of English as distinct from those of their native languages. As a result, I began teaching writing in conjunction with reading, and I worked to reduce the emphasis on vocabulary choice and grammar.

Influences of Kaplan in this approach can be seen in the heavy reading schedule that accompanies the writing activity and in the fact that the predominant question throughout the lesson is, "What are we trying to say?"

## Francis Christensen

A footnote in Kaplan's article refers to the work of Francis Christensen, and on a visit to States one fall I found a copy of his little yellow book, *Notes Toward a New Rhetoric* in a university bookshop (Christensen, 1978). I practically memorized whole chapters of that book because here at last was something specific to guide me in teaching "rhetorical principles." My efforts at teaching "above the sentence" had not been altogether satisfying. As I slogged through swamps of grammatically correct but illogically placed sentences, I began to understand why English teachers were loyal to the time-honored **awk** written in the margins of students' papers and why they cranked out masses of worksheets on sentence connectors, nonrestrictive relative clauses, and topic sentences. It is easier to work on something manageable than to struggle with the real problem faced by all composition teachers, whether their students are native or non-native speakers of English: Good writing requires the author to anticipate the needs of the reader and to build an essay by adding ideas (expressed, of course, in well-formed sentences) in a way the reader finds logical and convincing. Christensen's book provides the framework for teaching such writing.

I experimented with Christensen's ideas until I developed rules of thumb that students could apply to their writing and that I could use as the framework for in-class critiques of student papers and native speaker models. These rules of thumb were three principles:

1. The Principle of the Main Idea
2. The Principle of Addition
3. The Principle of Subordination and Coordination

My strategy was fairly simple. Rather than serve as the editor and proof-reader for students each semester, I attempted to teach them to consciously address a series of questions as they worked. The first question, to be asked again and again, was, "What am I trying to say?" The second question, "What information does the reader need here?" allowed them to build on the main idea by adding details, focusing on a specific quality, or drawing a comparison. The third question, which required the writers to scrutinize each sentence as they produced it, was, "How does this sentence fit?" According to Christensen's scheme, every sentence is either subordinate (semantically and syntactically) to the sentence immediately preceding it or coordinate with a sentence somewhere above it.

Writers who follow these rules of thumb may not win literary awards, but they will be guaranteed a level of consciousness about their writing that increases the likelihood of comprehensibility. It is fairly easy to produce work-sheets and models for focused classroom practice of the three principles, but the major advantage of this approach is that the principles provide a framework for the private and public critique of a piece of writing.

In the blackboard composition my questions concerning the main idea, my requests for clarity and focus, and my demands to know the function of a particular phrase or sentence all evoke previous lessons, worksheets, and homework assignments. In spite of the haphazard appearance of the lesson, the development of the paragraph on the board represents harnessed energy, an attempt to consciously apply a small number of rules in the development of an idea.

## Daniel Fader

By the time I began working on ways to teach writing to English language learners, I had spent two years studying the ideas of Daniel Fader, Professor of English at the University of Michigan, author, and school reformer. As an undergraduate, I had read his *Hooked on Books*, and in tutoring a group of inner-city Chicano adolescents, I had experimented with his suggestions for promoting literacy (Fader, 1976). Like many leaders in education, Fader advocates a functional approach to the teaching of reading and writing. He believes that students should have to read and write in all segments of the curriculum and that drills and worksheets should be replaced by activities that match students' interests and accomplish goals important to the students.

I have incorporated a number of Fader's ideas into my teaching—journals to encourage writing, paperback books to lure students into reading, discussions with students to find out what *they* think is important in their education—but the idea that is most obvious in the blackboard composition is the use of peer teaching. Fader avoids ability-grouping, and his respect for the teaching ability of learners is evident throughout his book. Class and small group discussions of ideas in class are products of this respect, and the peer review group is his mechanism for promoting peer teaching. By reducing the importance of the teacher in the learning process and by organizing an experience that shows students how much they have to offer each other, the teacher increases the probability that learners will acquire the skills and attitudes of literate users of language. They also are gradually nudged toward becoming their own authorities for their decision-making.

## Donald Murray

Donald Murray has a great deal to say to the writer-as-teacher about attitude, approach, and classroom technique, but the thrust of all of his work is that the writer must develop an appreciation for the process. Writing requires effort—we must work at a piece of writing until it satisfies us. But writing also clarifies our thinking. That is, in the process of trying to get our ideas down on paper, we begin to discover what we are trying to say. Murray asserts that in order to write well, we must develop a certain amount of respectful self-consciousness about the process. We do not all write well under the same conditions or with the same tools, and if we are to be successful as writers, we must work to produce the conditions that promote success for us. These same principles must be borne in mind as we teach writing (Murray, 1987, 1989, 2000).

I have used Murray as justification for a great deal that I do as a teacher, especially the explicit discussion of writing strategies with students, but his influence is most obvious in the laborious working and reworking of sentences as we develop our blackboard composition. When we begin, we do not know exactly what we are going to say, much less how we are going to say it. As we struggle to identify ideas and opinions, as we bicker over words and phrases to express them, we come very close to the process that, Murray argues, is the key to good writing: revising. Aspects of the blackboard composition that make it unattractive for many teachers—it is time-consuming, painful, and plodding—are precisely the qualities that recommend it to me. It is as close as I have been able to come to modeling the process of composing while actively involving the learners in that process.

### Earl W. Stevick

More than anyone else, Earl Stevick has influenced my understanding of language teaching and teacher education (Stevick, 1980, 1982, 1996, 1998). Two important influences are especially prominent in this lesson.

The first concerns the general atmosphere of the class. Whatever success I have had with group composing is due to the sense of security students have and the freedom that that security promotes. That is, I have worked to create an atmosphere that encourages student initiative and interaction. I explain the guidelines, and I provide feedback and encouragement to ensure the progress of the lesson; within those limits, however, students are free to do whatever is necessary to get the job done. This is my attempt at translating into practice Stevick's concept of the tension between control and initiative. He develops the metaphor of the jungle gym (Stevick, 1998, p. 34) to illustrate how a rigid structure can release the energy of the learner.

Stevick is also the primary source of my thinking about authenticity in language teaching. He advocates lessons that balance cognitive and emotional appeal and provide students with opportunities for interaction and self-committing choices.

I describe the goals of the process to the students at the beginning of the term. Because many of them come from cultures that emphasize the authority of the teacher, I do not merely hand the class over to them the first day we use the technique. Rather, I gradually recede into the background over a number of class sessions, explicitly stating my conviction that they must rely on their own judgment and exercise their prerogatives as they participate in class. I encourage them to suggest composition topics, I allow ample time for small group interaction, and I demand that they respect everyone's right to an individual opinion. In other words, I do not relinquish control of the class, but I do attempt to establish conditions that encourage students to take the initiative and to use the language skills they are acquiring to accomplish tasks that are important to them.

## Technique and Improvisation

So, there you have my annotation of the lesson—an apprentice's tribute to his masters.

Which reminds me of a story. My friend John Fanselow, professor at Teachers College, was accosted on the street by a former student who told him that his teaching had changed her life, and she insisted that he visit her classroom to see what she was doing. He was flattered, and he went, and although he was favorably impressed with what he saw, he confessed, "I have no idea what there was of me in those lessons."

This anecdote captures the relationship between teachers and their gurus. What we do in our classrooms is uniquely *ours*—no matter how much we admire the work of others, our teaching is *our* teaching, and this is the natural order of things. This is the truth that is obscured in professional and public debates about "the best way" of teaching or the most effective approach to a particular pedagogical problem. Methodological mandates and prescription of standardized approaches to teaching will never achieve the intended goals of standardization; all human interaction, including that encountered in classrooms, is unique to the moment.

To understand why this must be the case, let's examine the notion of "technique" more closely.

The term *technique* is transparent—it refers to any activity used in class to accomplish pedagogical goals. But in English language teaching it has acquired canonical status as a result of Edward Anthony's seminal 1963 article, in which he develops the case that classroom *techniques* must be consistent with *method*, which in turn must align with the philosophical tenets of *approach* (Anthony, 1963). H. Douglas Brown offers this summary of the distinction (Brown, 2000):

> In order to understand the current paradigm shift in language teaching, it will be useful to examine what is meant by some commonly used terms—words like *method, approach, technique, procedure,* etc. What is a method? Four decades ago Edward Anthony (1963) gave us a definition that has withstood the test of time. His concept of method was the second of three hierarchical elements, namely, approach, method, and technique. An *approach*, according to Anthony, is a set of assumptions dealing with the nature of language, learning, and teaching. *Method* is an overall plan for systematic presentation of language based upon a selected approach. *Techniques* are the specific activities manifested in the classroom, which are consistent with a method and therefore in harmony with an approach as well. (pp. 169–172)

This is the view that has dominated the profession for a generation—the assumption that there must be congruence between one's theory of language acquisition and language teaching, the curriculum that provides order throughout the school term, and the techniques that one uses every day in the classroom. This has led to assertions that a particular technique was out of date or ideologically inappropriate because it did not reflect tenets of the reigning theory. So, for example, during the heyday of audiolingual teaching, in which memorization of dialogues and pattern practice of key sentence structures were dominant, it would have been considered inconsistent to teach explicit grammar rules. As the profession moved into the "designer method" period (roughly, the 1970s and 1980s), discussions could be heard in language teaching centers about the innovative techniques associated with Suggestopedia, Counseling/Learning, the Silent Way, etc., and it was widely assumed that good teaching involved a search for exciting techniques.[2]

As a profession today, we are less caught up in this approach to teaching, but it is still widely assumed that some techniques are more effective than others or that techniques can be assessed on a scale of "theoretical rigor." And, most teachers are alert for new classroom techniques, for fresh and interesting ways of organizing class sessions. It therefore seems reasonable to pause a moment to explore the nature of the teaching technique.

*Technique* is merely a label for classroom activity, a sort of conversational shorthand that, among other things, allows us to negotiate professional discussions. At the copy machine before class it is not unusual to hear teachers exchanging ideas for how to teach the vocabulary in a required novel or how to foster student discussion of key concepts. Suggestions often come in the form of the convenient shorthand of the teaching repertoire—"Have you tried doing a *jigsaw* with that chapter?" or "I used an *information gap* approach last week and had good luck with it" or "I find that I can't get them to use those phrases in conversation until I run them through some *pattern practice* and *substitution drills* just to get their tongues wrapped around the words."

As with most labels, the words used to designate particular teaching practices leave much to the imagination, and neophytes may be more confused after the exchange than before if they are not familiar with the techniques mentioned. But in any case, the label is merely shorthand for the activity because a teaching technique, like all behavior, is not a *thing, an object*. Rather, it is an event, a moment in time when we orchestrate interaction among students with certain goals in mind. The label represents a bundle of options that we hope will nudge students toward mastery of the language. But we do not enter the classroom with a director's script and the intention of following every detail in lock-step choreography. *Technique*, therefore, is a series of decisions that we make as we go, depending on our assessment of a large number of complex, interrelated variables, among which the following would probably qualify for consideration:

- ❏ our theory of language learning and teaching
- ❏ the lesson plan
- ❏ the size of the class
- ❏ the ages, backgrounds, and interests of the students
- ❏ the quality and availability of teaching materials
- ❏ the material already covered and the content of future lessons
- ❏ the nature of tests and assignments required by the curriculum
- ❏ state and professional teaching standards
- ❏ the personal and professional characteristics of our immediate superiors
- ❏ the time of day and the day of the week
- ❏ the quality of the pasta and spinach salad at lunch

The variables are not all of equal importance, of course, and you may think me whimsical for mentioning lunch in the same breath as standards, but I doubt that many veterans would have difficulty remembering times when indigestion played as important a role in their decision-making as did curriculum mandates. The point is that our teaching is based on a wide variety of factors, among which the dicta of gurus are only one part.

This perspective has a number of important implications for teachers.

First, from this point of view, there is no such thing as a "good" or "bad" technique, at least not at the level of labels. That is, we cannot evaluate a lesson independently of the actual occurrence of the technique and the goals for the activity. Certainly we can reflect on a particular class session and proclaim the experience (and by inference, the technique) to be an unparalleled success or an unmitigated disaster. We form judgments concerning the technique that influence our attitudes and future behavior, but this will not constitute a blanket endorsement or rejection of the technique. It is entirely likely that a colleague could have radically different experiences with the same activities or that we could have more or less success on different days or with different students. We have to look beyond the labels to examine specific occurrences of techniques and to understand their strengths and weaknesses. The effectiveness of a technique is only visible *after* the activity has occurred, when we use our assessment of it to plan our next lesson.

A second implication is that any technique that you use becomes, by definition, uniquely yours. Your experience and understanding, your effort and energy during the activity, your evaluation of what is required at any moment—all of these factors make the technique your slice of reality. The technique is, therefore, only secondarily an example of the category indicated by the label we use to refer to it.

The third implication follows from the first two: In a consideration of teaching techniques and materials, or of classroom practice, there can be no prescription—only description and suggestion. In other words, as a teacher, you have to decide what will work for you and how you will use it, and you make your decisions both before the class begins, as you prepare lessons, and in the heat of the activity as the class unfolds.

Even if you see yourself as an orthodox follower of a particular approach, your day-to-day, hour-by-hour behavior will still exhibit the uniqueness that is characteristic of all teaching.

However, in spite of the conviction that teaching is largely idiosyncratic, I do not contend that skills and insights were acquired by revelation. As you reflect on particular lessons, you can identify people and experiences that provided inspiration for the choices you made. If you were to treat the transcript of a class session as a Talmudic exercise, you could trace most of your choices back to specific sources. These might be an article or textbook, a conversation with a professor, a hallway encounter with a colleague, or participation in a workshop at a convention; these are your authorities, the individuals you think of as you work to improve your teaching and whose work you cite in defending your practice to others.

So, how do we understand our classroom decision-making, and how do we account for our behavior?

Note the difference in orientation implied by the two questions. The first question revolves around the concept of responsibility. The second question aligns to accountability. The former is a matter of you and your standards; the latter has to do with how you justify your actions to others. I will not dwell on the matter here, but I contend that you need, first of all, to *believe* that the portrait I have painted is essentially accurate, that teaching is a matter of flexibly responding to events, of exercising your professional judgment, of personal decision-making. And, only secondarily but increasingly in today's climate, you need to be able to defend your decisions to others—administrators, policy-makers, members of the public you serve.

## Conclusions and Continuations

Just to be clear: I have not introduced any new concepts or proposals here—the argument I am making is one I have been developing throughout the book, that teaching is a matter of creating activities for learning and then nudging students toward our goals. The angle is slightly different in that I have addressed the issue of alignment to acknowledged gurus whose proclamations might be seen by some as prescriptions for good teaching, and I have presented a critique of conventional understandings of *technique*. I have urged an approach to teaching in which teachers are viewed as the experts in their own classrooms, the only individuals who have sufficient understanding of all the information to judge the relevance and appropriateness of instructional decisions.

In fact, the whole issue of what constitutes "good teaching" requires some attention if we are to understand how to nurture learning *and* balance the insights and admonitions of experts. My position is that this is an empirical issue—that we need to develop ways of paying attention to how students are adjusting to our demands, and that this needs to go beyond compiling lists—of attendance, of papers submitted, of grades on tests. Because learning is *change over time through engagement in activity*, we need to be able to see the changes, which means that we need to somehow plot the distance between the patterns of their behavior when they entered our classrooms and the patterns they exhibit after working with us for a while. I outlined one way to accomplish this on pages 62–83—action research—but the process is an ongoing one of reflective practice.

Here, the salient point is that, just as we need to acknowledge that teaching is not the smooth implementation of a particular set of procedures, we also need to understand that the evidence of learning is going to be far more ambiguous than conventionally believed. At first glance the three questions I posed at the beginning of the essay might appear to be unrelated, but I see them as pertinent to our efforts at understanding the connections between teaching, learning, and expert advice.

❏ How do we get students to take responsibility for their learning? How do we balance control and initiative in activities?

❏ How does one keep up with the scholarly work in the field? How do you integrate the advice of experts into your teaching?

❏ How does one respond to educational mandates from administrators and policy-makers?

The important insight is that we are all in the same bind—students, teachers, administrators, and policy-makers—everyone is adjusting to the demands of his or her position, attempting to solve the persistent problems of the day in ways that make sense both to us and to others. I have posed these questions as a teacher concerned about my students, but I could easily restate them from the position of the director of a school or a state education official.

Learning requires change, and this usually comes in response to external pressure. If we come to see the value of the change, we gradually incorporate the thinking and the behavior into our daily repertoire—we adopt the new ways of seeing and acting as our own. This is true whether you are learning the language or ways of teaching the language. It is a process of accommodation and assimilation, of adjusting to the pressures and gradually incorporating new repertoires into your daily routines.

Part of our responsibility as teachers is keeping up with the professional wisdom of the field—a difficult task, given the explosion of knowledge in the field. In this we are not very different from our students who know that there is far more to learn than about the language they will ever master. You read about a new approach to a familiar teaching problem, and you begin to adapt your practice to accommodate the potential it offers. Gradually, you come to see this as part of what you do, even though an independent observer—perhaps even the expert him or herself—would say that your adaptation is an imperfect rendition of the approach. So part of your responsibility is helping others understand how your practice aligns to expectations and mandates. How to accomplish this requires a book by itself—a combination of psychological support and political advice—because this becomes a matter of interpersonal negotiation among you and your colleagues and immediate superiors, and only you can judge how to proceed. However, in general, the best response is one of attentive and respectful attention to detail, coupled with the will to present counter positions based on the authority of the teaching masters you base your work on.

This leads us back to the discussions of theory and philosophy examined in earlier essays, the core argument of which bears repeating. Your first responsibility is to yourself—you have to be clear on what you believe and how that belief translates into effective classroom activity. Second, you need to be able to help others see how your effort aligns with contractual and professional expectations.

## REFERENCES

Anthony, E. M. (1963). Approach, method, and technique. *English Language Teaching Journal*, *17*, 63–67.

Berry, W. (1990). *What are people for?* New York: North Point Press.

Brown, H. D. (2000). *Principles of language learning and teaching* (4th ed.). New York: Longman.

Christensen, F. (1978). *Notes toward a new rhetoric*. New York: HarperCollins.

Clarke, M. A. (1984). On the nature of technique: What do we owe the gurus? *TESOL Quarterly, 18*(4), 577–594.

Cole, M. (1996). *Cultural psychology: A once and future discipline*. Cambridge, MA: Harvard University Press.

Fader, D. N. (1976). *The new hooked on books*. New York: Medallion Books.

Kaplan, R. B. (1968). Cultural thought patterns in inter-cultural education. *Language Learning, 16*(1), 1–20.

Murray, D. M. (1987). *Write to learn*. Stamford, CT: International Thomson.

———. (1989). *Expecting the unexpected: Teaching myself—and others—to read and write*. Portsmouth, NH: Boynton/Cook.

———. (2000). *The craft of revision*. Boston: Heinle and Heinle.

Stevick, E. W. (1980). *Teaching languages: A way and ways*. Rowley, MA: Newbury House.

———. (1982). *Teaching and learning languages*. New York: Cambridge University Press.

———. (1996). *Memory, meaning, and method*. New York: Heinle and Heinle.

———. (1998). *Working with teaching methods: What's at stake?* New York: Heinle and Heinle.

## NOTES

1. It is important to mention that the lesson described here did not actually occur as described; it is an account that consolidates experiences that I had during the year.

2. A number of good summaries of this period of language teaching exist. I recommend Earl Stevick's *Teaching Languages: A Way and Ways* (1980) and *Working with Teaching Methods: What's at Stake?* (1998).

# ❽  Teaching to Standards:
# How to and Why Not

In the distant past, *Teacher* was the word used for the older, wiser, more accomplished individuals who passed along knowledge, skills, and insights to callow youth in an apprenticeship relationship. They were usually relatives or members of the same clan. Expectations for appropriate conduct and learning goals were common knowledge but largely unarticulated. These were matters of cultural and family tradition, not codified in policy or law.

As the role of teacher became more formalized, professional standards developed and became the basis for retention and evaluation, although until recently, the focus was more on the process of teaching and learning, rather than the outcomes (Cochran-Smith, 2005). These days, with the institutionalization and increasing politicization of education, standards have become an apparatus of accountability.

If you teach in the United States you are familiar with this use of standards: They are explicit expectations for professional conduct, elaborated in minute detail in administrative memoranda and faculty handbooks. Intended as guidelines for the preparation of lessons and materials, standards are also increasingly used as objectives for teaching and benchmarks for evaluation of student learning and teacher performance.

The questions I am using to organize my thinking and to inform my interactions with students, colleagues, and administrators are these:

❏ What are standards? Where do they come from, and how do they influence our thinking and behavior?

❏ Whose standards count?

❏ How can I position myself to balance external mandates against my own sense of what is right?

Before we dig into these issues, however, it is necessary to lay the groundwork for the argument I want to develop.

All occupations require individuals to use their judgment to solve problems. The professions, in particular, require people to bring their training and experience to bear as they work on specific situations and encounter particular events. Teaching, certainly, requires this. However, the situations that teachers face every day are far too complex for formulaic solutions to problems. As a society, we have to rely on the training, experience, and best judgment of teachers in the classroom, as they respond to myriad situations and events of the typical school day.

The essence of professional conduct is characterized by an attitude of principled independence. Teachers, like other professionals—doctors, engineers, attorneys, etc.—accept responsibility for their behavior and conduct themselves according to guidelines developed by professional organizations in response to societal values. It is imperative that teachers assert their prerogatives and responsibilities in this regard. If educators do not take this seriously (both individually and as a profession), we will discover that others—politicians, pundits, publishers, and managers—are making all the important decisions and teachers will be left feeling frustrated and ineffective because they are merely implementing directives from above. Teacher discouragement and burn-out are the inevitable result.

Standards take many forms—program curricula and institutional guidelines, faculty handbooks, state and national policies for professional conduct, formal criteria for teacher conduct as developed by professional organizations, etc. So, it is important to build my case around an explicit example to assure that we are thinking of the same thing. Here are the sort of standards that I have in mind:[1]

1. Students will build vocabulary through use of dictionary strategies, context clues, and word analysis skills.

2. Students will develop command of grammatical structures to communicate effectively in academic and social settings.

3. Students will use English to research subjects, consolidate information, and present coherent arguments orally and in writing.

4. Students will use English to critically examine the claims of writers and speakers, to assert their own opinions, to disagree appropriately with others.

5. Students will interact appropriately in spoken and written English for personal expression and enjoyment.

Stated like this, "standards" seem reasonable. They provide clarity and focus, an organizing framework for teaching. Most teachers believe that it is important to be thoughtfully goal oriented in their work. But increasingly it is difficult to find teachers who believe that standards are, in fact, helping them as they go about their daily business. More and more standards are experienced as a mechanism for control in an environment of accountability.

But no matter where you teach, you are expected to perform according to institutional goals and mores, so it is not unreasonable to characterize the issue broadly as a tension between societal/institutional control and expectations on the one hand, and personal/professional discretion and responsibility on the other. In this essay I want to synthesize the argument I have been making throughout the book as I address that tension.

My point is this: Because teaching is a public trust, it is reasonable for teachers to be accountable to the community at large, and it is expectable that their conduct will conform to high personal and professional standards. However, ultimately, we have to trust teachers to do their jobs, because fine-tuned accountability mechanisms cannot *force* individuals to behave honorably. Therefore, what *is* required are clear guidelines and support, not prescriptions and micro-management.

So, the best way to "teach to standards" is to attend to your core values and the activities that move learners toward them, consulting the standards and adjusting your behavior *after the fact*, as you go, rather than starting with the standards and attempting to teach *toward* them. This approach results in a healthy cycle of adjustments that gradually nudge you and your students toward your goals.

But note the pronoun: *your* goals. You take into account the school's expectations as expressed in the curriculum and reflected in the norms established in the daily rhythms and routines of the school, and you develop lessons that reflect your understanding of the experiences, needs, and aspirations of your students, and you develop your goals for your teaching.

The *why not* of my title refers to the sorts of defensive maneuvers we engage in when we believe we might be guilty of infractions or transgressions. I'm thinking of the *compliance attitude* that often prevails when we are doing things because we "have to" or "it's expected of me" rather than because "it's the right thing to do." In the box, I've attempted to capture the most commonly heard reasons that teachers have given for teaching under duress.

---

### "Why not..." Principles

The following are *not* healthy or productive reasons for attending to standards as you teach:

I am teaching to the standards...

1. because I have to.... I am teaching this content or in this way in spite of my better judgment because I have been told I must do this.

2. because the teachers in the next level will wonder what I have been doing if the students do not know this material before they move on.

3. because I have to finish the book by the end of the term.

4. because it's on the test.

5. because the students expect me to cover the material.

---

This is the sort of behavior we see (and exhibit) when the locus of authority is external rather than internal, when we are deferring to someone else or some regulation rather than consulting our own core values and criteria for good teaching. It is neither appropriate nor productive to organize teaching merely to be in compliance with mandates, whether these come from the explicit demands expressed in state and federal standards or school curricula, or in the informal pressures exerted by your colleagues and administrators in meetings or the faculty lounge.

It is inappropriate to approach teaching this way because it abdicates the teacher's responsibility and defers important decision-making to individuals who, no matter how caring and responsible, cannot possibly know as much about the learners as the individual who is in the classroom with them every day.

It is unproductive because it will not achieve the results it is intended to achieve. People are not billiard balls or machines; they do not roll smoothly across slate tables or respond to tinkering with tools. Prescriptions from afar merely limit the flexibility and responsiveness of teachers. There is, however, a reasonable approach to standards, which I sketch here.

---

### "How to…" Principles

1. Know the standards you are expected to meet, whether these are explicitly articulated in documents such as curriculum guides or published guidelines, or merely part of the school culture. Be able to quote them on a moment's notice (to yourself and others) as rationale and justification for your actions.

2. Orchestrate lessons according to the principles elaborated in Bugs!

    a. **Core Values:** Be clear on what you are trying to accomplish.

    b. **Rhythm and Routine:** Establish a predictable pattern of activity.

    c. **Strong, Transparent, Light:** Modify the routine with improvisations that strengthen engagement.

    d. **Head and Heart:** Create activities that make students think and appeal to their emotions.

    e. **Interaction:** Provide opportunities for structured collaboration in pairs or small groups.

    f. **Self-Authorizing Choices:** Give students chances to make decisions that *they* believe important.

    g. **Feedback:** Respond throughout the lesson so that students know how they are doing.

3. Review the lesson and identify the standards you believe you achieved. Adjust your plans for the next lesson accordingly.

4. Repeat.

---

The list constitutes variations on a single admonition, which I attempt (not always successfully) to follow in life and work: Attend to what is important, and let the chips fall where they may.

This may seem hopelessly naïve (or suicidal, depending on your teaching situation), so I hasten to add that I am not recommending narcissistic self-absorption or blind defiance of authority. I am merely following the logic of an ecological approach to teaching and learning, a fundamental tenet of which is the recognition that there can be no unilateral control of human beings, whether we are talking about teachers or students. The best we can do is to create environments conducive to healthy goal-oriented activity, trusting that the individuals involved will conduct themselves appropriately.

There is another compelling reason for this stance: The fact of the matter is that teaching is a solitary endeavor. When it comes right down to it, the only people in the room most of the time are you and the students. You have to rely on your own judgment as you make the countless decisions that constitute the business of teaching. You do not want to put yourself in the position of second-guessing yourself by attempting to behave according to someone else's vision.

At the same time, of course, you have to come to terms with the tension created by external expectations and internal criteria for your behavior. It is for this reason that it is helpful to think through the relationship of general standards for professional conduct on the one hand, with the criteria that you use to assess your success in dealing with the minute particulars of the daily grind on the other. Let's get to the nub of the matter.

❑ What are standards? Where do they come from, and how do they influence our thinking and behavior?

Rather than merely accepting standards as given, we need to step back and examine their meaning and origins. Here are some definitions that might serve as useful points of departure for our contemplations:

1. **Dictionary:** "a level of quality or excellence that is accepted as the norm or by which actual attainments are judged"—(MSN Encarta®)
2. **Educational Policy:** Detailed descriptions of knowledge, skills, and practices by which teaching and learning are evaluated. This is an attempt to capture professional consensus and to develop policies and procedures that promote standardization across institutions.
3. **The ecological or anthropological view:** The observable evidence of individual and group commitment—what gets done. From a strictly empirical point of view, whatever can be observed in a school over a period of time reveals what the standards are for the people involved.

The three definitions vary only slightly—primarily in terms of emphasis. It can be agreed that standards represent norms for behavior and that they provide an important indicator of quality. But as we progress from the dictionary definition to the professional policy definition to the cultural definition, we are actually traversing the territory from abstract formulation to real life:

Definition #1 represents the clearest, most concise, most uncomplicated representation of standards.

Definition #2 could be seen as an attempt to translate the abstract definition into a working definition, the basis for policy and procedure.

Definition #3 represents the description that a group of teachers might achieve at the end of a typical week, reflecting on the messy reality of life in schools.

The three definitions delineate the common ground and contested territory of standards-based education. Let us imagine the situations in which the three definitions were crafted and who might have been involved in their development. The dictionary definition is clearest and most abstract, applying generally to all situations in which people might be expected to articulate their expectations for human behavior, written by lexicographers whose expertise is linguistic, not professional.

The second definition is the sort of result achieved when practicing educators are asked to help craft the standards for their work. The authors would be veteran teachers with years of classroom experience, and their efforts would reflect the realities of their own work in schools. They would have been convened by leaders in professional organizations or state policy-makers, and they probably work for several weeks in thoughtful contemplation and collegial interaction to come up with this definition and the details of the standards for their areas of expertise.

The final definition is the sort of rueful assessment that classroom teachers might produce if they were speaking honestly about the realities of their efforts with specific learners in real situations. Whatever their intentions were as they entered the profession (or even as they began a new school year) and however carefully they formulated guidelines for their own conduct, only clear-eyed observation over a period of time will reveal the norms by which they actually conduct themselves. This definition represents the unvarnished truth articulated by caring professionals who are doing the best they can with the situations in which they find themselves.

But the three definitions represent more than different approaches to understanding the expectations of teachers. They represent, in a nutshell, the dilemma that teachers face every day. You enter your classrooms to teach particular students, each of whom has his or her own personal history of problems and perplexities, and you attempt to organize their learning of specific curricular content according to your best understanding of the learners and that content. Your efforts are going to be most accurately reflected in the sort of attitude and approach reflected in definition #3. However, you are judged by others who will refer to the sorts of definitions articulated in #1 and #2. And this brings us to the second question of the essay:

❐ Whose standards count?

This gets us into some slippery territory because as I've indicated with my account of the definitions, we are all implicated in the construction of the standards, if only indirectly and remotely. That is, we are all members of the societies in which we teach and are active in the professions that hold us accountable for our actions. We are acting in good faith, doing the best we can with the tools and experience we bring to our work—teachers to classrooms, administrators to schools, policy-makers to laws—but given the institutional realities and locus of political power, it is teachers who are seen as responsible for whatever outcomes are achieved.

And, increasingly these days, given the diversity of students in schools and the pressures of budgetary constraints and scarcity of resources, the outcomes are seen as unsatisfactory. By everyone—teachers included.

But it is important that teachers not take on the burden of responsibility and blame for the situation. Things are the way they are *not* by accident. Systems function at all levels to produce the outcomes we observe, and although teachers are closest to the students and the nearest adults to the unhappy results, they cannot be held solely responsible for the problems faced by contemporary society and schools.

This is an important point, but the person who has to recognize it, accept it, and do something about it is, unfortunately, you.

Of course, what I mean is you and I and each of us as individuals and as members of the profession. And that fact permits us to move to the third question:

❒ How do I position myself to balance external mandates against my own sense of what is right?

As you attempt to organize your thinking and actions for the day (and week and semester) ahead, you need to find a comfortable space, psychologically, within which to work. At the same time, you need to develop strategies for interacting with others that will create the sort of flexibility required to do your job.

The first step is coming to grips with the fact that, whatever the pressures, you are going to be better off if you work from your own understanding of the standards and your own knowledge of your students. You must work to create the conditions for your own evaluation, and you must help others—colleagues, administrators, parents, and community members—understand what you are doing *from your point of view.*

Historian and philosopher Stephen Toulmin examines the dilemmas produced by this approach to evaluation, and he points out that your decisions will always be fraught with uncertainty, that you will never have the benefit of total information, and that you have to act in accordance with your own standards of conduct, not those formulated in distant boardrooms:

> The central issue is not the timeless question, "What general principles can be relied on to decide this case, in terms of binding on everyone who considers it?" but rather the timely question, "Whose interests can be accepted as morally overriding in the situation that faces us here and now." (Toulmin, 2001, p. 122)

The shift that is required by this approach to standards is not concerned with the content or the conduct of teaching; rather, what is required is a change in the relationship of the teacher to the standards and to the institutional authorities who mandate them. But it is more complicated than that, because it also requires the teacher to redefine him- or herself with relationship to values and authorities he or she has adopted.

This is a matter of (re)constructing oneself and one's experience of the standards so that you are in charge of the relationship. This requires a change in how you understand the world and your place in it, and it hinges on finding support within oneself—identifying core values and creating environments that permit you to achieve coherent alignments between your understanding of your practice and your employers' definition of acceptable work.

In other words, you need to distinguish between the position and the job. You need to take responsibility for the job and do the job that you believe important while meeting the requirements for the position. You need to become your own CEO, the individual to whom you answer on all aspects of your job.

## On Becoming Self-Employed

This is no easy task. It requires you to step back from your own experience and understand it as an observer of human behavior. It requires a certain amount of objectivity, of brutal honesty, of separation from the comfortable lessons of childhood and culture. Let me explain with the help of Harvard psychologist Robert Kegan.

As meaning-making organisms, we develop our understandings of self and the world from the messages we receive as we grow up in our families. These are the implicit and explicit lessons that we learn by being with our elders—the rules and regulations, the stories and admonitions, the verbal and non-verbal punishments, exhortations, advice, endearments, and chastisements that constitute the day-in-day-out experience of being a member of the family. Because we cannot *not* make sense of everything we experience, the learning is constant and insistent, unrelenting, inevitable, unstoppable. We have no choice but to learn these lessons. They are so powerful and pervasive that for most of our early years—through adolescence and perhaps well into adulthood—we do not even have the capacity to think that there might be another way of thinking, living, being. This experience is all there is; this is life and who we are in it is who we are.

When we become conscious adherents of these family-ordained standards, we enter into what Robert Kegan refers to as third order consciousness. When we develop the ability to critique this reality, we begin to move toward fourth order consciousness (Kegan, 1994). This does not mean that we have abandoned the family "line" or that we believe ourselves superior to the claims made on us by it; it merely means that we have achieved a new relationship to it. The authority of the family tradition is necessarily hierarchical because our position in it begins when we are helpless infants. And, even as we are socialized into responsible adult roles within the family, we continue to function in explicit and implicit hierarchical relationship to others. These relationships and meanings of the "clan" are extremely powerful; we never completely succeed in establishing psychological independence from the family, nor the culture of which the family is the most important institution.

It is important to clarify this view. "Family" does not refer specifically to the organizational unit of mom, dad, and siblings, although that might suffice for many individuals. It refers more generally to the significant individuals whose daily presence is the essential element of our awareness and with whom we negotiate every aspect of our selves, from the mundane requirements of making one's bed and taking out the trash, to the more encompassing responsibilities of caring for younger siblings or, later, for aging parents. This sense of connectedness would apply to all manifestations of the "modern" family, including the complex households of divorced parents and "parenting grandparents."

And culture, in this view, encompasses all the meanings conventionally conferred by anthropologists and popular understanding, although it takes on a slightly different meaning from conventional definitions; it is the context in which we live. Like fish in water, we have no understanding of life outside of culture, and although we may (through travel or friendships) develop an appreciation of other cultures and other ways of living and being, it maintains a pervasive pressure on our understanding and decision-making (Geertz, 1973, 1983; Erickson, 1992).

So, to return briefly to questions about the nature and origins of standards: Standards are the natural outgrowth of the culture's desire for certainty in an uncertain world. In the particular instance of a district or a school, individuals in positions of responsibility collaborate to articulate the ideal conditions for teaching and the desired trajectory of learning. Others participate in bringing the standards to bear on institutional practices of hiring, evaluating, and rewarding teachers.

What is difficult to understand is how individuals who appreciate the complexities of their own dealings with their fellow human beings can turn around and expect more precision of others in comparable situations. Even more galling are the times when we discover ourselves passing the pressure on to our students. But this is precisely the role we play when the reasons we give for assignments or activities are of the same ilk as those in the "Why not…" box on page 169.

So what is required is that we not uncritically accept others' expectations of us. What we need to be working on is creating the conditions for our own self-employment, working with colleagues and administrators to articulate standards that are reasonable for both us and our students, and to develop assessment policies and procedures that accurately reflect the learning that is taking place and that provide the resources for improvement of instruction.

Let me give one example of how this might happen.

## *Constructing Your Own Evaluations*

Perhaps the question is not, "Whose standards count?" but "How do we count the standards?" or "What counts for compliance with the standards?" That is, we have all been in the situation of believing ourselves unfairly judged by someone else who "doesn't have all the facts" or who "does not understand the context." What this usually means is that the events or data under consideration do not easily yield to the simplified, digitally organized criteria of "approaches standard," "meets standard," "exceeds standard." Consider this vignette.

### WHOSE STANDARDS

A young teacher of my acquaintance (whom I'll refer to by the pseudonym of Mary), working in her first year of teaching and attempting to control a particularly rowdy group of third graders, was chagrined to learn that her principal would be "dropping in" to evaluate her early in the semester. She had been given a large class (twenty-five students) with several "problem" students—English language learners and individuals who the system had identified as "learning disabled" or "behaviorally challenged." One boy in particular was difficult; he was given to temper tantrums during which he threw chairs, screamed obscenities, and lashed out at anyone within reach. Mary had managed, through a series of negotiations with parents, social workers, school psychologists, and other school personnel, to achieve a modicum of order and instructional routine in the classroom, but she was far from confident that she had established the sort of learning environment on which her teaching should be evaluated.

The principal was aware of the difficulties she had faced but had determined that it was time for the formal evaluation. So, Mary worked especially hard on her lesson plan and about halfway through an activity the principal did, indeed, arrive. She slipped in and sat at the back, took notes, and slipped out.

Well, that's over, Mary thought, and at least she came at a time of relative order and demonstrable learning. She was relieved to have the evaluation completed, and she was pleased that the lesson observed was a strong one. She knew that there was always room for improvement, but given the fact that this was her first year and that this was an officially recognized "difficult" class, she was certain she would receive good marks.

So it was with considerable distress that the only comment the principal had on the lesson was, "The three boys at the back were not engaged in the lesson."

What has happened here, and why is it a problem?

The principal, acting no doubt under pressure from above, has complied with institutional expectations to observe one of her teachers. But the observation merely fulfilled the most superficial and unimportant of the expectations; it was a pro-forma job, and whether intended or not, she merely passed the pressure on to the teacher. The problem is that what is likely to happen next is that Mary will merely pass the pressure on to her students, that is, create tasks and assignments for the "disengaged" boys at the back, "because I have to...."

And what are possible alternatives to this scenario?

The first step is to attend to the basic principles of instruction described—make sure that you are working from your core values and that you are carefully orchestrating experiences that you know will nudge your students toward your goals. In other words, concentrate on creating a healthy environment for learning.

Then, it is necessary to establish a principled relationship with your superiors, one in which you control the conditions of assessment of your performance and of the learning of your students. You need to identify the best time for a visit to your classroom, and give the observer a checklist of things to watch for, aspects of your instruction that you would like feedback on; choose both strengths and weaknesses, the former so that your accomplishments will be evident to the observer, and the latter so that you can get some feedback for improvement.

This needs to be a schoolwide effort—you do not want to be the only person who is stepping forward like this. And it is always helpful to use the procedure first with trusted colleagues in reciprocal feedback sessions before the formal evaluation session occurs. But in any case, you need to work to achieve control over the conditions of your employment.

## Conclusion

So, the answers to the question posed in the title of the essay, "how to and why not" can be succinctly summarized:

> By attending to what you know is important and not merely complying with authority.
>
> By engaging your colleagues and superiors in principled dialogue about how to improve the learning experience of students.
>
> By participating in the larger institutional sphere so that all teachers are supported in their efforts, not merely harassed by institutional expectations.
>
> In other words, by realizing that teachers today need to be philosophers, theorists, action researchers, and political activists.

Ultimately, what it comes down to is our ability to negotiate the multiple, conflicting demands on our time and behavior, and our ability to "live with ourselves." We cannot abdicate. The stakes are too high and the cause too important.

### REFERENCES

Cochran-Smith, M. (2005). Teacher education and the outcomes trap. *Journal of Teacher Education, 56*(5), 411–417.

Erickson, F. (1992). Ethnographic microanalysis of interaction. In M. D. LeCompte, W. L. Millroy, & J. Preissle. (Eds.), *The handbook of qualitative research in education* (pp. 201–225). New York: Academic Press.

Geertz, C. (1973). *The interpretation of cultures*. New York: Basic Books.

———. (1983). *Local knowledge: Further essays in interpretive anthropology*. New York: Basic Books.

Kegan, R. (1994). *In over our heads: The mental demands of modern life*. Cambridge, MA: Harvard University Press.

Toulmin, S. (2001). *Return to reason*. Cambridge, MA: Harvard University Press.

## NOTES

1. A complete text of standards for English language teachers and additional information and resources are available from the TESOL website: *www.tesol.org/*.

# 9 Changing Schools: Creating Disturbances and Alarming Your Friends

This essay focuses on the problems faced by English language teachers working in schools where the medium of instruction is English and English language learners are a marginalized minority.

But the issue is the same for everyone:

❑ How does one address systemic problems in schools and work for changes at the school and community level? In other words, how does one promote school-wide change to support English language learners?

❑ Another way of putting it might be—"How do I get my colleagues and administrators to adjust their thinking and behavior to align with what I believe to be important?"

"Absurdly self-centered!" you say.

And you are right. It's reminiscent of the remark attributed to Oscar Wilde: "Ah, civilization! That long steep road that leads to me." Very arrogant. So, why *should* you expect your school to be organized around your priorities?

I can think of three reasons.

First, and most important, your decision-making is based on a carefully developed theoretical and philosophical framework. Your conduct in the classroom and in school in general is guided by your commitment to values you hold dear and take seriously. And, while you understand that compromise is always necessary, you also know that you cannot teach in a school that does not subscribe to the same values. As a teacher of English language learners, you are an advocate for a minority in a democratic society, and no matter what other issues are being addressed in your school, equitable education for nonnative English speakers surely is an important one. So, assuming that you are working in a building where people share your values, it is reasonable to assume that you should be able to nudge important decisions toward your way of thinking.

Second, even if you see your primary task as getting your own classroom organized, you cannot accomplish this alone. Significant problems cannot be solved at the level they are encountered.[1] In the case of education this means that, because classrooms are nested within schools and schools are nested within communities, attempts at doing something creative in the classroom very often require attending to the constraints that arise from the "nesting" environments. For example, if you are attempting to orchestrate activities that get your students into the community to use their English in an authentic setting, or if you want to extend class time to work on projects, you will need collaboration from administrators and colleagues, and the policies and procedures at the school level will have to support the initiatives you are trying to implement.

Third, if you cannot influence the way your school functions, it may be time to seek a position elsewhere. Good teaching is more an institutional accomplishment than an individual *tour de force*, and if your goals are not viewed as important or worthy of support by your administrators and colleagues, it may be time to seek a position in another school.

Yes, yes—I know. You are saying to yourself that you have to be "realistic," that you cannot expect the world to revolve around your priorities. But if you are going to be effective, you must work to improve the environments within which you are working. And, you have to recognize that you cannot change the world single handedly. If you come to the conclusion that your current situation is not going to improve, you need to actively seek a school that is more in tune with your goals. It is really that simple.

And so, the two meanings of the title, "changing schools": You may be faced with the choice of changing the school where you work or changing schools so you can do your work.

This is a big topic and if you see your primary responsibility as orchestrating classroom instruction, you may be inclined to skip the essay and avoid thinking about these issues. Which is your prerogative, of course.

However, be warned: you can avoid *thinking* about the problems I examine here, but they will not go away. And many of the difficulties you face as a teacher of English language learners and as an advocate for linguistic and cultural diversity derive in large part from the way larger systems function. Societal attitudes and norms filter down to become school policies and procedures, and classroom constraints reflect these larger phenomena. It is in your best interests to participate in decisions that influence these constraints. The goal of this essay is to develop strategies for doing that.

It might help to focus the argument by elaborating on the questions given:

- ❏ How can schools adjust policies and procedures—and even more important, norms, routines, and daily rhythms—to provide healthy learning environments for English language learners?
- ❏ What are the roles and responsibilities of the individual classroom teacher in promoting the larger systemic changes of the sort required by these questions?
- ❏ How does one adjust one's thinking and daily activity to move oneself and the school toward these goals?

The assumptions behind the questions are deceptively simple: Schools exist to facilitate teaching and teaching is a matter of creating environments for learning. Discovering and adjusting to the experiences, needs, and interests of learners are therefore the first priorities. This requires almost constant adjustment as the demographics of the community change and as your understanding of the learners increases.

But, because it is human nature to slip into comfortable habits of thought and action, and because students come and go but teachers remain, schools become institutions that function for the convenience of the staff rather than for the benefit of the learners. So maintaining a stance of "student-centered" teaching becomes a matter of resisting the tendency toward comfortable routines. If you take this work seriously, you will find yourself in a state of constant perturbation and you will discover that you are also a source of alarm and disgruntlement for your colleagues and friends.

Hence, the coda of the title, "creating disturbances and alarming your friends," which contains a warning: If you take this work on, you will have to find ways of coping with the irritation of your friends and the aggressive response of your adversaries.

## Identifying Specific Initiatives

Let us get down to specifics. Nancy Commins and Ofelia Miramontes (2005) identify ten initiatives that every teacher can promote to improve the chances of success for English language learners in English-speaking schools.

## Things Every Teacher Can Do

1. Work toward equity in school policies and procedures and toward a climate of belonging for all students; incorporate aspects of students' culture and family in all aspects of school functioning.

2. Recognize that people's academic understanding always exceeds their ability to articulate what they know, and that English language learners have the additional difficulty of translating between languages; create activities that permit you to see what they know, regardless of the language in which it is expressed.

3. Organize instruction to build on what students bring with them from home; develop lessons that reflect the routines and rhythms of the family and that feature content familiar to the students.

4. Gather information about the learners' prior language and literacy experiences and use this to construct activities that are realistic and authentic.

5. Group and regroup students during the day to account for varying language proficiencies and grasp of concepts.

6. Balance your commitment to standards-based instruction with an understanding of the needs of students; that is, use student knowledge, skills, and interests as the starting point for planning instruction that moves toward the standards.

7. Adjust instructional activities to account for language proficiency.

8. Adjust activities to account for differences in first and second language literacy development. Work to assure yourself that all learners truly understand the concepts represented by text (rather than assuming that because they use the vocabulary they understand the ideas and experiences behind the words).

9. Modify the classroom environment so that both curriculum content and classroom rules are understandable to English language learners: pictures and graphics on walls, cabinets, cupboards, etc., to provide the information typically conveyed in print.

10. Develop activities that increase learner interaction around personally meaningful concepts and experiences.

*Source:* Adapted from *Linguistic Diversity and Teaching* (pp. 137–169), by Nancy L. Commins and Ofelia B. Miramontes, 2005, Mahwah, NJ: Lawrence Erlbaum Associates.

Indicate whether or not you find these suggestions reasonable:

_____ Yes

_____ No

_____ Not sure I want to commit to an opinion yet.

Indecision at this point is understandable. The initiatives in the box may provide a reasonable basis for a healthy educational environment, but depending on the situation in your school, the distance between this ideal and current reality could be significant. And the work required is not always immediately apparent. For example, it may seem a small thing to put signs up around the classroom that will help learners negotiate the daily routines (#9), but even this requires you to divest yourself of all the assumptions and understandings you use to operate every day in the world as a proficient, literate English language user. How do you convey the essence of a sign that reads, "Respect the privacy of others" or "Give your fellow students help when they need it but be aware that in this culture some kinds of help are considered 'cheating'?"

And what about initiatives that require collaboration? Adjustments in curriculum or evaluation procedures (#1, #2, #6, #7), for example, will require support of administrators and cooperation among faculty, even if everyone agrees on the importance of the work. And, of course, complete agreement is unlikely if significant changes to teachers' rhythms and routines are involved.

You may be wondering why all this tip-toeing around—why not just identify the work that needs to be done and then launch into the effort?

The answer lies in the fact that it is never clear what work needs to be done because there are as many opinions on this as there are participants in the school. Furthermore, even among English language teachers and others who are committed to these sorts of initiatives, there will be significant differences of opinion about the relative importance of different changes and the steps to be taken to accomplish them.

Which means that, even after you have launched seriously into a change effort, you will need specific strategies for proceeding. Because the details will vary with each initiative, and because circumstances change quickly, there are no simple prescriptions or easy formula to follow, but it is safe to assert that the kind of work you will be required to do falls into three categories—institutional, interpersonal, and internal—you will need to identify changes in the way your school functions, which will include negotiation with others, all of which is predicated on the assumption that you are able to adjust your own thinking and behavior. And, it is necessary to keep in mind that you will need to be working on all three all the time.

## Snippets of Reality

The argument is easier to grasp if we are working from specific examples. Ponder the vignettes that follow and jot notes to yourself about each situation. What is the problem? What might you do to solve it? What are the institutional responsibilities in each case (i.e., what changes in rules and regulations are indicated)? What would you do if you were the protagonist in the story?

---

### Vignette #1

A large (2000+ students) high school in a medium-sized university town has been experiencing significant difficulties as a result of changing demographics in the student population. The predominantly affluent, educated community has recently seen a dramatic increase in immigrant students from Mexico coupled with the arrival of Mexican-American working-class families. The staff responded by assigning students to classes based on English language proficiency as well as developing "sheltered" classes for English language learners (content courses such as math, biology, history, etc., that are taught with the needs of nonnative English speakers in mind). This has seemed to work for the immigrant students, but tensions remain and a number of flare-ups between Anglo and Latino youth have occurred where it is difficult to distinguish between recent arrivals and students who have lived in the country most of their lives. Gang-related disturbances have alarmed the Anglo community, resulting in public meetings in which parents have angrily demanded action. Central Administration has ordered the abolition of the sheltered classes in an attempt to integrate the English language learners into the mainstream of the school.

**Problem:** _____

**Solution:** _____

**Institutional Responsibility:** _____

**Your response:** _____

---

## Vignette #2

A middle school teacher steps into the hall during passing period just in time to see two boys square off. Faces contorted in anger, books and epithets flying, kids pushing back against the lockers to give them room to fight. One boy pulls a long key chain from his pocket and rears back gladiator fashion when the teacher pushes him up against the lockers and brings the fight to a halt. She pulls them into her classroom and makes them sit down and cool off. One of the boys is newly arrived from Mexico. The other is also Latino but was born in the country. The question is, "What to do next?" School policy states that fights are to be handled by the assistant principal and teachers are to fill out a disciplinary sheet describing the incident. Any involvement of weapons requires an immediate three-day expulsion from school, and key chains are explicitly listed as weapons. Three expulsions and the student is expelled for good. Failure to act in strict accordance to the rules could result in disciplinary action for the teacher.

**Problem:** _____

**Solution:** _____

**Institutional Responsibility:** _____

**Your response:** _____

---

## Vignette #3

Katarina dropped out of her ESL class at the local community college after the counselor told her that her English was not good enough for her to enroll in a computer class she wanted to take instead of the social studies class to which she had been assigned. She said she felt stupid in the social studies class and believed that the teacher did not take her job seriously because she was merely teaching immigrants. For example, as part of an assignment to talk about countries of origin, she gave a presentation on Peru. At the end of the class, the teacher summarized the presentations but did not mention Peru. When Katarina asked her why, she was told that the presentation was very good, but they could not spend more time on it because Peru was not in the curriculum.

**Problem:** _____

**Solution:** _____

**Institutional Responsibility:** _____

**Your response:** _____

---

### Vignette #4

José is a sixth grader and a conscientious student, but his family responsibilities often conflict with school tasks. He is expected to help out with his siblings when his mother has doctor appointments or chores that call her away from home. On one occasion he told his mother that it was very important that she attend a parent-teacher conference and that he had to do his homework so he couldn't run an errand. His mother shot back, "La maestra no manda aqui." (The teacher doesn't give orders here.) He ran the errand and didn't get his homework finished, and his mother didn't make it to school for parent-teacher conferences.

**Problem:** _____

**Solution:** _____

**Institutional Responsibility:** _____

**Your response:** _____

---

### Vignette #5

Marisa is a shy and quiet ninth grader who has always done well in school, but she is struggling with Social Studies this year. She seems to be missing the main points of projects—lots of work evident, but the main ideas are not nailed down and the misuse of key vocabulary in writing assignments indicates that she may not truly understand the concepts. After repeated phone messages and calendar conflicts, her teacher manages to make a home visit, where she discovers concerned parents who support their daughter's desire to go to college but whose English is not strong enough to help her with her studies. Marisa has adopted a complex strategy for dealing with the problem. She has been translating all of her homework into Spanish, discussing the concepts with her parents, then translating again as she completes the assignment in English. In spite of all the work, the results are indifferent because her translations are often inaccurate and her understanding of the concepts is not strong enough to overcome the linguistic problems. And, to make matters worse, she arrives at school totally exhausted.

**Problem:** _____

**Solution:** _____

**Institutional Responsibility:** _____

**Your response:** _____

These vignettes are glimpses of actual events and real people related to me by teachers or excerpted from situations described by Nancy Commins and Ofelia Miramontes (2005), Bonny Norton (2000), and Guadalupe Valdes (1996). They illustrate the need for school policies and procedures that support the learning of culturally and linguistically diverse learners. But more important, I think, they provide examples of the need to adjust our own attitudes and behavior to increase the chances of success of English language learners.

At first glance their similarity might not be self-evident. The need to respond to the mandate from central administration portrayed in Vignette #1 seems very different from the disciplinary decisions required in a middle school hallway (#2). And the student/teacher exchanges that led Katrina to drop out of her ESL class (#3) would seem to be much more straightforward than the kind of parent/teacher conversations required to remedy the problems described in #4 and #5.

But they all have this in common: If you are the teacher in each of the situations you will be affected by events and you will have to respond, either immediately or at some point in the near future, in order to contribute to the solution. And the chances for success revolve around calculated definitions of the problem and strategic approaches to the solutions. Let me elaborate on those two points a bit.

## Reframing Change Efforts

The key insight of this approach involves recognizing the importance of perspective. We cannot begin to understand what is happening or how we want to respond if we do not remember that everyone is operating according to his or her own perspective of the situation.

Most important, we need to remember that this applies to us as well. As we work we need to remember that the word *problem* is merely a label for a situation that we believe requires attention. Others may not be bothered by events and situations that we consider problems. They will have their own understandings of problems, and unless we can devise ways of discovering the extent to which our definitions overlap, we will not make much progress in solving them. So, as a starting point, we need to commit ourselves to focused, deep, and sensitive exploration of situations and understandings with others. We need to work to understand both our own perspectives and the perspectives of others. Then, we can begin to develop strategies for a commonly defined and constantly negotiated, ever-changing *group perspective* of the problems that we face. In fact, it is not an exaggeration to say that the most important aspect of our work is finding or creating common ground for decision-making of all the diverse stakeholders in the conversation.

I have found the concept of "frame analysis" developed by Erving Goffman and applied to organizations by Lee Bolman and Terrance Deal to be helpful in this endeavor (Goffman, 1974; Bolman & Deal, 2003). Imagine the world as grand theater and life as a series of performances. Goffman advises us to use the metaphor of the picture frame as we attempt to understand what is required of us. In order to avoid being distracted by the overwhelming complexity of life, you hold up frames of different sizes and different assumptions as you examine events and decide how you are going to respond. Bolman and Deal argue that, in attempting to change organizations, four frames suffice—the structural, human resource, political, and symbolic (Bolman & Deal, 2003, pp. 14–19):

❒ The *structural frame* emphasizes goals, specialized roles, and formal relationships. Structures—commonly depicted on organizational charts—are designed to fit an organization's environment and technology. Organizations allocate responsibilities to participants ("division of labor"). They then create rules policies, procedures, and hierarchies to coordinate diverse activities into a unified strategy. Problems arise when structure is poorly aligned with current circumstances. At that point, some form of reorganization or redesign is needed to remedy the mismatch.

❏ The *human resource frame*, based particularly on ideas from psychology, sees an organization as much like an extended family made up of individuals with needs, feelings, prejudices, skills, and limitations. People have a great capacity to learn and often an even greater capacity to defend old attitudes and beliefs. From a human resource perspective, the key challenge is to tailor organizations to individuals—to find a way for people to get the job done while feeling good about themselves.

❏ The *political frame* is grounded in the scholarship of political scientists. Organizations are portrayed as arenas, contests, or jungles. Parochial interests compete for power and scarce resources. Conflict is rampant because of enduring differences in needs, perspectives, and lifestyles among competing individuals and groups. Bargaining, negotiation, coercion, and compromise are a normal part of everyday life. Coalitions form around specific interests and change as issues come and go. Problems arise when power is concentrated in the wrong places or is so broadly dispersed that nothing gets done. Solutions arise from political skill and acumen.

❏ The *symbolic frame*, drawing on social and cultural anthropology, treats organizations as tribes, theaters, or carnivals. It abandons assumptions of rationality more prominent in other frames. It sees organizations as cultures, propelled more by rituals, ceremonies, stories, heroes, and myths than by rules, policies, and managerial authority. Organizations are theater: Actors play their roles in the organizational drama while audiences form impressions from what is seen onstage. Problems arise when actors blow their parts, when symbols lose their meaning, or when ceremonies and rituals lose their potency. We rebuild the expressive or spiritual side of organizations through the use of symbol, myth, and magic.

As you work, you shift from frame to frame as you talk to colleagues, parents, administrators, and policy-makers. You are working to craft flexible and creative responses to problems. For example, working with a *structural* lens, you might decide that a policy is too tight or rigid and is stifling creativity and engagement, or that another one is too loose and unpredictable, provoking defensive participation and withdrawal from the group. But if individuals are too immersed in the assumptions and routines of the organization to see the dysfunctionality of the established procedures, you may decide to promote conversations around the mission of the organization (*symbolic* lens), or the external opportunities and threats (*political*), or the particular skills and attributes of individuals (*human resource*) in the school. The key insight is that there are always many approaches to problems, and that often we cause more problems by failing to see that the solution chosen does not match the problem.

## Perspectives on "Problems"

The most important thing to remember is that "problem" is just a label for a situation that an individual finds irritating. It is highly idiosyncratic; one person's problem is merely "the way things are" for another individual. It follows, therefore, that deciding if there is a problem in the first place is an important step, and that framing the problem in a way that can be solved is also crucial. No sense spending time and energy on a situation that will not yield to a particular solution.

Let's consider each of the vignettes with this in mind. Using the four frames suggested by Bolman and Deal, I have identified a number of ways of characterizing the problem for each of the situations.

| Vignette | Labels for Problems | Solutions |
|---|---|---|
| **#1 High school mandate to abolish sheltered instruction** | Isolation of Latino students causing public relations, disciplinary, and instructional problems. | <u>Structural</u>: Work with student government to create programs for more inclusion of immigrant students in school life.<br><br><u>Symbolic</u>: Frame the problem as "school growing pains" with community and central administration; present a variety of responses that address disciplinary incidents involving mainstream youth as well as Latino youth. |
| | Central Office mandates that reduce local flexibility and professional discretion. | <u>Political</u>: Organize a group of teachers to create a variety of responses and meet with administration to explore options that give school staff more flexibility. |
| | The interim principal, hopeful of getting the permanent position, prefers to pass the pressure on from central administration rather than take a stand that supports teachers. | <u>Human Resource/Political</u>: Veteran teachers meet with principal to discover ways of solving problem that avoids eliminating sheltered instruction and helps him/her maintain positive relations with Central Administration.<br><br>Or a variation on the above, should the principal not cooperate: Veteran teachers bypass principal and go directly to central administration with solutions. (Generally, not a good idea as it creates ill will with principal, but it shows that you are serious.) |

| Vignette | Labels for Problems | Solutions |
|---|---|---|
| **#2 Middle school hallway scuffle** | Tensions between recent immigrants and "Americanized" Latinos | Structural: Teachers work with student government to create variety of programs that reduce cliques and promote community. |
| | Gang-related altercation; some sort of initiation ritual or dispute stemming from a gang member putting pressure on another student to join up. | Human Resource: Teachers and other staff members contact parents and older siblings; investigate details of pressures on young people to join gangs and tensions among youth.<br><br>Structural: Task forces of teachers and students created to address peer pressures and gang influence.<br><br>Symbolic: PR campaigns to affirm family values and heighten school community as alternative to gang community. |
| | Flaring of tempers; relatively minor event caused by the stresses of school, adolescent energy, crowded hallway, etc. | Structural: Building committee explores alternative bell schedules to reduce numbers of students in hallways at one time.<br><br>Human Resource: Student government and teacher task force create activities that assess and respond to student stress.<br><br>Symbolic: Teacher decides to call the incident a "difference of opinion" rather than a "fight," thereby avoiding the mandated disciplinary procedures and permitting her to cool the boys down. |
| **#3 Katrina's desire to take computer class** | Policies that assume that English language proficiency is required for students to benefit from all classes. | Political: Working within the school and district to create awareness that English proficiency is only one aspect of achievement and that people can actually know how to do something using another language.<br><br>Structural: Collaboration among teachers, administrators, and students to orchestrate projects that promote bilingual problem-solving and permit students to build on their strengths. |
| | Curriculum content is seen as the focus of instruction, rather than student learning, resulting in a lack of appreciation and understanding of student experience, interest, and ability. | Structural: Adopting project-based learning as a curricular approach; teachers are forced to adopt a different understanding of teaching, learning, and curriculum content.<br><br>Human Resource: Working with colleagues to create tools for discovering students' interests and to craft interdisciplinary activities that build on these.<br><br>Political: Building consensus among faculty to develop collaborative approaches to instruction. |

| Vignette | Labels for Problems | Solutions |
|---|---|---|
| | Teacher's lack of familiarity with students' experience, interest, and ability. | Human Resource: Identifying faculty and staff members who have interest in and awareness of the students and their families and using their expertise and experience to guide other teachers toward an understanding of students.<br><br>Structural: Developing data bases and activities that promote awareness of and insight into students' family and community situations. |
| **#4 Jose, his mother, and the parent/ teacher conference** | Faulty communication between home and school. | Structural: Home/school task force consisting of teachers, administrators, and students works for ways to increase communication. |
| | Cultural differences concerning the respective roles and responsibilities of parents and teachers in education. | Human Resource: Focused effort at helping teachers and parents understand each other, including cultural differences surrounding school and the role of parents in education. |
| | Differences in mutually agreeable schedules for parent-teacher conferences. | Structural: Teachers explore alternative days/ time for conferences. |
| **#5 Marisa's study strategies** | Large class sizes and demanding school schedules that make it difficult for teachers to work individually with students long enough to detect sources of learning problems. | Structural: Committee composed of teachers and administrators in charge of personnel (hiring and staffing decisions) and class composition; guidelines that encourage decisions that promote healthy learning environments.<br><br>Political/Human Resource: Identify individuals in central administration who are amenable to decentralized decision-making; identify individuals in the school who can work with them and brainstorm ways of getting smaller class sizes. |
| | Lack of bilingual staff and materials makes it difficult to differentiate between problems caused by language proficiency and those caused by other factors such as study habits, interests, abilities. | Structural/Human Resource: Committee whose task is to identify ways of getting more bilingual staff and materials into school.<br><br>Political: Task force to work on getting dual language programs.<br><br>Symbolic: School-wide effort at promoting pride in bilingualism—bulletin board competitions, heritage celebrations, etc. |

| Vignette | Labels for Problems | Solutions |
|---|---|---|
| | Miscommunications: Teacher who failed to understand the time, interest, and energy that a student put in on an assignment and/or student who failed to express her concerns to the teacher. | Structural/Political: Paraprofessionals to work in classrooms to help teachers learn about students.<br><br>Human Resource/Structural: Workshops and materials that help teachers improve their strategies for getting to know their students.<br><br>Human Resource/Structural: Student/teacher group that promotes activities to improve communication. |

What these alternative views of the vignettes reveal is that the nature of "problems" depends largely on the assumptions held by participants or observers. And, because we tend to operate from comfortable assumptions about the way the world works, once we have hit on a characterization of the problem in a particular situation, we tend to jump in with specific "solutions." This is unproductive for at least two reasons.

First, we probably have ignored viable alternative characterizations of a situation, which means that our search for responses will be myopic—we will tend to see only solutions that suit our view of the problem.

Second, focused, direct action rarely results in tidy solutions. From an ecological perspective, "problems" are understood to be merely the label we apply to irritating but expectable outcomes of the complex functioning of systems. They are identifiable points in a pattern of events, and unless we attend to all the factors that contribute to the pattern, our actions are not likely to have much effect. So, for example, an ecologically inclined observer might note that school failure of students is an expectable outcome if the language of instruction is different from the one they speak, or if there are no support services to compensate for the difference. Or, he or she might say that miscommunications between home and school are inevitable if the languages and cultures of the two are different. He or she might also conclude that achievement scores in a particular school will reflect the fit between the curriculum and the knowledge/skills of the students, and that this latter factor will change with the shifting demographics of the community (that is, immigrant students will have skills and understandings that reflect their experiences, which are different from the experiences of the students for which the schools are prepared).

One characteristic of this approach is that it does not "locate" the problem in particular individuals or groups of people. The problem is *not* the fact that learners are from another country/culture.

An important implication is that *everyone* involved—including teachers, administrators, and other school personnel—contributes in some way to the problems. This results in a shift in thinking: from problem-solving, program-oriented approaches that tend to limit the range of responses, to strategic approaches that encourage creative thinking, experimentation with different strategies, and action/assessment sequences. But this is a difficult argument to make in the abstract. Let us consider some specific suggestions that might provide focused movement toward such an approach.

## Identifying Specific Initiatives

Because people, schools, and society at large are all open systems functioning according to norms that are only partially explicit and imperfectly understood, efforts at achieving significant change require a different sort of logic than most of us are accustomed to. Contemplate the strategies in the box that follows.

These strategies are developed from the systems thinking of Gregory Bateson (1979, 1999) and the developmental constructivism of Robert Kegan (1982, 1994; Kegan & Lahey, 2001). The suggestions build on the assumption that we have to move from merely seeing the world toward seeing ourselves in the world, from being embedded in the problems we are trying to solve toward gaining perspective on them. We have to learn how to think differently about problems and solutions. Or, more precisely, we need to learn to see that what we experience on a daily basis are merely events and situations and that, depending on our understandings and commitments, we call some "problems" and others "solutions." The approach also assumes that an important leverage for this kind of change is how we talk—to ourselves and to others; for this reason, the strategies underscore the language we use as we work.

---

### Strategies for Organizational and Personal Change

1. Avoid reacting. Use any ritual or discipline that helps you create space to formulate a response.

2. Name the issue in focus. Generate at least three labels for it, not all necessarily problematic, and describe it according to these labels. Brainstorm appropriate responses to each of the perspectives.

3. Identify the patterns that produced the situation; look for other examples of the same situation.

4. Identify the factors that maintain the patterns, looking for your spheres of influence, your most effective leverage points.

5. Reframe the situations looking for connections between problems and solutions.

   a. Structural

   b. Political

   c. Human Resource

   d. Symbolic

6. Generate responses for each problem definition working under the assumptions of the appropriate organizational frame.

7. Identify the players you'll need to work with/influence.

8. Remind yourself of the primary sources of authority for your work.

9. Understand your own contributions to the problem.

10. Identify the sorts of events or situations you'll take as evidence of progress.

❶ **Avoid reacting. Use any ritual or discipline that helps you create space to formulate a response.**

Whether you are breaking up a fight in the hallway or responding to an administrative memo, you need to give yourself time to think before you act. Remember the adage, "Sin in haste; repent at leisure"? Well that applies to all of life's conundrums, especially in this age of sound-byte instant messaging.

We are looking for solutions that are both rational and reasonable, that is, responses that conform to policies and procedures that were formulated by thoughtful people far away from us, *and* that take into account the messy details of the situation as we encounter it.

For example, you may agree in general with the need to refer fighters to the assistant principal (Vignette #2), but if you know the boys involved and you believe you can work out a better solution without kicking the bureaucracy into gear, you will want to ponder your options before you write them up.

❷ **Name the issue in focus. Generate at least three labels for it, not all necessarily problematic, and describe it according to these labels. Brainstorm appropriate responses to each of the perspectives.**

This follows closely from Strategy #1. It is important to approach situations in ways that permit you to see all sides of an issue, including how some people might not view it as problematic. Most problem-solving involves working with others, and very often a part of what you will be trying to do is change their minds and behaviors. By disciplining yourself to come up with several labels for the situation, you will find that it is easier to see things from others' points of view.

I'm not suggesting that you sit down immediately and write out three names for every situation you face, although on the bigger issues—discipline and attendance policies, relationships between administrators and teachers, home/school connections, etc.—this is certainly possible. But most important is that we face potentially problematic situations squarely and come up with ways of dealing with them.

Labeling the difficulty of getting parents to school for conferences (Vignette #4) as "cultural differences" is a good start, because it is highly likely that this has something to do with it. But there is not much you can do about culture, so you are left feeling frustrated by the situation. However, if you label the situation, "communication difficulties caused by cultural differences," you can begin to think of things you might do to improve your ability to communicate with the parents.

❸ **Identify the patterns that produced the situation; look for other examples of the same situation.**

From an ecological perspective, all situations are local instances of larger patterns, the inevitable result of systemic functioning. This means that you can save yourself time and frustration by recognizing how the situation you are dealing with is part of larger patterns of organizational life. Vignettes #4 and #5, for example, might best be seen as variations on the same pattern, rather than distinct situations that require specific attention to José and Marisa. If you are the teacher involved in both cases, it may seem more direct to call their parents or to work with the students to improve parent participation in improving their school work. However, if José and Marisa are having these sorts of difficulties, it is a safe bet that other teachers are dealing with them as well and you will be doing everyone a favor if you are able to muster organizational energy and resources to address them.

❹ **Identify the factors that maintain the patterns, looking for your spheres of influence, your most effective leverage points.**

The only problems that can be solved quickly and easily are small, unimportant ones, and we are interested here in the big ones. So this means that you will need to be content with nudging the systems within which you work toward the solutions you envision.

The most significant step you can take toward successful change efforts is to recognize a profound truth of nature: Simple, straightforward causal explanations for human phenomena are rarely useful. People are complex, and organizations even more so. Whether you are attempting to understand a particular event or situation or trying to change something, you need to abandon causal thinking—Event A causes Event B—and adopt ecological thinking—Event B can be understood as the (expectable) outcome of a convergence of factors. How to influence these factors to create an environment for change becomes the focus of your efforts.

And this means looking for the factors that contribute to your problem and seeking ways of adjusting them in ways that improves the situation. For example, hallway scuffles such as the one described in Vignette #2 occur because of multiple factors, only a few of which are described in the "Vignette/Problems/Solutions" chart. By working on several simultaneously, you greatly increase your chances of success.

❺ **Reframe the situations looking for connections between problems and solutions.**
   a. **Structural**
   b. **Political**
   c. **Human Resource**
   d. **Symbolic**

Particular understandings of situations will result in identifying them as problems with corresponding solutions. What is important here is making sure that you do not merely revert to defining situations as "problems" with "solutions" with which you feel most comfortable.

Take, for example, the "solution" of restructuring. You have no doubt been part of some organizational restructuring effort in your career as a teacher. This is because restructuring is the easiest thing for a new administrator to do when he or she arrives. It is also one that feels important. But my guess is that it is appropriate in only a fraction of the cases in which it is done.

Another example: A number of the solutions listed in column three of the chart will result in "passing the buck" if you do not continue to work on reframing the problem and searching for coordinated solutions. This is true whenever you form "task forces" to look into problems. Very often this results in others believing that the problem no longer relates to them, and they feel free to ignore situations that they should, in fact, continue to work on.

The same is true when you identify individuals as "solutions": Hiring paraprofessionals from the same culture as the students is the most common error we see in this category. Every time a problem arises, the paraprofessional is called in to solve it, and teachers and administrators believe they have been relieved of the responsibility to learn more about the students and their culture. The problem is compounded by the inevitable differences of power and prestige between professional and paraprofessional staff that often result in exploitation of the paraprofessionals or power struggles between teachers and paraprofessionals.

**❻ Generate responses for each problem definition working under the assumptions of the appropriate organizational frame.**

Conversely, there are times when a structural response solves what might otherwise appear to be a problem amenable to a human resource solution. For example, some schools require all teachers to make home visits or other kinds of parent contact in an effort to address the sorts of problems described in Vignettes #3, #4, and #5. However, it may be that particular teachers are more suited for interacting with parents because of linguistic or cultural skills or merely because they are jovial people who enjoy talking to parents. In such situations, creating committees and dividing the labor permit teachers to work from their strengths.

Here again, it is important to remember to continue exploring responses after you have crafted definitions of the problem and to maintain a flexible attitude as you approach the work so that you do not mistake mere action for "commendable solution."

**❼ Identify the players you'll need to work with/influence.**

All change of the sort we are discussing here requires people to change, and as you wade into the strategies you have identified, you will need to decide who among your colleagues are likely to become your allies and who are more likely to emerge as adversaries. You have more leverage with people who agree with you, and so you will want to figure out ways of getting them to sign on to your agenda. Individuals who have a different view of the situation than yours will require more thought on your part; it may not be worth your time or effort to try to change their views, but you want to avoid irritating people or making enemies if you can help it.

### ❽ Remind yourself of the primary sources of authority for your work.

I am speaking here of "authority" in the grand sense, harking back to the philosophy work in the essay on pages 84–110. It is true that your department chair or school director/principal also has authority over you (not to mention more distant individuals such as superintendents, governors, etc.), but I am advocating a view of teaching in which teachers identify the ultimate authorities that guide their decision-making. These may be your parents or revered ancestors, a favorite teacher or esteemed philosopher, the leader of your religious community or a distant guru. It may include research findings or inspirational texts.

The point is, we are all seeking coherence in our work—ways of aligning our behavior with our convictions—and we want to avoid being compromised by the pressures that seem to dominate the profession these days. Because our students' welfare is at the heart of our personal and professional commitments, and because English language learners are marginal participants in the culture and in schools, we will find ourselves crosswise of the system on many occasions. And on those occasions, we need to remind ourselves of the reasons we got into the profession. This will not automatically yield solutions, but it will keep you going.

### ❾ Understand your own contributions to the problem.

An important aspect of this sort of work requires us to examine our own reactions to situations and the hidden motives of our participation in particular solutions. It is easier to use the labels "parental indifference" or "cultural incompatibility" when confronted with home/school miscommunication than it is to admit that you would rather not make home visits or return to the building for parent conferences later in the evening when parents are off work. It is easier to complain about administrative mandates that make your life difficult than it is to volunteer for committee work required to change school policies and procedures.

The fact is that we all have our comfortable rhythms and routines, and if we are not diligent we will find ourselves merely following those rather than doing the difficult work required for significant and sustained change.

⑩ **Identify the sorts of events or situations you'll take as evidence of progress.**

From an ecological perspective, there are no "bottom lines," or "final products." Things are never "over"; life keeps on happening, and so we need to be content with marking how far we've come rather than moaning about the fact that we have not reached the final goal.

It is impossible to get whole-hearted and effective participation by all parents in their children's school lives, but we need to monitor our record over the semesters so that we have a basis for decision-making that keeps us on track. Twenty percent attendance at a back-to-school night may not sound good, but it represents progress if you only had 10 percent before you changed the day and time, for example.

## Conclusion

This is slow work, and patience is required. You'll become discouraged if you keep looking at how much work remains. Rather, focus on the progress you've made and rejoice in the small victories.

I realize that there is not much immediate comfort in this approach. The list of initiatives and the strategies for accomplishing them will strike some as common sense while appearing to others as quixotic, and it would not be difficult to find individuals who wonder why this is even a concern—after all, shouldn't immigrants be expected to learn the language of their adopted country? Why should we change the system to accommodate them?

In addition, an ecological perspective of change may seem frustratingly complex and non-prescriptive. It does not conform to our take-charge attitude toward change. Some will view the approach as hopelessly naive, others will find it tactically ineffective, and still others will wonder why we should make it so complicated. I have no responses to these points that would add significantly to what I have already said, nor, however, do I offer apologies. This is the way the world works, and if we are to accomplish long-term results this is the way we need to proceed.

I view the effort as both common sense *and* quixotic. I look around me and see the numbers of English language learners growing, and it seems inevitable to me that something has to give, yet I can see that change will be difficult and time consuming. The ecological perspective of the world is complex, but it is far less complex than the reality it attempts to describe.

I am not content with responses to situations that begin by ignoring the complexity in order to make problems easier to solve.

## REFERENCES

Bateson, G. (1979). *Mind and nature: A necessary unity.* New York: Dutton.

——. (1999). *Steps to an ecology of mind.* Chicago: University of Chicago Press.

Bolman, L. G., & Deal, T. E. (2003). *Reframing organizations: Artistry, choice, and leadership.* San Francisco: Jossey-Bass.

Commins, N. L., & Miramontes, O. B. (2005). *Linguistic diversity and teaching.* Mahwah, NJ: Lawrence Erlbaum Associates.

Goffman, E. (1974). *Frame analysis.* New York: Harper Colophon Books.

Kegan, R. (1982). *The evolving self: Problem and process in human development.* Cambridge, MA: Harvard University Press.

——. (1994). *In over our heads: The mental demands of modern life.* Cambridge, MA: Harvard University Press.

Kegan, R., & Lahey, L. L. (2001). *How the way we talk can change the way we work: Seven languages for transformation.* San Francisco: Jossey-Bass.

Norton, B. (2000). *Identity and language learning: Gender, ethnicity, and educational change.* New York: Longman.

Valdes, G. (1996). *Con respeto: Bridging the distance between culturally diverse families and schools.* New York: Teachers College Press.

## NOTES

1. This relates to the phenomenon of "scale," which I discussed in detail on pages 19–32. We cannot escape the fact that we live in a world of nested systems—systems within systems within systems—and that enduring problems are those that are supported by conditions that exist at many levels. A detailed discussion would weigh the essay down in technical details. Suffice it to say that I am defining "significant problems" as irritants that you decide to work on but that you recognize cannot be solved in a quick and efficient fashion because they are too big. So, my working definition of scale is: the physical and/or temporal characteristics of a situation that must be taken into account as we attempt to address problems.

# ⑩ It's All One Thing

The argument developed in this book is the essence of simplicity: There is only one thing, and that is life. All we have to do is figure out how to respond to it.

All human beings and all enduring collections of human beings—families, communities, classrooms, schools, etc.—are open systems functioning according to a handful of principles. Because the principles are the same regardless of scale, they provide guidance as we negotiate our daily challenges. I have articulated the following principles in a number of ways throughout the book; it is helpful to consider them again.

1. **Systems function toward stability.** People and institutions develop comfortable habits and routines, and they resist change. This is natural and expectable. We should not be too critical of ourselves or impatient with others for desiring things to remain the way they have been; we all enjoy the comfort of routine to some extent.

2. **Systems function in response to internal and external messages, adjusting to signals received from within as well as information from the environment.** The internal vibrations are metabolic and psychological. There is a genetic aspect of human behavior, an inheritance from ancestors, the collected bundle of traits sometimes referred to as "personality." The external messages come in the form of all the demands that bombard us every day from all sides. We will improve our chances of happiness and

effectiveness to the extent we become aware of the patterns of responses—ours and others—to internal and external information.

3. **Systems respond to disturbances in ways that, if not precisely predictable, are patterned and therefore expectable.** Change is gradual, and we can learn a great deal about individuals, schools, and communities by observing and taking note of cycles of activity and the adjustments we and others make to them. Even sudden, unforeseen, dramatic changes have been a long time coming; they have surprised us because we have not been paying attention to the signals.

4. **Systems cannot be changed unilaterally (because such efforts are only part of the information on which they function—the external messages mentioned in #2); the conditions for change must be present.** Our efforts to change the patterns of responses of our students, for example, that we call "teaching," can best be understood as creating environments for learning. And the same thing is true for our attempts at changing the way the school operates or the way we interact with the community.

5. **The world consists of systems within systems within systems.** Predictably, the environment we are most concerned with is the classroom, but classroom events are influenced by school policies and procedures and by the characteristics of community and society. All systems are nested within other systems, and significant, sustained change at one level requires changes in the larger systems; if you are attempting something even remotely radical in the classroom, you will need to create the conditions in the school and perhaps the community to sustain your effort.

From this perspective effective teaching must be understood more broadly than generally assumed, and teachers must look beyond the classroom as they work to improve their teaching.

This graphic, introduced on page 28, is an attempt to capture these insights in a single illustration.

The tall person in the middle represents you, and the group of smaller figures represents the individuals over whom you exercise some influence. As

a teacher, you have the greatest influence over the students in your classes, but you also have some influence with your colleagues, administrators, and community members. You need to see yourself as a teacher in any situation where your commitments are at stake.

The ellipses to the left represent the past. Where they meet is the present. The future extends to the right. The smaller the ellipse, the more immediate the feedback loop, that is, the shorter the cycle of activity you need to attend to.

The graphic helps us remember that life is both cyclical and negotiated. The patterns of today are visible in the days and weeks just past and expectable in the future. The cluster of figures reminds us that all experience is constructed with others.

This vision of reality is elegant and all encompassing, but it can also be overwhelming. Coming to an understanding of the complexity of life does not necessarily mean that we will be more adept at dealing with it. But it does mean that we are at least operating with all the data—or, at least, with an awareness of the extent of the information we should be attempting to understand. It also means that we have a principled basis for understanding the dismay and frustration we experience as we attempt to cope with problems, and it gives us a way of selecting the problems we are going to work on and the way we are going to approach them.

Even more important, this perspective emphasizes that the problems are all variations on the same themes. This is a crucial realization, because if we are clear on our core values and if we work toward coherent responses to the problems that assail us, we stand a chance of nudging the systems within which we live and work toward healthy conditions for learning.

We cannot reduce the complexity of the world, but we can exercise some control over ourselves as we confront it. Here are three principles for coping with the complexity:

1. Identify the boundaries of your efforts.

2. Work within yourself.

3. Focus on what you are doing *now*.

The looping ellipses that represent the clusters of systems within which we live and work are an illusion of the graphic; in fact, there are no concrete boundaries between systems, which means that one of the greatest challenges we face is determining the limits of our efforts. But it is essential that we consciously identify the size of the territory we seek to influence. The majority of the time this will coincide with our institutionally sanctioned responsibilities—

the classroom—but when we shift our efforts to larger systems—the school or the community, for example—it is important that we clearly delimit for ourselves and others the limits of time, energy, and geography of our work.

A corollary of this principle is the requirement of identifying your own limits. This means being clear headed in assessing your strengths and brutally honest in identifying your weaknesses. It means constantly talking to yourself, reminding yourself of your core values and the big picture as you work on the task at hand.

And finally, the logical consequence of these two, we need to discipline ourselves to focus on the task at hand. It is easy to become distracted by the details of life that assail us on all sides, so it is imperative that we push the world away and do the best job possible of whatever we are working on. It is also important to recognize that "best job possible" may fall short of our own expectations for the task; small steps toward our goals *are* progress. We have to focus on how far we have come rather than how far we have to go.

If we take this view and bring it to bear on the ten essays of the book, it is possible to gain a bit of perspective on the issues examined and at the same time recover some composure in the face of the daunting challenges that we face.

The chart that follows presents a summary of the arguments made in each essay and indicates the roles that teachers play in different situations.

| Essay | Argument |
|---|---|
| **Introduction:**<br>**Whose Questions Count?**<br><br>**Teacher Role: Reflective Practitioner** | These are contentious times with powerful players clamoring for a say in educational debates. Teachers need to raise their voices and be heard, and the questions that matter to teachers should be the ones that schools and society attend to. |
| 1. **Ecological Perspectives of Teaching: Making Choices in a Complex World**<br><br>**Teacher Role: Ecologist** | Teaching is a function of relationships and good teachers make good choices, choices that reflect their awareness of the nested contexts of school, community, and society. Gwen Hill responds to students' alarm over pending immigration legislation by organizing a lesson from the newspaper story that has upset the students. The success of the lesson derives in large part from Gwen's sensitive awareness of the larger contexts in which she works. |

| | |
|---|---|
| **2. On Learning and (Therefore) Teaching**<br><br>**Teacher Role: Theorist** | Human beings cannot NOT learn, but whether our students are learning what we want them to learn is a matter for reflection. Aimee Trechock orchestrates a successful reading lesson that could be based on a number of theories, illustrating the assertion that teachers need to craft their own theories, balancing insights from scholarship with their own personal experience. Theory is used both to guide and defend classroom practice. |
| **3. Teaching as Learning, Learning as Life**<br><br>**Teacher Role: Action Researcher** | Significant problems can rarely be solved at the level they are encountered. The changes in Maria's school work lead her teacher to collect information about the family responsibilities of the students and to develop programs that connect the school and the community. Teachers may be reluctant to cast themselves as action researchers, but they are the only professionals in position to leverage change based on the needs of students. |
| **4. Philosophy as Autobiography**<br><br>**Teacher Role: Philosopher** | Who we are as teachers is a variation of who we are as human beings. We need to combine the wisdom of scholars with our experiences as learners to craft a philosophy of teaching that will guide us both in the classroom and beyond. A working philosophy provides for principled connections between core values, the authorities on which these are based, and classroom practices. |
| **5. Authenticity in Language Teaching: Working out the Bugs**<br><br>**Teacher Role: Reflective Practitioner** | Authenticity has long been a goal of language teachers, but too often it is cast in such ambitious terms that the classroom seems the last place we might find it. The key to organizing authentic lessons, however, lies in creating structures and procedures that permit you to relate to students in ways that they find personally meaningful. The lesson plan consists of scaffolding within which we vary the rhythms of activity to engage students' heads and hearts, create opportunities for them to interact in meaningful ways with others, and position themselves as the authorities of their own actions. |

| | |
|---|---|
| **6. Authenticity Revisited: Rhythm and Routine in Classroom Interactions**<br><br>**Teacher Role: Reflective Practitioner** | Authentic teaching is a matter of interpersonal negotiation in which we connect with individuals through small variations in the classroom routine that permit us to know our students and permit our students to exercise some agency in the classroom. The important work is done by the teacher shifting consciousness; permitting insights into students' experience, needs, and aspirations; and permitting meaningful lessons to be negotiated. |
| **7. Teachers and Gurus**<br><br>**Teacher Role: Reflective Practitioner** | We all stand on the shoulders of our mentors and scholarly forebears, but good teaching is an interactional accomplishment; the success we have is a result of our ability to negotiate the exigencies of the moment, not follow a script. |
| **8. Teaching to Standards: How to and Why Not**<br><br>**Teacher Role: Reflective Practitioner** | We need to align our teaching to the standards of the profession and to the institutional expectations, but we need to maintain our independence and exercise our judgment as the lesson proceeds. Evaluation of the extent to which we have met the standards comes after the lesson, as we assess how things went and adjust our plans for the next lesson. |
| **9. Changing Schools: Creating Disturbances and Alarming Your Friends**<br><br>**Teacher Role: Activist** | "Problem" is merely a label for a situation that we do not like, and one person's problem is merely "the way things are" for someone else. How we define problems will affect where we search for answers—in structural, political, symbolic, or human resource solutions. The key is to remain flexible and to organize allies to work with us at different levels of scale. |

## It's All about You

Early on in the writing of this book, my long-time friend and colleague Ann Johns of the American University in Cairo and San Diego State University agreed to read the manuscript and give me feedback on it, but after a few weeks I received an email: "Can't do it, Mark. There's too much Mark Clarke here for me," she said, and begged off.

You may have had the same difficulty. Although I *say* in the Introduction that this is not personal memoir, you might be forgiven if, like Ann, you found too much of me in these essays. I didn't plan it that way, but as the pages rolled off the printer it seemed clear to me that I had to ground the argument in my own experience. Luckily, I had Ann's accusations ringing in my ears, and I hope I have toned it down a bit so that you can find something of yourself in these pages as well.

The danger of the argument I have made here is that it will collapse of its own weight. You picked up the book thinking it was about teaching English language learners and then quickly discovered that I have cast teachers as theorists, philosophers, action researchers, school and community activists, and reflective practitioners who acknowledge no authority except their own.

It *is* daunting, but the fact of the matter is, we cannot understand the world if we do not make an attempt to understand ourselves; any concerted effort at crafting a place to stand in the contested territory of education will require some degree of self-analysis. And because all understanding emerges from experience, our change efforts will be marked by our very personal approach to problem solving.

We have to tell our own stories—if only to ourselves—if we are to understand where we stand and where we are headed.

Best of luck.

# ACKNOWLEDGMENTS

Family, friends, and colleagues:

You will recognize the arguments developed in this book, and I hope you will also see your contributions to my thinking. As you know, this is my world view, and I have difficulty seeing alternatives to the position I have developed. It is not surprising, therefore, that some of the most valued contributions have been made by friendly skeptics. But whether you agreed with my position and were helping me clarify it and figure out applications and implications, or providing balance to my zealous energy, I understand that whatever there is of value in these arguments derives in large part from our interactions.

Patricia Barr Clarke: Your commitment to community and your tenacious pursuit of justice and fair play, your relentless research and archiving, your consistent critique, and your generosity of spirit have provided me with a model and a standard for what I call action research.

Julian Edge: Thanks for careful reading of all these essays, several of them more than once, for thoughtful word-smithing, long walks, and pub seminars. I have not always heeded your calls for moderation, but I have benefited from the professional and considerate approach you take toward scholarly debate. I live in fear that you will call in my debts for your contributions to this book.

Alan Davis: Our weekly conversations in the Lab of Learning and Activity, and the frequent plunges into pasta and problems at The Market, have provided a constant in the disequilibrium of the changing university. The original title for the manuscript that would become this book was *Surviving Innovation*. It got demoted to a subtitle for the series, but I continue to believe this is an accurate way to sum up the work of teachers today. Your consistent friendship and collegial dismay at my proposed projects have helped me remain confident of the value of community in these troubling times.

Kelly Sippell: Where to start? I appreciate your careful reading of the manuscript and your critical editorial skills, but far more important have been your partisan loyalty to the project and your tenacious efforts at making the essays strong, transparent, and light. You had confidence at times that I did not. Thanks for seeing this through.

Viola Moriarty: Your enthusiasm for the project was very much needed, especially in times when I doubted that classroom teachers would welcome such burdensome scrutiny of their work. I will save your detailed annotations of early drafts with the boisterous exclamations, multiple question marks, and detailed suggestions for turns of phrase and refer to them in moments of doubt.

Tom Scovel: I owe you for much more than the many breakfasts, lunches, and dinners you wouldn't let me pay for. I took to heart all of your questions, comments, and quibbles, and even though you may still find an unrepentant exuberance, the arguments here are far sharper for having had your careful scrutiny.

Earl W. Stevick: You have been model, mentor, and mensch for me since your visit to the ELI in the early '70s. Through most of the book I have felt like Charlie McCarthy, chattering away on your knee. These are themes that you have developed with far more authority elsewhere. Your recent phone call, out of the blue on a Saturday afternoon, reassured me of the importance of this work and of the need for calm and thoughtful contemplation. The lessons of the Utopians and Arcadians are more urgently needed than ever.

Jeanne Hind: You truly understand "all one thing" and "total learning environment." I have been lucky to collaborate with you on a decade (and counting) of Rocky Mountain TESOL Institutes, the closest thing there is to an example of the sort of teaching-learning experience I advocate in these essays.

Lola: You are the environment within which I have made productive steps toward an ecology of mind. Many thanks to Elaine DeLott Baker, Cathy Bodine, Ruth Brancard, Stephanie Dewing, Venita Doughty, Kathie Goff, Jeanne Hind, J. Franklin Horn, Dan Jesse, Kristen Kaiser, Larry Linnen, Joanne McLain, Marge Mistry, Karen Myers, Honorine Nocon, Judy Northup, Gene Plampin, Lee Ann Rawley, Jennifer Rudkin, Sharon Sherman, Maria Thomas Ruzic, Corrie Santos, James Mark Tafoya, Dana Walker, Kim Walter, Natasha Watson, Phillip White.

Colleagues and friends at Spring International Language Center: I have appreciated your patience and good will for the past ten years as we orchestrated the chaos of Rocky Mountain TESOL Institute, and I look forward to another ten: Karen Barker, Lauren Brombert, Chris Crupper, Gavin Edwards, Kelly Foster, Richard Gaines, Dana Harper, Sara Holzberlein, Barbara Kessler, Katherine Kouris, Cara Martinez, Judy Okamoto, Nada Petrovic, Tom Rohrbach, Shoko Sato, Heather Torres, Laura Vance.

This book, like its predecessor, *A Place to Stand,* is an attempt to translate systems theory into a tool for everyday living. My understanding of this arcane science rests heavily on the little yellow book *Steps to an Ecology of Mind* by Gregory Bateson, which I purchased in Ann Arbor in 1973 at the suggestion of Pete Becker. I've been reading the book ever since. Mary Catherine Bateson and Peter Harries-Jones, have helped me understand Gregory's ideas and his approach to this work. In particular, I have appreciated your efforts at helping me understand the importance of the problem that time presents in unraveling the conundrums of scale and the logical categories of learning and communication.

I was introduced to the work of Robert Kegan by Jeffrey Miller, science educator at Metropolitan State College, and I have benefited from conversations with Wayne Gilbert, Community College of Aurora, as I have attempted to use Kegan in my classroom. Ruth Brancard, Community College of Denver, has led my thinking on the use of Keganesque ideas and research methods to understand learning as a change in identity.

Amy Clarke Moore, thank you for the bead embroidery on the cover and for many conversations about office drama that helped me clarify my thinking.

Ann Johns: I taped your email above my monitor as I worked: "Too much Mark Clarke!" Trust you to put advice succinctly and memorably.

And Chris Cupper, thanks for this, ever appropriate reminder: "To the making of many books, there is no end, and much devotion to them is wearisome to the flesh." *Ecclesiastes* 12:12

Sue Wharton: I appreciate your thoughtfulness in reconnecting with me and exchanging ideas about teaching and teacher education.

Gwen Hill and Aimee Trechock: You invited me into your classrooms on ordinary days, and I left with indelible images of artistic accomplishments in teaching.

Bill Goodwin and Kenny Wolf: Thanks for the careful read of "On Learning—and (Therefore) Teaching" and energizing conversations around the details of classroom maneuvers.

A much earlier version of Essay 5, "Authenticity in Language Teaching: Working Out the Bugs," first appeared as Clarke, M. A. (1999), "Gregory Bateson, communication and context: An ecological perspective of language teaching," in D. J. Mendelsohn (Ed.), *Expanding our vision: Insights for language teachers* (pp. 155–172), Toronto: Oxford University Press. This was an emerging version of an address delivered in various guises to the following audiences: AzTESOL Convention, Flagstaff, April 1983; Rocky Mountain TESOL, Salt Lake City, October 1983; University of Zagreb, Yugoslavia; English Language Institute, American University in Cairo, Egypt; and CoTESOL Convention, Denver, November 1983. The file for this essay is three inches thick, an indication of the struggles I had in its writing. If I succeed at all in making connections between the abstractions of systems theory and the details of language teaching, it is because of the patience and effort of colleagues who read and commented on the manuscript over the years. Thank you Karin Bates Chen, Julian Edge, Kathie Goff, and Tim Murphey for your detailed responses to a desperate email in the spring of 1998 that contributed substantially to whatever clarity I accomplished. David, thank you for organizing the book that prompted me to put the ideas on paper.

The excerpt in Essay 6, "Authenticity Revisited: Rhythm and Routine in Classroom Interactions," was published in a section of the ESL textbook, *Choice Readings* by Mark A. Clarke, Barbara K. Dobson, and Sandra Silberstein, Ann Arbor: University of Michigan Press: 153–156. The exercises emerged from my own teaching but took their final form through the rhythmic rituals of co-writing with Barb and Sandy. I have continued to use exercises from *Choice Readings* in workshops and classes, but in the summer of 2006, in one frenzied marathon session of revision and adaptation, I brought the Bugs! chapter into my methods class at the Rocky Mountain TESOL Summer Institute in response to questions and critique raised by the teachers. You were a tenaciously thoughtful and focused group, and I will always remember with a smile our sessions in that cramped classroom over the gym: Paula Adamo, Nicole Avery, Desiree Back, Denice Botten, Megan Collins, Amber Dryer, Susan Feinglas, Anne Flemming, MJ Kim, Courtney Kingsley, Juila Lamb, Stella Lee, Kathy Lewis, Kait Martin, Jan Montassir, Makailah Perkins, Alicia Privitt, Mike Rowe, Kent Talmage-Bowers, Wendy Thompson. The excerpt is reprinted with permission of the University of Michigan Press and the Associated Press/A. P. Images.

A much earlier version of Essay 7, "Teachers and Gurus," first appeared in 1984 in the *TESOL Quarterly, 18*(4), 577–594, as "On the nature of technique: What do we owe the gurus?" The article represented my effort to understand the relationship between theory and practice in second language teaching, especially as it related to the preparation of teachers. My thinking was been greatly influenced by discussions and epistolary exchanges with numerous individuals, and I remember fondly our conversations. Thanks particularly to Jean Handscombe and Sandra Silberstein for insightful and thorough critiques of early drafts. Others who worked on these ideas with me were Patricia Barr Clarke, John Fanselow, Norman Gary, John Haskell, Debra Jackson, Lynn K. Rhodes, Connie Shoemaker, Earl W. Stevick, Marie Wirsing, and as always, the teachers in my graduate classes. Thanks also to the *TESOL Quarterly* editors, Barry Taylor and Stephen Gaies.

Mark A. Clarke
October 2006

# INDEX